ENTRY LESSONS

ENTRY LESSONS

THE STORIES
OF WOMEN
FIGHTING
FOR
THEIR PLACE,
THEIR CHILDREN,
AND
THEIR FUTURES
AFTER
INCARCERATION

JORJA LEAP

BEACON PRESS | BOSTON

BEACON PRESS
Boston, Massachusetts
www.beacon.org

Beacon Press books
are published under the auspices of
the Unitarian Universalist Association of Congregations.

25 24 23 22   8 7 6 5 4 3 2 1

This book is printed on acid-free paper that meets the uncoated paper
ANSI/NISO specifications for permanence as revised in 1992.

Text design and composition by Kim Arney

Many names and distinguishing characteristics of people described
in this work have been changed to protect their identities.

Throughout the book, the words "gang," "hood," "neighborhood," and "barrio"
are used interchangeably, depending on the individual's terminology.

Library of Congress Control Number: 2021050581
Hardcover ISBN: 978-0-8070-2287-0
Ebook ISBN: 978-0-8070-2288-7

This book is for Karrah Lompa and Elie Miller
and in memory of Thea Ernie and Beatriz Solis.
It is also for all the women in these pages who
gave me their time and their trust.

I didn't need reentry services. I needed *entry* services—like how do you enter into a normal life? Reentry is a lie; it's the wrong word. What we need is help on how to heal, how to live, how to enter this world.

—DENISE MARSHALL

Put simply, we know that when we incarcerate a woman we often are truly incarcerating a family, in terms of the far-reaching effect on her children, her community, and her entire family network.

—LORETTA LYNCH, former US attorney general

CONTENTS

PART ONE

THE JOURNEY IN

ONE

SLEEPWALKING

*At Homegirl, we all understand each other. We're
a family. There's so much pain and so much love.*

—SHAYNA WELCHER

The Homegirl Café was operating with total efficiency. That could only mean something was really wrong. The homegirls were ordinarily the liveliest—and worst—waitresses imaginable, full of laughter and chatter while ignoring the customers who waited patiently for their water or their food or their check. Usually this only got worse before the last table was cleared and the doors were locked for the night. But today was different. The atmosphere in the café felt more like a prayer meeting than a party, the women delivering plates and checks with silent precision.

Erika Cuellar, one of the café directors, wasn't on the floor, which made the ballet of organization even more alarming. I found her in back, outside the building, behind the kitchen. When she turned toward me, I saw she'd been crying.

"So. You heard what happened?"

"No. You're scaring me—what is it?"

"It's Janeth. She got locked up." I looked at Erika closely. This news was not exactly remarkable. We were at Homeboy Industries, for God's sake.

"For what?"

"Murder. You know—they've been trying to find who killed that church deacon. Now they know. Pedro Martinez shot him. Ivy and Janeth were with him. I'm not sure what happened. But that's why they arrested Janeth last night. Elie thinks her bail is going to be over a million dollars."

Erika started crying again while I stood still, trying to make some sense of her words.

I was used to people getting locked up. While criminal justice reform had growing support on both sides of the aisle—or so we kept hearing—evidently the Los Angeles Police Department and the Sheriff's Department hadn't gotten the memo. Instead, almost everyone in law enforcement had only one thing on their minds: how to maintain the 40 percent drop in crime that in late 2012 was being touted as a historic low. So, people got locked up on suspicion. A crime was reported and then it was time to "round up the usual suspects"—particularly if they had tattoos and were hanging out in an area under a gang injunction. More often than not, after a few days passed, they were released. Invariably, it all came down to a technicality: "It was a DA reject," or "They found the right guy," or "The charges wouldn't stick." Actually, the reality was that there just wasn't enough room in the LA County jail to detain every suspect, particularly for cases that were weak or lacked physical evidence. On any given day, twenty-two thousand men and women were locked up in some part of "CJ," as the homies referred to the county jail, most of them awaiting the disposition of their case. Because of this, there was constant pressure to sort cases out. Additionally, if an arrest involved drug possession, the person charged would most likely go to drug court and then a rehab program. Cases rarely went to an actual trial. But a charge of homicide was different. And this one involved a church deacon, a violent gang member, and two women who were on the scene during the commission of the crime.

Everything about it was different.

No one ever thought of homegirls as murderers. Gang life was gendered, and women played supporting roles. They were girlfriends, or hood rats, or baby mamas. They were extensions of the male iden-tity—readily available, on call as accomplices, personal assistants, char-acters in the gender cartoon of criminal behavior. "Y'know, women are supposed to be baby mamas. Maybe they do a little dealing on the side. But come on, they're not criminals; *they're women*," one gang member had patiently explained to me, as if talking to an idiot. Their drug dealing sounded as innocent as having a Tupperware party or selling costume jewelry to make extra money. For women, crime was not a ca-reer—it was just a practice to generate petty cash, some pin money for the little lady. "I hid my dope in my baby's diaper bag and even right in his diaper," Joanna "Bright Eyes" Carillo once told me. "I just made a little money on the side—I could buy baby clothes or a dress, and I wouldn't have to ask my man for any money. I could get something for the house." When women talked about the minor crimes they engaged in, it all sounded so domestic, not worthy of any major public policy intervention.

If a woman actually engaged in violent activity—even murdered someone—it was usually *with cause*. I had already heard three separate stories from women at Homegirl. Each of them knew a woman who had killed a man because he had raped her, or sexually abused her, or repeatedly beaten her. Or all three.

Given all that, what could explain the run-up to this particular mur-der? Both women were mothers, both had experienced major traumas, and both struggled with their trauma and their recovery. So much had already happened to them in their lives. I knew Janeth had been in-volved for years with Luis, who'd fathered her daughter, Angelina. He was involved in gang activity, cheated on her, and beat her repeatedly, but she always wound up taking him back—she felt she had no one else in the world.

I also knew that Carlos, the father of Ivy's son, Jessie, was locked up long-term, and Ivy had been alone for a long time, insisting she didn't want to be involved with anyone. Ivy herself had been locked up, and when she was released from prison, all she cared about was Jessie and being a good mother to him. No one knew why she'd ever gotten involved with Pedro Martinez, the alleged shooter—who wasn't part of the recovery-based world of Homeboy Industries. Even if he was attractive, as many of the homegirls found him, he was older, he'd been locked up, and he was still an active gang member. The women in the café worried about Janeth's and Ivy's involvements with such troublesome men—especially Pedro. While some of Luis's behavior was blamed on his youth and stupidity, Pedro was judged more harshly when it got out that he'd been beating Ivy. In gang life, you were supposed to handle your business, take care of your family, keep everything under control. You weren't supposed to beat your lady. Because of this, the homies had no love for Pedro, while the homegirls all worried about the pain both men inflicted and its impact on Ivy's son and Janeth's daughter.

"Was it just the two of them? Was anyone else with them? What happened? Who got picked up?" I kept asking questions without waiting for Erika to answer. Something inside of me just didn't want to know. I knew Ivy and Janeth were both struggling, trying to recover from trauma, not get involved in more of it.

"Pedro was the shooter; Ivy was driving the car. Janeth was tagging the church wall. I think Pedro killed the deacon. The deacon's wife is pregnant."

As soon as she delivered this verbal telegram, Erika started crying again.

Janeth and Ivy had hit the trifecta of crime: homicide, an innocent victim, and an unborn child. I knew what this meant. Barring a miracle, they would be incarcerated for a long time. Right now, Los Angeles had an aggressive DA who might even seek the death penalty. What was worse, up until a few weeks earlier, when she quit working as a waitress, Ivy had been one of the most beloved women in the café. Janeth was younger and more of a wild card; the women had worried about her. Ivy was older and committed to her recovery; everyone adored her. Customers came in and asked to sit at her table. She was a source of the warmth the café exuded. Even though she'd left Homegirl, everyone, including me, believed Ivy would be back sooner or later. She was too much a part of life at the café not to return.

The Homegirl Café had long existed as a sanctuary for women within Homeboy Industries. It was where women felt protected. Where, even if their relationships were failing or their kids were acting out, they could come, earn decent money, talk with the staff—feel seen, feel understood. I couldn't imagine what had happened with Janeth and Ivy. Right now, Erika was way beyond answering any more of my questions. But I knew what I had to do. *I had to find Elie.*

Elie Miller understood better than anyone else the struggles women confronted as they made their way through the thicket of the criminal justice system. Before becoming Homeboy's resident lawyer, she'd worked twenty years as a public defender. Elie was the homie whisperer—a combination legal authority and mother confessor. She loved the men and women at Homeboy while refusing to be manipulated by them. I'd gone to court with her when she was defending a former gang member allegedly operating a large-scale drug distribution network. On the way to the courthouse she was complaining, "I don't know what I'm going to do about this case. Shorty had a fucking pharmacy in his house—he had to know he was going to get caught. And he told me he cared about being a good father. What's going to happen to his kids now? He's got five of them. He's a complete idiot." Following her train of thought, I tried to empathize.

"You probably can't stand him right now." Elie looked at me, puzzled.

"What? I love Shorty—I really do. I just can't figure out why he did this."

That was the quintessential Elie. She loved the homies; she just bemoaned what they did—and hated how they got into trouble over and over again.

Elie already knew Janeth was locked up; she was down at the clerk's office at the courthouse trying to find out what the charges were, if bail had been set, and when she'd be arraigned. The women at the café were certain that Elie would save the day.

"We just have to wait for Elie."

"Elie will know what's going on."

"Elie will get her out."

It was a Friday night and, if the story was true, I knew Janeth would be in custody at least over the weekend. There wasn't going to be any last-minute arraignment, bail wouldn't be set. And even once bail was set, how on earth could Janeth afford it? Erika had one thing right—bail for a crime of this nature would be set at a minimum of a million dollars. My questions begat more questions.

And there was still the biggest unanswered question.

Where was Ivy?

Back inside the café, the "closed" sign had been hung on the door, and the women were sleepwalking through cleanup. One by one they came up and asked me: "Did you hear?" "What's gonna happen?" "Does Janeth have a lawyer?" "Is she gonna be all right?"

I had no answers; all I could repeat was the mantra "Wait for Elie."

In a few days, the story of the murder was all over the news.

"I heard something happened in Westlake with two of the Homegirl women. Didn't you live there once?"

The question—well-intentioned but tone-deaf—was coming from one of my UCLA colleagues who knew all too well the comings and goings of my personal life but who wasn't as well versed in the cross-hatch of communities that made up Los Angeles. He had only part of the story right.

The Iglesia Principe de Paz—the Church of the Prince of Peace—was located in the heart of the Westlake neighborhood of Los Angeles. With a congregation of Central American immigrants, this white-washed evangelical church was like a storefront, its windows guarded by a foldable iron gate. It looked like so many other establishments that rose up from the sidewalks throughout LA—in Watts, Boyle Heights, and Rampart. This area was often confused with Westlake Village, where I'd briefly lived, a bleach-white planned community at the western edge of Los Angeles County, right next door to Calabasas and the plastic-coated wonders of the Kardashian family. Westlake, near the Pico-Union district in Central Los Angeles, was a multi-ethnic enclave, home to many Central American immigrants and Filipino and Korean families. Churches formed the center of community life, and the Iglesia Principe de Paz was no exception. However, its congregation was too poor to support anything resembling full-time clergy. Alongside a more senior priest, Andres Ordonez volunteered as a deacon at Principe de Paz. His roots at the church were deep—he'd attended services there from the time he was ten years old. He'd married the granddaughter of the church's pastor. As deacon he'd stand at the church door, welcoming parishioners and offering each one a blessing.

Ordonez's backstory was deeply poignant, a narrative guaranteed to mark the murder as a tragedy and render Janeth and Ivy completely unsympathetic. His parents had migrated to Los Angeles from Guatemala when he was a toddler. He now worked as a restaurant cook but had bigger plans, greater aspirations. A shy and serious child, Andres had dreamed of someday being a police officer. There was no barrio for Andres, no tagging, no acting out. As a teenager he'd enthusiastically participated in the LAPD Police Explorer program, and it had reinforced his desire to serve his community. At twenty-five he was closing in on obtaining citizenship and applying to the LAPD. Andres was also focused on family as well as on his dreams: he was the father of a one-year-old son, and his wife, Ana, was three months pregnant with their second child. On this day Ana hadn't been feeling well. She'd left the church service and was sitting in the family car, parked in a nearby lot. Andres and another parishioner left during a break in the church services to check on her.

The precise details surrounding Andres's murder remained—for the moment—ambiguous. In the early evening of November 4, 2012, around five thirty, Janeth began tagging the walls of the Principe de Paz in the growing darkness. The graffiti included the typical tagger roll call, beginning with the symbols for her gang, Rockwood, followed by her gang moniker along with Pedro's and Ivy's. Janeth was claiming territory for her gang in enemy turf: Rockwood operated in the surrounding area, sandwiching their rival gang, Temple Street, between their original territory one mile to the east on Rockwood Street and the territory controlled by one of their cliques to the west at Westmoreland. Law enforcement was well aware of the conflict between the two gangs. In fact, the LA city attorney had already filed a "nuisance abatement" notice against Rockwood, spurring the LAPD to crack down on gang activity. Janeth knew this—it was probably why she was tagging. At twenty-two she was the youngest of the threesome in the car and the likeliest choice to tag the territory.

Inside the church the congregants were singing while food was set up in the parking lot for dinner once the service ended. A parishioner stepped outside to gauge the food preparation and saw Janeth spray-painting the wall. He asked Janeth to stop, and she did—long enough to walk over and push him to the ground. At the same time, Andres, who'd gone back to the church, was on the phone talking to his wife and heard noises. He emerged from the church and joined the group. Andres and another parishioner—a woman—tried to help the man up and told Janeth to stop what she was doing. *Why didn't she simply respond? Or run away?* But instead, as a group gathered around Janeth and the others, Pedro jumped out of the car with a shotgun and opened fire into the crowd. Ordonez and a woman parishioner fell. After spraying the area with bullets, Pedro jumped back into the car, where Ivy waited behind the wheel. Janeth ran to the car, jumped in, and the three drove away. Someone called 911 as the parishioners surrounded Andres—some kneeling, some standing, all of them praying.

The shooting took place in the Rampart district—long a battleground for gangs, including MCS-13—Mid-City Stoners 13 ("13" signifies the gang's ties to the Mexican Mafia, which made them the object of LAPD gang units like their rivals, MS-13), 18th Street, the Bounty Hunter Bloods, and the Rollin' 20s. In the Westlake neighborhood, where the church stood, gang rivalries had been linked to five homicides that had taken place over the past year. Residents had painted over gang graffiti, but their community-based efforts had incited gangsters, who threatened future violence. The walls of the evangelical church were thick with paint applied over previous tagging. In a neighborhood dense with apartment buildings, residents' fears multiplied. Witnesses didn't want to talk about what or who they'd seen at the church. There were rumors of gang retaliation if anyone spoke up. On top of that, many residents were undocumented. Nothing in this atmosphere lent itself to cooperation with law enforcement.

———

The shooting occurred on a Sunday. Four days later, on Thursday morning, the LAPD held a press conference. The deacon's widow, Ana, looking like a grief-stricken Madonna, asked the public to help find her husband's killer. Andres's father-in-law, Cirilo Mendez, asked for justice for his fallen son-in-law, "He has been in this country since he was a boy. From the bottom of his heart, he was American. He felt American. His wife was an American citizen. The life he was going to make was going to be made here."[1] There was talk of a reward for information but nothing definite. In the meantime, no one was talking to the police.

Not that there weren't stories about what had happened. The homie communication system had always functioned better than any intelligence operation, and rumors had started flying. While the media covered the press conference and entreaties from the LAPD, Homeboy was rumor central. Everyone was clear that Pedro was the lone shooter. Then there was word that police had raided the house where Ivy and her son, Jessie, lived with the couple she considered her in-laws. News of the police search lent credence to another story circulating, that Ivy and Janeth *might* have been involved in the murder. Early Thursday two homegirls reported that they'd seen Janeth. "I didn't kill anyone, I'd never kill anyone, I can't even shoot. I don't want to. Believe me," she'd reassured them, and it made sense. Women didn't kill anyone unless there was a reason.

And still the women in the café wondered, where was Ivy?

Five days after she was arrested, on Tuesday November 13, Janeth was officially charged with suspicion of murder, two counts of attempted murder, and vandalism. Given that she was described as a "reputed gang member," gang allegations would be added to her charges later. Her bail was set at $2.5 million. Ivy and Pedro were still at large.

TWO

PARTY BUS

It is the mission of the Custody Division to serve the best interest of Los Angeles County by providing a secure, safe, and constitutionally managed jail environment for both staff and inmates.

—LOS ANGELES COUNTY
SHERIFF'S DEPARTMENT[1]

It is January 2013, and Janeth is still locked up; Ivy and Pedro are in Mexico, according to the latest rumors. Although Janeth has been formerly charged, a trial won't be scheduled until all three are apprehended. After spending the morning with Elie, monitoring the progress of the case, I leave for a professional commitment bordering on the surreal. I've been enlisted to accompany a group of philanthropists as they tour the Los Angeles County Women's Jail. "Maybe I'll see Janeth," I grimly joke to Elie, knowing she's in a high-security lockup, cloistered away from any VIP tour.

The tour organizers had invited me along so that I could speak to twenty funders traveling to the Century Regional Detention Facility, the euphemistically named women's jail. The group was made up of representatives from private and family foundations from northern and southern California. Each day, these individuals oversee the awarding of millions of dollars of philanthropic funding dedicated to criminal justice reform. Their current interest stems from their dawning realization that so far, criminal justice reform has been almost entirely focused on men.

By the second decade of the new century, philanthropy was slowly catching on to this lopsided situation—and the reality that justice was gendered didn't fit with most foundations' emphasis on equity and access. Funders were recognizing that things needed to change. As a consequence, this group wanted to see a women's facility "up close." The sheriff, ever in search of funding and political connections, had responded to their interest by granting unusual unlimited access to the women's jail. The philanthropists were scheduled to tour the facility and talk to guards and incarcerated women, directly observing how detention operates. I'd been asked to offer what is called "context": information about women, gangs, and crime. I was also supposed to reinforce the fact that the jail was originally designed to "detain" individuals while they awaited trial. Detention wasn't incarceration, which occurred in the state and federal prison systems after trial. I knew that today's visitors often mixed up the two, an honest confusion they shared with most of the public. This confusion was further complicated by the current instability of California's overcrowded carceral system. With the exception of federal crimes, which are subject to an entirely different system, jails operated by city or county entities are supposed to serve as *pre-trial* facilities. Prisons, in turn, are *post-trial* facilities and are administered at the state level. But in California, many jails, including the one we're scheduled to visit, house individuals who are post-conviction and serving time. This is only the first of many complicated issues that will have to be explained during the tour.

We travel to the women's jail in South Los Angeles on a luxury bus, with the group scheduled to eat lunch while I talk. The tour organizer passes out boxed lunches, and everyone spreads themselves comfortably around the upholstered seating. We look like we could be traveling to the Napa Valley for a wine tasting instead of going to a detention facility.

As the participants eat, I offer an overview of the specific dilemmas that women face. I talk about the types of crime women are most frequently charged with (drug-related), their changing roles in gangs (more active), and the dramatically increasing numbers of women being incarcerated. The funders listen as the bus rolls along, moving south on the 110 freeway, bypassing the marginalized Los Angeles neighborhoods many of the women we're going to see call home. I pause to take questions while I wonder, *Wouldn't it be better if the funders could at least see the areas these women came from? To understand how their individual lives are intertwined with their communities? Is this group really going to grasp the inequities that lead to mass incarceration? Is anyone thinking about the voyeurism—going on a "field trip"—of privilege?* As my internal monologue runs on, the funders ask questions, mainly about the role girls and women play in gangs. This has captured their attention—I'm not sure why. It's probably easier to deal with women in the outside world, in the streets, rather than face the narrative that surrounds their incarceration and its aftermath.

Still, I can't let this go. I ask the group, "What do you think happens to women after incarceration? What's their place in the criminal justice landscape?" No one responds. Finally, one woman asks what programs exist for women caught up in the criminal justice system. We're nearing our destination as I briefly explain that for so long both girls and women have been "included" in or pasted on to male-focused community-based programs, without a thought for their own experience of criminal activity and gang membership, their own struggles, their specific needs. Instead, they continue to be the object of an all-purpose strategy, with programming that has been developed for men frequently reconfigured for women. And this lack of insight into the issues that women face begins with their detention—in an overcrowded, understaffed, and antiquated facility that everyone on the bus is about to see.

In the beginning, jails were designed to hold people *briefly* until they could secure bail or until they were tried and sentenced. Today, because of prison overcrowding, they have turned more or less into ad hoc prison facilities where a stay in jail might last "two days or two years."

There's a reason for these two extremes. Up to the present moment, individuals were usually kicked out immediately for lower-level crimes or due to what was termed a "DA reject"—based on a lack of enough evidence to hold them. However, if they were formally charged with a crime, bail would then be set. This was where the problems began.

The Los Angeles County Sheriff's Department currently operates the largest jail system in America—it is the twenty-fifth largest correctional institution in the world, consisting of seven separate facilities. Out of the more than twenty thousand individuals LA locks up on any given day, a little over two thousand are women, and the numbers are rising as part of a national trend. But what's more stunning is that almost half, 46 percent, of these women are in jail simply because they can't afford to post bail. They're locked up on what's categorized as "pretrial status," and the vast majority of these women, unlike Janeth, have *not* been accused of violent crimes. If they're mothers, their children can be taken away from them at this point and forced to enter the child welfare system and foster care, just because they can't make bail.

The remaining 54 percent—women no longer awaiting trial, who have cut a deal, or who have had their day in court—are still incarcerated in the Los Angeles County jail system because of a shift in public policy. In 2011, to address overcrowding in the state prison system, California voters passed Assembly Bill 109 (AB 109), which approved a practice known as "realignment." The bill didn't affect individuals who'd been convicted of serious offenses such as violent crimes—they stayed in prison. But individuals convicted of less serious felonies were diverted from state prison to county jails. The trouble with realignment was that jails were designed for detention, not incarceration, and these pretrial holding facilities assumed responsibilities they were never intended to fulfill. Now, with the women's jail hopelessly overcrowded, the Los Angeles County supervisors had to consider building more jails in outlying areas far from where families lived, instead of funding community-based alternatives to incarceration. As a result, women who couldn't afford bail or due to AB 109 were literally withering away in overcrowded, often violent settings for weeks on end, either awaiting trial in an equally overcrowded and understaffed court system or counting the days until their release.

But the problems didn't end there. At least one in ten of these women—this is a low estimate—didn't belong in jail or any kind of detention facility. These were women classified as suffering from a severe mental health condition. There were other unintended consequences of overcrowding: contagious illnesses and racialized violence. Additionally, in any given year there were at least 175,000 children who required county services because they had a parent who was incarcerated or on probation. This posed an additional strain on the Department of Children and Family Services as well as on the Probation Department and made absolutely no sense. This was why, as we embarked on our jail tour, one question circled round and round in my head: *Where was a pretrial release program?* How much better would things turn out for these women, their children, and their families if some sort of mental health diversion, some sort of family-strengthening effort, was funded instead of the county's gearing up to spend two to three billion dollars on a jail in the middle of nowhere?

It all felt so counterintuitive. In ever-expanding ways, the jails made women's problems worse. The majority of women in jail had encountered and been victims of violence throughout their lives. They didn't suffer the effects of an isolated incident—which was traumatic enough. Instead, most women who were locked up experienced an ongoing "relationship" with violence resulting from childhood abuse or domestic violence. Or both. And then they were confronted with more violence in jail.

I'm thinking about how to convey all of this to the group when we arrive at our destination, a standard-issue government building—nondescript, gray, and timeless. In reality, the jail was built in the 1950s, but it wasn't until 2006 that it was designated as a detention center exclusively for females. From the outside it doesn't look so much like a prison facility as a post office, its courtyard surrounding a centerpiece: an American flag whipping in the wind. Then, once inside the door everything changes. The group passes through the metal detector—sans purses, bags, tablets, cell phones, and laptop computers. All the accoutrements of our wired age are turned over. Once through the metal detector we navigate increasingly smaller, darker hallways—the finished walls give way to cinder blocks, the lighting becomes dimmer, the ceilings lower.

Today's visit is rigidly structured. Everyone is silent while we're divided into two groups. Already I feel trapped. It's not going to be possible for me to separate myself, to step outside, to leave early, to answer emails while I pretend to take notes on my laptop. Prison is the ultimate existentialist exercise. You're forced into the here and now with no escape. I keep thinking about one former gang member I've gotten to know well while working in the community, Donald "Twin" James. It's no coincidence that during his thirty-two-year stretch in San Quentin, Twin learned all the speaking parts in *Waiting for Godot* and read everything he could about Samuel Beckett.

I'm assigned to the first of two groups, led by Susan Burton. Because she operates one of the few reentry programs in California exclusively for women and is formerly incarcerated herself, Susan is more than a guide—she's the expert our group desperately needs. She promises to talk with us when the tour is over. In the meantime, a deputy sheriff appears to instruct us that we're supposed to move together as a group and follow the directions of the deputies within each area. Finally, we're admitted to the first cellblock area. It's small and strangely intimate. This isn't the grid layout of a maximum-security prison. Instead, there's a central desk and observation site on a raised platform in the middle of the room. The guards sit there, almost royal, perched on their Aeron chairs, watching the women. All around the observation desk, the women's individual cells rise up in tiers, almost like the seats in a concert hall. They are stacked in three vertical rows and form a semicircle facing the desk. The cells are behind thick doors with a window set at eye level in each door. We're on the unit where women who represent behavioral problems are isolated in single cells. "Is this solitary confinement?" one of the tour members asks and I nod while we're shushed by a guard who wants to talk to the group. She gives us a brief orientation—jail cell etiquette 101. We are not to touch anyone. We are not to reach through the bars. There is a subtext the guards are communicating to the group: *Remember, no matter what they look like, these women are dangerous, they are criminals, they can attack at any minute.*

As I approach the first woman I want to talk with, I look beyond the door. There are bars and behind them, the tiniest of all possible spaces, just enough for a small cloth cot and, six inches away from the cot, a metal toilet with sink on top of it. There is no floor space. It is beyond claustrophobic, beyond containment, beyond description. And it is dark. There are no signs of the sky. It could be eight in the morning or midnight—there is no sense of time. The dim light, somehow worse than darkness, feels oppressive. There is sweat everywhere—on the walls, on the women, on my body.

The women talk through the bars as if it's the most natural thing in the world. And their concerns are elemental. They need "sanis"—they don't have enough sanitary napkins. One woman is recovering from having given birth two days earlier and can't stop bleeding. They are sick. They haven't seen their children. They talk about things women everywhere on earth talk about. Their kids. Their men. Their women. Their longing to return home. Their periods, their aches and pains, their bodies, their feelings that they aren't attractive, that they are ugly. And they are hungry.

I'm an inveterate talker, but here words fail. The women keep talking to anyone who will listen. Again, and again, they talk of hunger. Withholding food is the most potent form of punishment the guards employ indiscriminately. We've already heard that when women misbehave or break the rules, their meals are stopped. Instead, they're fed two "jute" balls a day. One guard helpfully supplies a photo of what the jute balls look like—supersized non-meatballs that our group is assured possess all the daily calories and nutrients required for good nutrition.

I ask one of the women about this system of punishment.

"They get you for anything they want. Even if you talk back—they cite you. It can add days to your stay. You lose your visiting privileges. And you have to eat those balls. They're all the scraps left from the food they make. Like if you peel a carrot, the peel goes in a pile they use for the balls; you take the skin offa something, the skin goes in. Then they pack those balls together and freeze them. You gotta gnaw on the ball until it gets warm. I'd rather starve than eat that shit."

I'm thinking about a friend who feeds her cats broiled lamb chops for dinner. I feel like I'm going to throw up. The guards repeat their warning that this is the high-security area for the most difficult prisoners, even though all I see are deeply depressed women. Then, before we can have any more meaningful conversations, our group is moved to lower security, where the women actually walk around in the area outside of their cells, interacting with one another. Some of them work at jobs in other parts of the facility—in the laundry, in the kitchen. It is not lost on me that they're engaged in what is traditionally categorized as "women's work" inside as well as outside the jail walls.

Susan Burton moves through each of the low-security spaces and disobeys the rules, hugging women and talking to them in a low voice. The deputies ignore her while warning our group not to touch anyone. As we are looking—*not touching*—proof of overcrowding is unapologetically on display. Instead of a single cot, there's a three-level bunk in one tiny cell. Susan explains what she learned from being locked up multiple times: the top bunk is the most desirable; the bottom bunk is referred to as "the coffin." And even with three women to a tiny cell, there are additional three-level bunks set up outside the cells—all highly desirable because they're "out in the open."

Our tour group is led into a small area next to the low-security cells and organized into six smaller discussion groups with two detained women assigned to each. It's announced that this arrangement will allow us to talk more personally. It would be laughable if it wasn't so oppressive. There's no privacy—guards are stationed a few feet from us. As the women begin to share their experiences, everyone is aware that we're being carefully monitored. So much for the "unusual, unlimited access." In each group, the incarcerated women are talking, answering questions. But despite their carefully scripted accounts, their problems sound so complex, interrelated, and unsolvable. And they appear in multiples. There is a collective feeling of being overwhelmed.

I'm sitting next to a small, thin woman who looks straight ahead and pretends she's listening to another woman who's talking. Then she starts speaking to me, barely moving her mouth, and for a minute I feel like she's Edgar Bergen and I'm Charlie McCarthy. Her voice is so quiet that I strain to hear her.

"I'm not supposed to tell you stuff. They warned us about what we should say. We're not supposed to say anything bad about what's going on in here. We're supposed to talk about our crimes and how they're helping us to get ready for when we get out. But it's all bullshit. And the worst part is not knowin' what's gonna happen when we get out. I've been locked up three times. I got nothin' waitin' for me on the outside. I don't know where I'm gonna live. It's bad in here and it's even worse out there."

I quietly tell the woman that when she gets out, she should call UCLA information and ask for Jorja Leap.

"Can you remember that? 'Leap'?"

"Like leap year. I'll remember you. Don't forget me."

I reach out to hug her.

"I've gotta pretend I don't want you to hug me," she whispers, making a show of her rejection.

We're leaving and I'm the one with nothing to lose. She tries to push me away, but I hold her close.

The lead deputy barks that the tour is over, then adds, "Wait! There's one more part of your visit!" In an exercise that seems half public relations and half madness, our group is now guided into the deputies' roll call room to debrief us on the visit. And we're *still* not alone. Several sheriff's deputies sit in on the discussion.

After we find our seats, Susan Burton stands up in front of the shell-shocked group.

"I always cry when I leave here," she begins. "We need to do something for these women, for their children. Did you see any children's visiting areas in the jail?"

The group all shake their heads, "No," comes the answer, in unison.

"This is one of the worst things—it's not the only bad thing—but it's one of the worst. Do you know that none of these women get to see their children? And they haven't even been found guilty. The only thing they're guilty of is not having enough money for bail. We see poor women, Black women, women of color, women who can't afford to pay the rent, let alone bail out. And if they do get out—there's nothing waiting for them. Most of the time, by the time they get out, their children are gonna be gone—either staying with family or in the system. We have to stop this. Now. We gotta think about taking care of these women—while they're locked up and once they're out."

The group is listening, nodding and murmuring to one another about their next steps.

As she winds down, Susan is joined at the front of the room by a late arrival, the man invariably introduced as "the producer of the *Hangover* movies, Scott Budnick." Despite being in his early forties, he has the infectious energy of someone much younger. Scott appears everywhere—even at formal affairs—in dark-colored tennis shoes, his personal interactions often marked by the preoccupied attitude of an overactive child. But this lack of attention isn't in evidence when he's concentrating on the nonprofit organization he founded, the Anti-Recidivism Coalition (ARC), and when he is trying to help the young men who gather around him for support and guidance. After just a handful of years running ARC, Scott is now appearing in prisons alongside public figures like Richard Branson, who trumpeted via social media and at national convenings that Scott was one of his seven heroes (along with his mother and the Dalai Lama). Still, there's no denying Scott's passion. He is the *Hangover* franchise crossed with criminal justice reform. He can twist arms, schmooze, connect, raise money, and change social policy, sometimes all at the same time.

Scott is in rare form. Alongside Susan, he criticizes the deplorable conditions at the jail, announcing, "We're gonna do something about this." While Scott talks, one of the ARC members accompanying him, James Anderson, pops up next to me and grabs my elbow.

"Did you see those jute balls?"

"I'm still trying to figure out how they get away with calling that nutrition—"

James interrupts me.

"Scott and I are on it. We're getting rid of them."

Scott yields the floor to Susan, but I can't take my eyes off him. Despite the edict banning all electronic devices, Scott is tapping madly away on what appears to be an iPhone while James whispers in my ear, "He's texting the governor." It appears that Scott Budnick probably has a direct line to Jerry Brown, Barack Obama, and God himself. I am certain, in that moment, that if I walk into the jail kitchen I will see the jute balls magically disappearing into the trash can.

Susan tells the group that everything they've just observed today is a microcosm of what is occurring with women in jails and prisons throughout the country. Judging from their rapt attention and the expressions on their faces, every funder in the room has been affected by the women's stories and their needs. Yet, there's still no discussion of a path forward. And the issue of funding for women's programming remains unresolved. There is a great deal of work left to be done. And no one knows more about the deficit in action and the unaddressed needs of formerly and currently incarcerated women than Susan—Ms. Burton.

Susan Burton was born in Los Angeles, living first in an East LA housing project, Aliso Village. Alongside poverty, her childhood was punctuated by trauma, beginning with sexual abuse by her aunt's boyfriend when she was four years old, and a family life that was beyond dysfunctional. As she moved into adulthood, she swung between criminal behavior, mainly drug dealing, and conventional family life. But tragedy stopped the clock. In 1981, her five-year-old son was killed after being hit by a car, driven by an off-duty LAPD police officer. In the aftermath of the accident there was no prosecution, no public apology, no response to the trauma she'd endured. She didn't remember seeing LAPD chief Daryl Gates at the funeral, although her daughter Toni later told her he'd attended. After that, there was never any official response to ease her pain or address the tragedy that had occurred. Instead of therapy or religion, Susan turned to crack cocaine, smoking it and developing an addiction that landed her in jail and in prison. Worse yet, this kicked off a cycle of substance abuse and incarceration that endured for fifteen years.

In Burton's beautifully written memoir, *Becoming Ms. Burton*, she likens those years to moving through a "turnstile" she was powerless to escape. Finally, in 1997, Burton entered rehab at the CLARE Foundation in Santa Monica, a facility that largely served residents of the coastal communities that were predominantly white and affluent. Her friend Joe had recommended she try this program, and her brother Melvin had paid for her treatment. While in the process of ending her dependence on drugs, she experienced an awakening about the purpose of her life. Having struggled with the revolving door of incarceration, she became committed to helping other women reenter mainstream society once they left jail or prison. She also knew that women leaving incarceration needed more than a place to sleep—they needed the level of services she'd seen provided to the more privileged women on the west side of Los Angeles.

To fund her dream of providing such a haven, she worked as a live-in caregiver, saving the money necessary to buy a house in Watts. She maximized sleeping arrangements and turned her dining room into an office-bedroom, a layout that lent new meaning to the term "multi-use structure." She opened A New Way of Life in 1998 and never looked back. The house has always been full, and the waiting list is long.

By the time of the jail tour, Susan had already begun collecting the awards that accompanied this kind of commitment: she was named a Top 10 CNN Hero, received a Soros Fellowship, and accepted a Citizen Activist award from the Harvard Kennedy School. Two California governors, Arnold Schwarzenegger and Jerry Brown, appointed her to serve on state commissions on sentencing reform and gender-responsive strategies. She was, in short, a person with gravitas, whose impact on the treatment of women paralleled what Father Greg Boyle had accomplished for male gang members all over the world.

But right now, she wasn't interested in accolades. She was, as always, interested in change.

"Everyone ignores these women," she told the group. "Today that has to stop."

At that moment, I *knew* I wanted to understand what women caught up in the criminal justice system experienced. I knew their stories needed to be told, framed in terms of the issues they faced. I also knew there had to be a way to address their plight, to change their fate. I just wasn't sure what that might be.

THREE

PERSONAL STATEMENT

For a long time, I didn't tell anyone what happened—he told me no one would believe me. I knew he was right. Nobody would trust a little girl who said her father and her brother were molesting her. They'd say I was making it up. And I wasn't.

—DIONNA JEFFREYS

What I'd seen at the women's jail lingered within me for days afterward. I couldn't still the voice of the woman who'd whispered how bad things actually were at the facility. Her words, coupled with what I'd witnessed, had put me in a state of both intellectual and emotional dislocation. In the truest sense of the cliché, I was in unfamiliar territory. When I'd visited women in jail or prison before, I was always accompanied by an attorney and our meetings were held in interview rooms. We'd talked about their cases and how I might help. I only thought briefly what each woman confronted after I left; I was focused on their case, thinking about their judge and what I'd say as an expert witness. But up until the philanthropy field trip, I'd never actually seen the conditions incarcerated women were forced to endure.

My ignorance and inexperience were a microcosm of how much I didn't know about women and the criminal justice system. Up until this point, my work had focused on boys and men and the overwhelming problem of gang violence. I'd long wanted to understand why boys as young as ten or eleven years old had been driven to join gangs and risk spending their lives in prison, along with enduring the trauma of killing and the threat of being killed. It was if they had no agency, only despair—their violent fates were predetermined. As I learned about the twists and turns of their lives, I wanted to find out how any of these same boys and the men they became ultimately left gang life. I needed to understand how a small and steadily growing group of men had survived incarceration, returning to the communities they'd terrorized, struggling to reconnect with the children they'd been separated from, all while creating lives of purpose and meaning.

It wasn't that I'd completely ignored women as I navigated gang culture. In reality, I had grown close to several women who associated with gangs because of their families, the fathers of their children, and just their basic economic need. This had all occurred because, with the blessing and approval of G—Father Greg Boyle—I had the extraordinary experience of being embedded at Homeboy Industries for almost four years. I sat in G's office, "a fly on the wall," as he labeled me, watching how he applied his overarching philosophy of kinship in real time. I witnessed both the hard-won successes and the struggles the leadership staff faced trying to keep Homeboy running as they dealt with ongoing financial pressures. Alongside this work, I spent weeks sitting in the Homegirl Café, charting the lives of the women who worked there—the "waitresses with attitude," as G called them—recording their histories and learning about their children, boyfriends, families.

At the time, Homegirl had an exclusively female staff, and its approach combining employment and wraparound services had proved highly successful. Because of the ongoing struggle for more funding, its reach was confined to business hours. After work, an ad hoc support system existed among the women there, but it was not supported financially. Additionally, Homegirl could not meet one of the most critical needs formerly incarcerated women confronted: housing. This lack of housing was part of a vicious cycle trapping women into dependence on men, prostitution, substance misuse, drug dealing, and other criminal activity. There were "halfway houses" scattered throughout Los Angeles County where women could live once they exited prison. Yet, all too often, these so-called houses were set up to control, not rehabilitate, and offered little to no reentry services, leading to recidivism and more pain.

There were some reentry organizations that tried to help women as well as men dealing with life after incarceration. The problem was that, however well-intentioned, the programs that included women pretty much followed a "one size fits all" model—and the size was usually men's, extra-large. Most significantly, in retrofitting men's programs to include women, the role of children was rarely considered—and even when children were mentioned, they were more of an afterthought. Few reentry programs were specifically designed for women and their families. Homegirl struggled to respond to this problem, but it wasn't enough. It couldn't help all the women who'd finished serving their time, who were trying to reenter their families and their lives.

Now, to add to what I'd learned at the Homegirl Café, the trip on the bus had raised a new series of questions: What had these women endured? And how had they ended up entangled in the criminal justice system? Just as I'd once asked why men became deeply attached to gangs, I now needed to understand how women became involved with gangs and criminal activity. And more than anything, I wanted to grasp what happened to women after incarceration: How did they remake their lives? Or were they even able to remake their lives? The visit to the jail had only highlighted how much I didn't know.

I wasn't alone in my ignorance. While *Orange Is the New Black* was "flavor of the month" on HBO for a while, gaining critical acclaim and millions of viewers, the actual lived experiences of women who'd been incarcerated still received little attention from practitioners and policymakers. I didn't think that a one-day visit by philanthropists to a detention facility was going to change that. There might be a lot of handwringing and a series of declarations, but what exactly was going to happen to make the lives of these women any better? The only response to the increasing numbers of detained and incarcerated women was that the Los Angeles County Board of Supervisors was moving toward construction of a new county jail specifically for women, to the tune of approximately $1.2 billion to $1.5 billion. The ridiculousness of the cost was eclipsed by the insanity of where the jail was going to be constructed: in the middle of the city of Lancaster, over eighty miles from the neighborhoods of South Los Angeles County, where most women at risk for incarceration and their families lived.

These major policy concerns are crowded out of my attention when I call former homegirl and my unofficially adopted daughter Joanna Carillo, to see what's going on in her life. She tells me that a mutual acquaintance, Sonya, has been locked up for drug dealing; right now, Joanna's trying to get enough money together to bail Sonya out. I tell Joanna to come over to UCLA, and I'll give her $200. My husband goes to the ATM several times a week and silently adds cash to my wallet because he knows of my ongoing efforts to bail out the ocean of need with a bucket. I wonder if there is any hope of Joanna actually getting together the $5,000 that is needed. Uneasily, I shift my attention to the other part of my life, teaching.

In my office on campus, I'm trying to ignore what feels like my own version of multiple personality disorder. This morning, alongside my work partner Karrah Lompa, I've been spending time in Watts, meeting with local leaders, interviewing residents, and trying to get people the resources they need. Now, in the afternoon, I'm at UCLA, lecturing to undergraduates about the problems confronted by individuals enmeshed in dysfunctional systems. This is followed by office hours, where students sometimes want to discuss my least favorite part of the job: grades.

Most of these students are extraordinary people who care deeply about inequality and social justice; they make my life a joy. During office hours, I relish talking with them and never want them to leave. But it's the students in search of their A, who don't want to talk about learning, who drive me crazy. Today, the students have just received their midterm grades, making office hours an exercise in anger management (mine) until—in the midst of all the complaints about grades and the excuses about why they missed six classes in a row—a student appears who is neither obsequious nor maddening. She is strong, tough, defiant. I'm not sure how to react to her yet I know, in an instant, what thirty-seven years of teaching has equipped me to see. She is special.

Denise Marshall has already emailed me several times asking me questions about the course and social welfare. Still, I don't recognize her name—maybe because all I know is her email handle, China Girl. I later learn that this was her gang moniker as well. I can see why her name has endured—Denise is a beautiful Black woman with a dark, unblemished complexion and a small compact body, a little over five feet tall. She is dressed strikingly, wearing a scarlet blouse with nails to match. The minute she tells me her full name, I know she has been incarcerated. This isn't due to any sixth sense; it's because I serve on the faculty advisory board of a campus organization, the UCLA Underground Scholars Initiative. Founded by Danny Murillo at UC Berkeley, the group is composed of formerly incarcerated students devoted to helping one another navigate the challenges of undergraduate study. In this on-campus organization dominated by men, Denise is one of very few women who participates, consistently and vocally. She's clear about the depth of her struggles as a formerly incarcerated woman, writing about her experiences in a paper she submitted for my class. But this is the first time we have met in person.

Interacting with me, Denise is full of contradictions. She is warm yet guarded. The phrase she uses almost reflexively is "What do you mean by that?," delivered with the slightest edge. She's not going to be easy, and yet I welcome her attitude. I'm wary of students who either seek my approval or approach me with a playlist of a sycophant's greatest hits—flattery, hyperbole, you name it. Not Denise.

"I want to talk to you about your class," she tells me. "And I want to talk to you about graduate school."

"Okay . . . let's start with the class."

"I think there's a lot of fools in there. There are students, they don't have any idea about what it's really like out in the world." She leans in for emphasis, "You've got some students saying, 'There's discrimination here at UCLA.' Discrimination! Get the fuck out of here! What type of rock do you live under? You're so lucky to be here—we're all so lucky to be here. I know what discrimination feels like—I just couldn't articulate it. What UCLA has given me is the opportunity to learn. That's the start of change."

Denise barely stops to breathe.

"The students and even sometimes the administration—they worry so much about things that don't matter. I thought I wanted to get a master's and then a doctorate, but I don't know; there's just so much bullshit. I want to go on with school. I want to change my life. I just don't know if I can put up with all of this. I don't know if I want to."

The air is thick with Denise's hostility. I've seen students like her in the past, similarly full of anger and plans, who didn't follow through on anything they claimed they wanted to do. I calculate the depth of her recovery, her dedication, her ability to succeed at UCLA. It's my white privilege on parade and I check myself. I also know there's a deeper story here, but past failures have taught me to just shut the fuck up and allow Denise to tell her own story, at her own pace. Instead of asking about her background, I will wait. That information is for another day. For now, I cut to the future.

"I think you've got what it takes to succeed here, to graduate—"

"I know I do."

"Okay. So you will have to put up with the bullshit to get your degree."

At this, Denise starts laughing. "Okay."

"So, what do you want to know about graduate school?" I ask.

"I want my MSW. I know I want that."

"Why?"

"Because I want to help people—my people—the ones no one helps. The girls. The women who've been in prison. The men get everything. Why is that? The women need help too."

"What's your GPA?"

"A 3.9 since I got to UCLA. I've been in the honors program. I know I can do graduate school. Now are you gonna help me?"

"You gotta do what I say—and I will work to help you get in."

"Okay."

I wasn't making an empty promise and I wasn't going to have to ask any special favors to guarantee her admission to the MSW program. Denise was close to graduating UCLA with a very competitive GPA; the little I knew of her personal history would reinforce her already strong case for admission. But after setting up our next meeting, Denise had a parting shot. "I know you're trying to tell me I've got to understand your world. I don't know if you can understand my world. Unless you've been through it, you don't understand what it's like to try making your way in this world after living in that other world. Being here—it's like landing on the moon."

Denise and I meet several times in the weeks that follow. Slowly, her edgy wariness diminishes. She trusts me, to a point. She has to. As part of her graduate school application, she's knee deep in the daunting process of amassing her paperwork, her letters of recommendation, and the most difficult task of all, writing her personal statement. The more we talk, the more I'm convinced she has the makings of a social worker, combining intellectual talent with lived experience. "Lived experience"—how I hate that phrase. Is there such a thing as unlived experience?

I'm thinking about this as I drive to a community meeting being held at Dorsey High School in the aftermath of yet another school shooting. I'm traveling north on Crenshaw Boulevard, which crosscuts the Thirties, a series of residential streets beginning with Thirtieth Street. All around are the signs of slowly emerging urban development and gentrification: townhomes are under various stages of construction, and a new shopping center surrounds USC, a few blocks to the east.

But appearances are deceiving: this is Rollin' 30s gang territory in the city of Los Angeles. At a stoplight I peek at my phone and see an email from "China Girl," asking me to read her personal statement. If I believed in the paranormal, I'd swear Denise is psychic—I'm driving through the neighborhood where she grew up. When she came of age, the Rollin' 30s Crips were already notorious as a violent, multigenerational street gang claiming a membership of around seven hundred, broken into three major cliques. Things haven't changed. Even now, with its base of operations in South Los Angeles, the gang remains a target for the LAPD. Although tied in name to other Crips sets, this association never stopped the Rollin' 30s from engaging with their supposed allies in often lethal disputes, some of which raged for days in the surrounding streets during the 1980s and '90s. That was Denise's first exposure to gang violence.

The presence of the Rollin' 30s didn't shape Denise's childhood as much as the violence at home. Over the past few weeks, she's begun to open up, telling me she was the child of a relationship that was "troubled from the beginning; my father was abusive, and my mother wasn't strong." After her parents broke up, her mother married the man Denise still considers her father, explaining, "When I talk about my father, *that's* who I am referring to—my stepfather." The union endured for about ten years, until her stepfather began smoking crack, becoming a victim of the drug epidemic that was laying waste to the Black community in South Los Angeles in the late 1980s and 1990s. This community-wide tragedy came to play a specific role in Denise's family life—one with lasting impact.

"Around the time he started smoking crack, he just disappeared. Then my father's family—his mother, his two brothers, and his sister—all came from Alabama to stay with us. Their father had been a child molester. He molested all of his children, including my dad. That kind of trickled down because my uncle Marcus, my dad's brother, molested me and my sister."

I'm sad to say her account didn't surprise me. Based on nationwide data, the National Center for Victims of Crime reports that one in five girls is a victim of childhood sexual abuse. Due to shame, fear, and other factors, this number is most likely low, the incidence of sexual abuse underreported. So many victims of childhood sexual abuse want to forget whatever happened. Sometimes their families insist that they are lying. This conspiracy of silence affects the rest of these children's lives. And so many simply don't want to talk about it.

Not Denise. She described this traumatic turn of events matter-of-factly. I worried she was pushing her emotions away—so many women who'd experienced sexual abuse did. But while her story had similarities with the narratives of other women, it came with a slightly different twist.

"Uncle Marcus was a teenager. My sister and me were his first victims. It started when I was six or seven, and it stopped when I was eleven—that's when I told my mom. She went crazy because her family has a history of molestation. So, when it came out, it was a big ball of shit." Denise revealed everything to her mother because of "that stupid-ass commercial that said, 'If someone touches you in your private places, you need to tell somebody.'

"My mom told my grandmother, who was absolutely devastated. I was a minor and he was a minor, and things could happen—we could get taken away." Any involvement with the child welfare system was to be avoided at all costs. Her mother forbade her to discuss Uncle Marcus with outsiders. There was no one Denise could turn to. And there was nowhere she felt safe. In school, Denise was a "fuck-up from day one." She says, "I ditched all the time. I didn't like school—it wasn't challenging. The teachers were mainly babysitters."

She was just an eleven-year-old, "trying to put it all together—the shit with my mom, my dad, not really being able to figure out why the hell my dad disappeared; being sexually aroused and not knowing what to do with that. I was a mess."

Denise couldn't concentrate and was failing her classes. It was apparent something beyond academic difficulties was in play. In the midst of all the trauma and the toxic stress it engendered, one teacher tried to help her. "I can't remember what his name was," Denise told me. "I wish I could thank him." He gave Denise a glimmer of hope, offering to take her home to stay with his family if she was having problems. Ultimately nothing changed. I'd heard stories like this, classroom teachers who cared deeply for their students. But, all too often, no one from the ironically named Children's Protective Services connected the dots. Why didn't someone intervene to help place Denise in a better situation? I instinctively knew the answer. The child welfare system was frequently as much a source of trauma as the family.

Ultimately, Uncle Marcus disappeared, and the family moved forward as if nothing had happened. This silence blocked any conventional pathways to healing, and Denise's problems multiplied. Her sister, who was three years older, internalized the molestation both girls had experienced at the hands of Uncle Marcus: she began molesting Denise as well. At the same time, after multiple absences, academic failures, and acting out in the classroom, Denise was expelled from the neighborhood school she'd attended since kindergarten and wound up being bused to junior high school, then high school, an hour away in the San Fernando valley. In the meantime, the family moved from the Thirties to Inglewood. It was here that Denise's life changed drastically.

It's hard to describe what Inglewood was like in the 1980s. It had transitioned from a small, predominately middle-class community in South Los Angeles to ground zero for gangs. The houses, once tidy with rose bushes and green lawns, now sold crack and sheltered teenagers active in the world of guns, drugs, and prostitution. Denise was one of those teenagers. She joined a hood at the height of the gang violence epidemic in Los Angeles. Three decades later, in 2018, there were fewer than 300 homicides a year, 259—still too many. But in 1989, the year Denise turned thirteen, the city of Los Angeles and its nearby areas recorded over 1,200 homicides, many of them gang related. It was a violent place in a violent time, and Denise Marshall was, in her own words, "off the chain."

"When I was a little girl and we lived in the Thirties, I was already attracted to gangs—they did shit that I didn't do, and I wanted to join. The neighbor who'd babysit me was an active member with the Rollin' 30s. I admired her because she was always dressed nice. Like, Gucci outfits and the fly-ass hair. It's all I could see. Later, I also realized that she did drugs with my mom and dad—they'd party together."

Denise's desire to join the Rollin' 30s was short-circuited when the family moved to Inglewood. Instead, she joined the Imperial Village Crips, a Black gang operating in the streets that bisected the Imperial Highway. Today, they're recognized as a Crips gang that has endured in Inglewood, well known for their connection to Tupac Shakur. One of their high-profile homies, Big Syke, was part of the rap group Thug Life, founded by Tupac. "We were Inglewatts," Denise explained, and I knew just what she meant. Because Inglewood was dominated by the Bloods, her hood wanted to reinforce its alliance with the Watts-based Crips and their leadership.

I understood the gang alliances and beyond that, I felt a strange sort of kinship with Denise. The streets she mentioned, the territory she mapped, were as familiar to me as the lines in my palms. It was the community where I was born in a Catholic hospital across the street from Inglewood cemetery. It was where I'd grown up, in the heart of my extended Greek family, twenty years before Denise. My family had moved away, but in the end Watts had called me back. It was where I'd returned while in graduate school and then after that, first as a social worker, later training newly hired social workers, and finally as a community-based researcher and activist. It's an understatement to say that Denise's experience was different from mine: she had not been part of Inglewatts through a privileged life; she was there because it was her hood.

The reasons she joined the gang were all too familiar. After her stepfather left and after Uncle Marcus had also disappeared, her mother's new boyfriend molested Denise. When Denise disclosed what happened, her mother called the Los Angeles County Department of Children and Family Services. A social worker arrived, picked up Denise, and placed her in foster care. She immediately ran away—right back home to her mother. There was no follow-up.

This happened more often than not, back in the day when DCFS workers' responsibilities stretched to the point of absurdity, with caseloads consisting of as many as eighty families. There was absolutely no way for children's social workers to track what was going on when they were carrying caseloads of that size. But returning home didn't mean the family was joyfully reunited. Denise and her mother were "physically fighting by this point. She would put me out and I would be walking down the street in boxer shorts and a T-shirt and no shoes. That was my mother. She put me out of the house. On. The. Street."

Denise had started telling me about her involvement with her hood and crime over several afternoons, talking in my office. Today was different. Today was about her need for her mother and the pain that created. She paused and looked away, out the window. Both of us were crying, tears streaking Denise's face. We agreed it was time to stop.

The personal and environmental violence so many incarcerated women encounter from childhood on deeply affects both their emotional and social development, shaping the trajectory of their lives. Prior to incarceration, from the time they are girls, women are frequently subjected to multiple adverse factors, among which the most notable is the exposure to ongoing threats and constant violence. There is no respite from the violence, and for many girls and women, no respite from the violation of their bodies. You don't need an advanced degree to intuit that this ever-present exposure to negative and frightening experiences results in long-term consequences for women's mental and physical health.

In recent years, psychologists and physicians have begun to examine "adverse childhood experiences"—ACEs—and how they affect child development. More specifically, research focuses on how harmful childhood experiences negatively affect a child as she develops. Dr. Vincent Felitti created the ACEs scale, which measures ten types of childhood trauma; these describe the experiences of most of the women I have gotten to know. Five types of ACEs are personal: sexual abuse, physical abuse, verbal abuse, physical neglect, and emotional neglect. Five concern family members: a parent who is an alcoholic or addict; a mother who is a victim of domestic violence; a family member who is incarcerated; a family member diagnosed with mental illness; and loss of a parent through divorce, death, or abandonment. Each of these ten types count as one experience and a total of four appears to be a kind of threshold. One researcher, Christine White, explains that "compared with someone who has an ACE score of zero, a person with an ACE score of 4 or more is twice as likely to have heart disease and cancer, seven times more likely to be addicted to alcohol, and twelve times more likely to attempt suicide."[1]

Building on the work of Felitti, White, and several others, the pediatrician Nadine Burke Harris has connected adverse childhood events to what she labels "toxic stress"—the chemical, psychological, and neurodevelopmental response to child abuse and violence that has deep and perceptible consequences for brain development. How does this all happen?

The brain's natural ability to be alert to danger is necessary to human survival. But this is not the same as toxic stress. I value how Burke broke down toxic stress when she talked with Ira Glass on his radio show, *This American Life*: "If you're in a forest and see a bear, a very efficient fight or flight system instantly floods your body with adrenaline and cortisol and shuts off the thinking portion of your brain that would stop to consider other options. This is very helpful if you're in a forest and you need to run from a bear. The problem is when that bear comes home from the bar every night."[2]

For a person who has suffered childhood trauma and toxic stress, the brain trains itself to be on alert all the time. According to Harris, the brain's alarm system, the amygdala, actually increases in size and may be activated more often during traumatic experiences; what scientists refer to as "the architecture of the brain" is literally changed. After repeatedly responding to threat, the brain doesn't know how to differentiate between a real and an imagined threat. Alongside this "high alert" status, children and adults suffer with stress dysregulation: they're uncomfortable in their own bodies and relive this feeling through impulsive and aggressive behavior. This dysregulation haunts individuals throughout their lives.

Susan Burton ruefully reports, "I aced the ACEs—I've got a score of ten—and that's one test I didn't want to pass." As I listen to Denise's story, I feel certain that if someone administered the ACEs scale to her she too would probably score a perfect ten. While much of her experience is unique, in other ways, she wouldn't be alone. Every woman I know has either experienced toxic stress or knows someone who experienced it because of sexual abuse or harassment.

I keep thinking of Ernestine or "Thea Ernie," my father's sister, who was my beloved aunt. We didn't really develop any sort of relationship until late in her life, when she was fighting the cancer that was over-taking her body. I'd always worshipped her. There was *something* about Thea Ernie. She was strong and sexual—she appeared in a television documentary about menopause where she explained that she was deal-ing with hot flashes by learning to belly dance. By the time she died, she'd outlived five husbands—and her fifth had been over a decade younger than she. Yet, several months before she died, this beautiful, tough woman broke down over lunch, swore me to silence, and then told me how a family friend had fondled her on the "back porch of Dunsmuir Street," the house where she and my father and their sister and brother had grown up. "Everyone thought he was so good, so kind. No one knew he trapped me back there and felt my breasts and stuck his tongue in my mouth. Then he told me it was our little secret, to keep it between us."

When she told me this story, she was eighty-four years old and had carried this "little secret" with her for seventy years. "I thought about telling Mama, but I knew it would break her heart. I decided I just wouldn't talk, I'd just keep going." I asked if I could tell her story when I wrote about other women who'd experienced sexual abuse and she told me, "If it helps someone, go right ahead, you should!" adding, "Just don't tell anyone who it was."

There's something in Denise that reminds me of Thea Ernie. Her toughness and resilience shine through, even as she describes something brutally heartbreaking. Denise and Thea Ernie both possessed the same hopeful determination. As we are saying good-bye, I tell her that.

"Well, maybe I got your aunt's spirit in me," Denise says, smiling.

"She would have loved you. She would have wanted to mother you. It was sad, she never had kids of her own."

"I hear that," Denise tells me. She looks at me carefully. "I'm trying to decide if I should tell you something."

I am silent.

"I want to have a baby."

INTERLUDE

While Janeth is locked up, Ivy and Pedro remain at large. The Los Angeles City Council is offering a $50,000 reward for "information leading to the identification and arrest of the persons responsible for the murder of Andres Ordonez." Rewards like this are rarely offered in local homicide cases, but these were unusual circumstances and, as the motion noted, "What happened to Mr. Ordonez was an especially disturbing crime."

In the meantime, Elie has uncovered more details surrounding the LAPD investigation. "This doesn't look so good," she warns me before sharing the most damaging information. Evidently, gang detectives from Rampart Division arrived on the scene soon after the shooting and recovered three shells that could be traced to a semiautomatic weapon, along with a spray-paint can near the curb. Janeth's fingerprints and DNA were on the can. The detectives also picked up a broken beer bottle from the gutter close to the spray-paint can, and this had Ivy's fingerprints and DNA. On top of that, graffiti on the wall included three names: Wicked, Looney, and Ivy, along with the words "Fuck Tampax"—"Tampax" being code for the Temple Street gang.

Elie is right, none of this looks good. The rumors are flying that Pedro and Ivy have gone to Mexico in Ivy's BMW. Then a homie tells me that Pedro forced Ivy at gunpoint to sell the BMW to finance their escape. The women in the café are worried about what Pedro is doing to Ivy now. "He used to beat her, and we knew it," Carla, a young homegirl, tells me. "Pedro was mean, we kept telling her to leave. Ivy didn't want to, she thought she needed him. Ivy acted strong but she really didn't think she could make it without a man. She hadn't learned she was beautiful, just alone, without anyone." I'm thinking about what Carla said and what kind of trauma would keep her tied to Pedro. And I wonder if the couple will disappear permanently in Mexico. Elie doesn't think so. "Trust me," she says quietly. "They're going to find them."

FOUR

I DIDN'T HAVE ANY TEARS

The one person that I thought really cared about me and was supposed to nurture me and make sure I was safe was my mom, and she wasn't there. So why would some stranger care about me if my mom never did?

—EVELYN LOPEZ

As my eighty-nine-year-old mother deteriorates in the grip of age and dementia, I think a great deal about our relationship, a bond that has been both caring and troubled. As with all human connections that are uneasy, part of this is her responsibility and part of it mine. She sometimes drifts into my thoughts after I listen to formerly incarcerated women talk about their mothers. While describing the passage through youth to adulthood, nearly all of the women talk about their struggles trying to find some kind of meaningful connection with their mothers. And yet, they also recall how their mothers failed them—their experiences of betrayal and rejection often turning into expressions of anger and despair. But there is one common theme that weaves in and out of these accounts: their feelings of abandonment and their unvanquished longing for their mother's love.

Interestingly, I hear very little about fathers in their stories. For most of these women, while they were growing up, their fathers were altogether absent—victims of the new Jim Crow, many incarcerated for decades, a handful for life. Some came to know their fathers in adulthood, while others never knew who their father was. Sonya, who had cycled in and out of prison for fifteen years, ruefully explained, "My mother was a whore, and I don't know who my father was. She told me she was sure it was her pimp because I look like him. I don't know if she said that to make me feel better." For most of the women I spend time with, their fathers were offstage and did not loom as large in their lives as their mothers.

As they dealt with their feelings of abandonment and loss, some women decided to cut off all contact with their mothers. Others reported relief that their mothers had died, while a small number remained attached, even taking care of the mothers who had once abandoned them. But repeatedly, there was the unanswered need for love and approval in the mix. In turn, these deep-seated feelings affected their life trajectories. After listening to these stories of love and longing and the major role they've played in formerly incarcerated women's lives, it's surprising that there's been very little research on the impact of the mother-daughter relationship on women's pathways into the carceral system. The lack of knowledge surrounding women's relationships with their mothers forms a significant part of the attention deficit surrounding the journeys and needs of women reentering life after incarceration. It also is yet another difference in understanding the lives of formerly incarcerated women and men.

In recent years, a great deal of attention has focused on what has been termed "the father wound" and how this often acts as a precursor to boys becoming involved with gangs and ultimately ending up in the criminal justice system. Researchers have studied the impact of father loss on individual development, especially for young males, with studies revealing a heightened risk of psychiatric disorders; problems with reasoning, processing, and memory; and overall long-lasting effects. These studies have also found that the younger the individuals, particularly boys, the more severe the impact of the father loss. But most significantly, research has shown that the impact of father absence is greater for young men than for young women. The National Institutes of Health have weighed in and reinforced the existence of this gender-based difference, observing that the effects of father loss have been shown to be stronger in boys than girls. Even I'd been swayed by this emphasis: my own research had examined how the lack of a father figure deeply affects young men, shaping their identity and activating their search for a substitute father in gang life.[1]

The absent father, the missing father, the father who wove in and out of a son's life was a source of sorrow, rage, and ultimately often criminal activity. Aside from my research, I'd learned this lesson first-hand in Watts when I co-facilitated a men's group through the Project Fatherhood program. My experiences with the formerly incarcerated men who formed that group eventually became a book that contributed to the growing literature on the impact of absent fathers. The men in the group, like the men I'd gotten to know at Homeboy Industries, idealized their mothers while at the same time working through their feelings of loss and anger at their fathers. Now I was discovering how most of the women I was talking with expressed similar feelings toward their mothers. They even used words that echoed the men's feelings toward their fathers: they felt alone, they needed a role model, they needed someone to nurture them, to show them how to be women. Where was their mother? They also lamented how their mother was supposed to protect them and didn't, particularly when it came to shielding them from physical and sexual abuse. But instead of openly expressing rage, as the men had felt comfortable doing toward their fathers, women repressed their anger, which was frequently eclipsed by feelings of responsibility. Conflicting life histories emerged: while boys ran in the streets, girls frequently became "little women," taking the place of mothers in their families. There was a price for all this. Years later, the deep sadness of their lives floats in a reservoir of unexpressed rage.

Little attention has been paid to the "mother wound" and how so many young women were forced to fulfill an adult role while longing for the mother who simply wasn't there. There were even a handful of formerly incarcerated women who experienced the extreme: their mothers not only failed to fulfill the maternal role; they actually exploited their own daughters. Some looked the other way when boyfriends or family members molested their daughters. And there were other maternal failures, maybe not as excessive, that still had deep implications for their little girls once they grew up. As these mothers struggled and often failed to fulfill what was required, their daughters stepped into their mother's role. They became the de facto parents, describing lives in which they never experienced a childhood. Their life histories were individually unique, but no matter who the woman was, no matter her color or her crime, there was one experience the majority of formerly incarcerated women shared: they functioned as adults early in life, most frequently taking on the roles and responsibilities of their mothers. I thought of Denise, of Joanna—both women I had come to know and love. Long before any of these women were adults, each had to fulfill parental roles and responsibilities in a destabilized family system, taking care of parents as well as children.

This dynamic is often referred to as "parentification." Most people are aware of the process of parentification without knowing the exact terminology. I was no exception. Growing up, I never understood the division of labor at my friend Mandy Lewis's house. While we played Barbies in her bedroom, it seemed like her mother spent a lot of time in bed. Her father was never around. And whatever the circumstances, Mandy invariably had to put her Barbie away right at five o'clock to cook dinner and make sure her younger sister and brother were doing their homework. Watching all of this, I was torn between admiration and discomfort. Mandy Lewis's mother wasn't majoring in incompetence, I now realize. She was probably chronically depressed as well as alcoholic. But this was the early 1960s, before therapy, before chemical imbalances, rehab, and recovery became part of reality TV and daily experience. Back in the day, when women retreated from the family, a child—usually a daughter—was left to pick up the slack.

My family moved to another neighborhood, yet I often wondered how Mandy was doing. I intuitively knew it was somehow wrong that as a little girl she was forced to take on adult responsibilities. Later, in graduate school, I learned the formal explanation for the process of parentification, how children literally pushed away their own needs to care for their parent and their siblings. The "psychopathology" texts we used—how I hated that word—said that parentification usually occurred in "disorganized family systems." This made me uncomfortable. Intuitively I knew that blaming the family didn't always make sense. As a young social worker in South Los Angeles, I saw that parentification took place in completely functional families that were economically and structurally pressured to the max. In these families, the parents were not dysfunctional or mentally ill; they were simply poor. The parent or parents were holding down two or three jobs, just trying to meet the rising costs of living, determined not to apply for welfare and live "on the county." The single-parent families, usually headed by mothers, faced the biggest economic obstacles. One parent was the only source of economic and emotional support. Whatever the configuration, the parents were loving and responsible, yet they were strung out over the economic needs of the day. Still later in my personal life, I got an up-close and personal look at the wounds of parentification when I began to understand just what my husband had encountered growing up with an alcoholic mother. He was completely parentified and early in our marriage tried taking responsibility for the fate of everyone in our household. He was a deputy chief in the LAPD, and his professional life reinforced his need to control every situation. None of this boded well for our marriage or our daughter, but we were a middle-class couple who could go to therapy; the economic wolf was not at the door. Our family dynamics might have been difficult; still, we faced what our daughter called "first-world problems."

This was not the case for the women getting out of jail or prison. Along with their trauma and their feelings of abandonment, many were parentified. While conducting a case study of women at A New Way of Life, I had found that the most universal experience for women who entered Susan Burton's program was the parentification that occurred during their childhood. Literally every woman interviewed talked about fulfilling a parental role in relation to one or more family members, from young siblings to extended family. And in these women's lives, parentification wasn't a matter of taking on household duties while a parent or parents worked. They weren't just babysitting or preparing meals. The women all felt they had to protect the sisters, brothers, and family members they cared about; some placed themselves in harm's way, trying to intervene in partner violence and child abuse. Others worked to help support their families financially.

For someone like Denise, all of these demands colliding at once was not unusual. She was practically the walking, talking embodiment of the parentified child. As her mother drifted into relationships and breakups, Denise was invariably the one holding things together because "my mother just wasn't there. I wanted her to take care of us, but she just didn't or couldn't. To this day, I don't know why." When her sister became pregnant, her mother didn't respond to the situation, and Denise knew what she had to do. "I turned my first trick to get money for my sister's abortion," she told me matter-of-factly. There was a problem, and she found a solution.

Denise's problem-solving was extreme and tragic, but in this she wasn't an exception. So many of these women have been intuitively parental and protective of their siblings, as well as of their parents. This doesn't end with the onset of actual adulthood. Once these children who have been functioning as parents grow up and make their way in the world, they feel guilty trying to save themselves; they continue to focus on and prioritize the needs of others. What results is a particularly potent form of survivor's guilt. These women are never able to mourn the loss of their childhood. Instead, they remain literally trapped in a cycle of taking responsibility for others, with no time or space for themselves.

The results of emerging research in this area were disturbing: parentified children were at a high risk for developing mental health and substance abuse issues. Researchers also concluded that these children developed a strong internal locus of control—they continue to feel responsible up until adulthood for both their family and the conditions that created their parentification.[2] On top of that, the women I was studying faced yet another conundrum: how did they react to the external control exerted over their lives both during and after incarceration? Their loss of autonomy was directly counter to the responsibility they had shouldered throughout their lives; they had gone from controlling literally everything to controlling nothing. There was so much to factor in to fully understand their struggles. It felt like everywhere formerly incarcerated women turned, they faced another stressor. Along with poverty, ACEs, and trauma, there was also the impact of parentification. *How on earth did anyone survive?*

As if this wasn't complicated enough, formerly incarcerated women had to find a way to cope with their feelings of abandonment, most frequently alongside the wounds of parentification. After cycling in and out of jail for over a decade, Anika Johnson was in recovery and putting her life together. She was now in her early forties, had given birth to three children, and had functioned as a single parent from the time she was sixteen. Her only outlet was drugs, men, and criminal activity. And because, as she told me, "I gotta admit, I really never had a real childhood—I had trouble growin' up, because there was no time to grow up." Even now, she still longed for her mother to come and take care of her. "My mother just wasn't there," she explained. "I was raised by my grandmother and my auntie helped out. Now I know, it was really my grandmother who brought me up, and if she couldn't always be around watchin' me, I know she tried the best she could." Her testimony to grandparental devotion left out one important fact. While raising Anika, her grandmother ran one of the biggest and most notorious dope houses in South LA. When I asked what drugs her grandmother trafficked in, she laughed and told me, "Everything." It was the only life Anika knew, and she accepted it. But what Anika couldn't accept was her missing-in-action mother. "I never really knew my mother—she'd come around for a few days, then she'd be off with a boyfriend, doing crack, gambling, going to clubs. I wonder how I would have turned out if she'd been around. Sometimes I still wish she was with me even now. She's dead. Sometimes I still dream she comes home to me."

The absence of a mother is the hole in their heart these women want to fill. *Most significantly, many formerly incarcerated women feel emotionally abandoned by their mothers. So many still seek their mother's love—setting them up for a cycle of more pain.* Some women tried to rationalize their mother's abandonment, often with little success. Anika told me, "I knew my mother loved me, but she had me too young. Sometimes I do think, if she had this baby, why didn't she stay with me? She just dumped me with my grandmother." Another woman, Estella, told me, "My mother was never there when I was growing up." Yet, she insisted, "I'm trying to forgive her—even now I still want her in my life." Many women understood that their mothers were trying to cope with their own issues—trauma, poverty, and substance abuse. The problem was, whatever had caused their abandonment by their mothers, that loss meant that there was no space for their daughters to develop a secure sense of self or a stable identity.

I knew that the earliest trauma both Ivy and Janeth had experienced occurred because their mothers had abandoned them. Ivy's father and mother were both drug addicts raising two children in a chaotic household where Ivy had matured beyond her years by the time she was five years old. Her family wasn't stable; she lived in a party house where substance abuse and drug dealing were the order of the day. By the time she turned thirteen, her father was long gone, signing off on a divorce and completely disappearing. Her mother was lost to the streets, addicted to cocaine and slipped back and forth between drug dealing and prostitution. While her mother was gone for days at a time, Ivy felt responsible for her brother, Guillermo, and developed a deep bond with him. Still, even this could not heal the trauma she'd experienced, and she began to self-medicate, developing an emotional and physical dependence on drugs. Still, even as Ivy struggled, she always held out hope that her mother would get clean, settle down, and take care of the family. But there was no mother to take care of her children and Ivy and Guillermo both became increasingly caught up with gangbanging, drugs, and partying. Ivy was a child of the hood, absent from school, high on cocaine, kicking it with her homies. By her sixteenth birthday, she was constantly using drugs and committing petty theft to support her habit. There was no one to take care of her and, like so many other women, she found her way into an abusive relationship where she stayed trapped for eight years, because she had nowhere else to go. The mother she hoped would someday return finally died, and Ivy felt she'd lost her hope forever.

Unlike Ivy, Janeth never nurtured any dream of seeing her mother again. Growing up in Mexico, she'd never known her father, and even there, her mother was in and out of her life, focused mainly on using and dealing drugs. Instead, Janeth's strongest support came from her aunt, her mother's sister, who truly loved her and helped to take care of her as she grew up. However, she was forced to leave her aunt's care when she was ten. Her mother had turned up and announced she'd decided to cross the border into California illegally. She insisted that Janeth and her two brothers come with her, promising them that life would be better in Los Angeles. Frightened to leave her aunt and the only family she'd ever really known, Janeth didn't trust her mother's words, and her misgivings soon proved true.

Life was hard, and expensive, in LA, and the family scraped by on money made from drug dealing, with much of the earnings used to feed her mother's addiction. Janeth had trouble in school; she was hungry, she was frightened, and she could barely speak English. She began acting out, disrupting class and getting into fights. Ultimately, she wound up in Central Juvenile Hall, detained for a few nights until she was released to her mother's care. Soon after that, she was assigned to a school-based probation officer who had little interest in her struggles or her attendance at school. The streets were calling and Janeth was rarely at home, cycling through Juvenile Hall on low-level charges such as being out past curfew.

Meanwhile, her mother's drug dealing activities soon attracted the attention of law enforcement. Once her undocumented status was discovered, US Immigration and Customs Enforcement (ICE) got involved, and days later Janeth's mother was deported back to Mexico with the two boys—but not Janeth. She returned from spending a couple of nights with her new boyfriend, Luis, and the apartment was empty. In that moment she realized she was on her own. Her family was gone, without even leaving a note. She was sixteen years old and undocumented and had to avoid any authorities or she'd be deported. She managed to call her aunt, who urged her to come home to Mexico. But her aunt had children of her own and barely enough money to take care of them, and Janeth didn't want to be a burden. For Janeth, there really was no choice. She turned to Luis and his gang, Rockwood, and they became her family; Luis's mother, Myra, took her in, and she had a place to live. The situation was not ideal—Luis could be cruel. Still, he understood what frightened Janeth: he and his brother were undocumented as well. "I knew he'd take care of me," she told Erika at the café. A few years later, she learned that her mother had been killed in Mexico; the homegirls whispered to me that "it had something to do with the cartel." Both Ivy and Janeth were motherless; this loss had marked their lives.

Despite abandonment and the trauma caused by their mothers that so many of the women I knew had experienced, I *still* was finding that there was almost no research focusing on how mothers impact the development and identity of their daughters who either are or have been incarcerated. Instead, the studies that do exist examined one facet of this topic: the relationship between women and their mothers when they serve as surrogate parents for grandchildren while their daughter is incarcerated. One pilot investigation focused on how positive co-parenting relationships between incarcerated mothers and maternal grandmothers translated to children experiencing fewer "externalizing behavior problems."[3] Other research discussed how incarcerated women experience interrelated feelings of gratitude for and jealousy of the bond that developed between their mothers and their offspring.[4] Aside from these studies, there appeared to be no other research exploring the emotional complexities that arise between formerly incarcerated women and their mothers. I kept reviewing what had been written, trying to uncover the hypotheses, the data, the empirical findings. And I kept coming up empty-handed.

But still, after whatever research I'd read and whatever stories of parentification and maternal abandonment I'd heard, nothing prepared me for Rosa Lucero. We connected at Loyola Law School's annual conference about life in a gang, "Guilt by Association." This event was the brainchild of Sean Kennedy, who, along with heading up Loyola's Center for Juvenile Law and Policy, championed the need to understand the nexus between gangs, criminal activity, and trauma. Every year in Los Angeles, he created a space for professionals and formerly incarcerated individuals to examine how these forces all fit together and affected one another. This year, the conference included a focus on "Women, Female-Identifying People, Gangs and Trauma." I was part of a panel along with a female gang interventionist, and the main speaker, who was a female former gang member. That was Rosa. Standing in front of a room filled with lawyers and law school students, she quietly detailed what had happened to her, something far beyond "lived experience." The more accurate words to describe Rosa's life can be found in the reports of Amnesty International: torture, imprisonment, and, at the very least, a profound violation of human rights. The room was silent when she finished. The gratitude and admiration of everyone present was boundless.

I'd first met Rosa during my research at Homeboy Industries. She was being mentored by one of the senior staff and working as her administrative assistant, helping in the front office. She never worked at the Homegirl Café, and her stint in the office didn't last long. After a few weeks, Rosa flunked her drug test and faced Homeboy's zero tolerance policy. There were immediate consequences for using. Instead of firing people, trainees who "tested dirty" were told they could return to Homeboy once they completed rehab. Some refused, but most enrolled in treatment. After she relapsed, Rosa went to Royal Palms, the rehab facility that had a contract with Homeboy and treated trainees for free. I lost track of her once she left.

This had all occurred a decade ago, before anyone understood that Rosa's substance abuse at Homeboy was part of a bigger problem. This was neither Homeboy's flaw nor its responsibility. In its early years, Father Greg Boyle led an agency that worked to replace the despair that led to gang membership with hope and pro-social activities. Homeboy's priority had been employment training and job placement, reflecting its mantra, "Nothing Stops a Bullet Like a Job." That was the whole idea that gave birth to the "Industries" in its name—a logical focus for what rapidly became the largest program for individuals seeking to leave gang life in the country. The need for jobs was reinforced in many sectors. I climbed on to the bandwagon as well. Whenever I talked about my community-based research designed to understand how men (and later, women) navigate the process of reentering mainstream society after incarceration, most people assumed that the answer could be found in employment. Repeatedly, I'd be told, "Those people need jobs." While there was a partial truth to this reentry prescription, "those people" also needed to address the trauma that landed them in jail or prison in the first place. And the unaddressed trauma continued to affect formerly incarcerated women—even if they successfully confronted some of the obstacles facing them when they reentered their lives. They may have jobs, they may have housing, they may be trying to raise their children and create a home with a spouse or a partner, but always, lurking in the background, lies the trauma.

Ironically, Father Greg Boyle was among the first to realize the critical need to deal with the trauma these men and women had experienced; a job alone could neither facilitate nor guarantee their recovery. This was the reason so many homies and homegirls relapsed: *their underlying trauma had never been addressed and treated. There were never any resources available to them. No one was even talking about trauma.* This was particularly true for formerly incarcerated women, who were often labeled "unstable" or "emotional" or—stupidly—"hormonal." Their behavior wasn't "hormonal." It was the result of trauma, trauma with its roots in the places where women should have found sanctuary: their homes and families. What G discovered at Homeboy was also being confirmed in other criminal justice sectors. Right around this time, the groundbreaking research on the impact of childhood trauma was emerging, shining a light on the impact of adverse childhood experiences.

Alongside these developments, lawyers were lasering in on trauma and its meaning for the entire criminal justice industrial complex. The focus on trauma at the Loyola conference was not a one-off; similar convenings were occurring across the US. A few weeks earlier, I'd been at a conference in Miami, presenting on the significance of trauma in capital cases and sentencing mitigation. But much of that discussion was theoretical; Rosa's narrative offered something completely different: it cut through concepts, with a story that was deeply personal and, for most of us, unimaginable.

Rosa and I connected a few weeks after the conference. We agreed to talk at a coffee house after she texted me, "If you come over to my house my kids will literally scare you and we won't be able to focus on anything. LOL."

We meet up at Terra Mia, a coffee house in Lynwood a few blocks east of the Los Angeles County women's jail. Rosa is beautiful. Small and thin, she wears a sundress and walks with a purposeful stride. Ordering coffee, we make small talk, discussing her interest in learning to be a computer programmer. As we stand in line, my mind wanders. Rosa was once somebody's daughter, somebody's little girl—what happened to her? I don't have to wait long for an answer. In a few minutes, we're sitting on the patio, and as Rosa sips her latte, her softly rounded face grows serious. She takes a breath and starts talking.

"I was born in Honduras—I don't really remember anything about my life there other than short visions of my past." Her mother left shortly after she was born, then her grandmother raised her until she was seven, when she traveled with a coyote to Los Angeles to join her mother and stepfather. "I just wanted to be with my mother," she tells me. "This was all I thought about—and when I got to America, I felt like my dreams had come true." That didn't last long; soon after she arrived, her stepfather "forced himself on me—he molested me. It went on for some time. I don't know what happened. . . . I guess I thought it was normal."

Rosa's voice trails off for a moment, then she adds, "I didn't say anything. I didn't want to go back to Honduras. I just wanted to stay with my mother. I loved her so much." Rosa was not her mother's only child; she had two older sisters she'd never met. "Right about the time I was eleven or twelve, my mom told me both of my sisters were coming over. I was so excited to be with the two of them—I thought they were older and so smart." Rosa remembers how thrilled she felt when her two sisters offered to help her dress in grown-up clothes. "They were giving me so much attention. I was feeling so good and so excited, but it was the day of, like, a horror movie. It all begins so happy. Then things started to change." After helping her dress up, her sisters offered Rosa "this special drink." She didn't want it. Still, her sisters insisted, telling her it would help her relax. "Relax for what, I wondered."

She goes on, "Then they took me to a bar and a man was waiting there. He said I was pretty. Then he took me to a house attached to the bar. It was a brothel. He had sex with me. It took me a while to figure out what was going on. I knew, but I didn't want to know. My parents were trafficking me for sex."

These are Rosa's words. This is the terminology she uses, the way her life should be honored. Beyond that, how can anyone adequately label Rosa's experience? There are formal definitions that are essential to our understanding. In *Ending Human Trafficking and Modern-Day Slavery*, the groundbreaking book edited by Dr. Annalisa Enrile, she defines trafficking as "the recruitment, transportation, transfer, harboring or receipt of persons, by means of the threat or use of force or other forms of coercion, of abduction, of fraud, of deception, of the abuse of power or of a position of vulnerability or of the giving or receiving of payments or benefits to achieve the consent of a person having control over another person for the purpose of exploitation."[5] The statistics are staggering. At any given time, in a global industry that generates $32 billion in profits, there are 2.5 million human trafficking victims, with women making up 76 percent of this total. Enrile goes on to say that—at a minimum— the exploitation includes prostitution or other forms of sexual exploitation. It's clear that Rosa experienced sexual exploitation, becoming one of the ten million girls and boys that the United Nations estimates are involved in child prostitution globally, in both developed and underdeveloped countries. However, what's not included in the definition or in these statistics is the impact of having your mother being your trafficker, the person who has consented and in this case facilitated her daughter's being sexually exploited.

In acknowledging her exploitation, I found the enormity of Rosa's betrayal to be unlike anything I'd heard before. Rosa's mother persisted in selling her daughter and pocketing all the money she earned. As Rosa grew older, she continued to regularly "take the special drink," and it made her feel better, "especially when I was with men, because it was mainly like a dream—like I was in a Nintendo game. It felt like it wasn't real—I was hoping it wasn't real."

Rosa describes a life where she was simply an object to be used and discarded, with no one caring for her. "I didn't even have a designated place at the brothel, like my sisters did because they were older. There was always a guy waiting for me at the bar, and we'd find an empty room. My mother or my stepfather would hand me off." In between these assignations, her mother kept all three girls barricaded at home. "We were all prisoners," Rosa recalls. One day, her two sisters escaped through the window, but she didn't make it out—her parents caught her.

"I was this little girl that was just literally hurting inside. And I couldn't defend myself. And the person who was supposed to protect me wasn't there." To this day she has difficulty in her relationships with women, saying, "Sometimes it's really hard for me to trust women. In my mind, I think—what do they want from me?" When Rosa muses about whether this is an aftereffect of being trafficked throughout her childhood, I can't tell her what I'm thinking: *I wouldn't have trouble trusting women—I would hate them.*

She gave birth to her first child—a son, Arturo—when she was thirteen years old. "Now I think, where was social services? Where was child welfare? Didn't anyone notice that a thirteen-year-old was pregnant?" I have so many questions of my own as I listen to her talk. I can't ask; I don't want to disrespect her story by inserting myself into it. There's another reason I can't ask any questions: *I just can't take it.*

"When I finally had my little boy, DCFS took him away," Rosa says. It's unclear how the LA County Department of Children and Family Services finally arrived on the scene. Rosa thinks her parents may have called them. Once Arturo was taken from her, Rosa felt she had nothing to lose; she was willing to risk her life to get away. A plan began forming in her mind. Her mother and stepfather had taken to simply dropping her off at the bar to fend for herself; this ultimately provided her with the means of escape. There was a park next door to the bar where she'd hang around between clients. "A guy that was part of a gang took me in." Here her story is echoed in the accounts of other women. "People make it seem like gangs are bad. Gangs weren't my nightmare—they helped me to escape, and they helped build my identity so I could react and respond."

Rosa joined MCS, the Mid-City Stoners 13, a group that started out as a Mexican American stoner barrio and evolved into a violent Sureños street gang. As a gang member, Rosa was fearless. She was unafraid to go into other hoods, including those claimed by rivals. Still, she's quick to point out that this was not because she was courageous.

"I should have been afraid," she tells me. "I just didn't have remorse; I didn't have empathy. I had already cried so much as a kid, I didn't have any tears."

Rosa was still a prisoner. Gang life had replaced being sexually trafficked, but the outcomes of this trade-off weren't positive. She became deeply involved in drugs, gangbanging, and criminal activity in exchange for her freedom. "That guy from the park, he was broken just like I was. I went to work in a strip club to feed our addiction. I didn't feel bad; I got through it. My image now was at least I was somebody's somebody." The hood mentality was attractive to Rosa; she needed to be protected. And working in the strip club was still a far cry from being sexually trafficked. "No one was touching me—it wasn't like my mother pimping me out. I was doing this with my man—he wasn't forcing me into it. He didn't betray me—my mother did that."

When formerly incarcerated women describe their lives, there is often an explosion of emotion and pain. Still, with Rosa there is something beyond the emotion; her narrative is laced with deep understanding. She knows she has to titrate her experience for certain audiences. "You know they tell me on panels sometimes—your drugging, your gang involvement, keep it limited. I don't always listen when they say this. Sometimes I just can't limit it or not talk about what happened to me because gangs helped me survive. They gave me this identity. They gave me so much power. And I also understand why people can only listen to so much. So, I try to tell about what happened to me slowly. They have to get used to my story." The terrible trauma Rosa endured has not robbed her of her empathy today, even for the anonymous audiences listening to her story.

And yet. As Rosa sits in front of me sipping her coffee, she doesn't only talk about the brutality and loss that had long characterized her life. She also talks about her love for her children. She worries about the job interview she has the next day at Watts Labor Community Action Committee. She promises she'll tell me what happened to her when she was repeatedly incarcerated, as well as the hope she discovered. But that is for another day. For now, she has to pick up her son from school.

I keep thinking of Greg Boyle. I keep thinking of how he has struck a chord in me and so many others when he says he stands in awe of these individuals. I keep thinking, how are they doing it? And I keep thinking about Ivy on the run, and of Janeth, locked up and alone in the women's "detention facility" just a few blocks from this coffee house.

INTERLUDE

Law enforcement, frustrated for months in their search for Ivy and Pedro, finally catches a break. Someone—no one knows who—has tipped off the cops that they are in Tijuana. All the media reports is that an anonymous source is set to receive $20,000 as a reward for the information and that an arrest warrant has been issued. In February, almost four months after the shooting, Ivy and Pedro are found in Mexico and extradited back to Los Angeles.

At Homegirl, the women wonder why Ivy got involved with Pedro. She'd always been so strong. Ivy hadn't known Pedro for very long before the deacon was murdered. Pedro was a few years younger than she, and most of her friends considered him immature, beneath her. And he was abusive—Ivy had confided in some of the women in the café that the beatings were getting worse. They saw the bruises. They couldn't understand why Ivy stayed. Still, one of the women at the café, Adela Juarez, understood. "Ivy never faced her trauma. She always got involved with men who were abusive. They were cruel. That's all she thought she deserved—these were men who beat her over and over again. She couldn't escape." Ivy had turned her back on gangbanging, but Pedro was still active—he'd just gotten out of prison and rejected the idea of accessing any services at Homeboy when the two of them hooked up. Ivy always insisted their relationship was casual. But Adela knew more than anyone about the vectors of the relationship. "Ivy just couldn't escape. She was still scared no one would want her, no one would take care of her. She knew Pedro was bad, but her fear was worse."

Now, when Adela visits her at jail, Ivy explains how she told Pedro, "We gotta turn ourselves in because I can't deal with this." Adela knows that "they had nobody in TJ; they were running out of money." She says, "I'm sure Pedro was abusing her and Ivy couldn't take it anymore. So, they were coming back, and when they came across the border, that's when they got arrested."

It doesn't matter now why Ivy got together with Pedro or how he abused her, or if she started using drugs again, with her trauma increasing. Law enforcement wasn't thinking about her trauma when they brought the couple back to Los Angeles and locked them up in different facilities. In Lynwood, in the women's county jail, Janeth and Ivy are finally reunited, facing multiple charges and unaffordable bail; all they have are the services of two court-appointed attorneys.

FIVE

I THOUGHT HE WOULD
TAKE CARE OF ME

*I never had anyone I could trust. I never had anyone who said
they'd be there for me. Then he told me that no matter what,
he'd take care of me. I believed him. I gave him my heart.*

—VALERIE VELEZ

"Well, I got a surprise for you." Denise is in my office, and she
wears a look of mischievous joy. I wonder if she's found out
that she's been accepted into the MSW program.

"Have you heard from UCLA?" I ask.

"Nope." She giggles.

"What is it?"

"I think I might be pregnant. I don't know for sure. I gotta go see a
doctor. My home test came out positive."

I'm anxious that this is going to be a challenge, to say the least. But
for just one minute, I forget my misgivings about Denise juggling graduate school and motherhood. The possibility of a child is her hope. Her
dream. It's a flesh-and-blood statement that her life has truly changed.

"And if I'm pregnant, I'm gonna be the best damn mother I can be.
I've been thinkin' so much about my own mother."

I look at Denise carefully. I can't stop thinking about what she's already shared with me and how she, along with women like her, have looked for help to deal with the trauma they continue to endure. They didn't think of counseling or therapy; nothing like that was readily available to them. Instead, each woman's response was the most natural one in the world: they wanted to find someone—anyone—to protect them from further trauma. And more often than not, this led to the inevitable conclusion that men had the strength and the resources—a man would protect them. This is what so many women had been told and had come to believe: that they couldn't really protect themselves, that they needed a man to take care of them. I kept hearing the same stories over and over from the women who were part of my work. This was a message they'd received as girls: men weren't just a source of financial support; men would stand up to threats, they'd protect their woman from danger and from pain, whether it came from the homes they grew up in or the community that surrounded them. From the time they were young, even before they were adolescents, girls believed that their personal safety could be found in relationships with men. "First it was my daddy, but pretty soon I learned that wasn't true. So, then I told myself, I'd belong to someone and he'd take care of me," Blanca Ortega, who been involved in gang life, remembered.

Blanca wasn't alone in that conviction. Many others were convinced that a man would stand up for his woman, he wouldn't let any outsider abuse her. If someone did—if a woman was attacked—it would be dealt with; street justice was the mechanism men used. Ella Jones, who'd been incarcerated ten years for gang-related crimes, explained it all to me. "I was in Athens Park, sitting with my babies, and two homies grabbed me—took my purse, my rings, my jewelry. Scared the shit out of the kids. I couldn't believe it. I told my boyfriend what happened when he came over the next morning. By the time the sun went down, those two boys had been tuned up. They weren't gonna be walking for a few days." Ella later went on to explain that it didn't matter that her boyfriend constantly cheated on her. He was there when she needed him.

I kept hearing these stories. I even experienced the promise of some "protection" myself. When I told two gang members I'd known for several years that I'd once been involved in an abusive relationship, they both demanded I share the man's whereabouts. "We're gonna mess him up," one told me. "We'd never let anyone hurt you." While I quickly told them that I didn't know where the man was now, I momentarily experienced that feeling of care, however violent its direction. It also frightened me. But my response was irrelevant. What was critical to understand, and I did, was that all of this made women feel safe, that there was someone who was going to watch out for them, take care of what scared them.

Still, this protection comes with a price. For many women, violence and gang involvement make up part of that price.

This is true for Denise. "What happened after your mom kicked you out?" I ask, reassuring her she doesn't have to talk about it if this isn't a good time. She starts shaking her head, "Nooooooo," drawing the word out like a blues singer. "I *want* to talk about it. I *need* to talk about it." After her mom's rejection, Denise was homeless—another part of many women's experience that remains unacknowledged, even today. She'd stay in abandoned apartment buildings or go to the house of a man she knew and "he'd look out for me. I trusted that man to take care of me. I needed to feel safe and I *knew* he'd be there. He wound up being the one who led me to the gang. He was like, 'You want to be from the hood?' and I was like, 'Hell, yeah.' That's how it happened."

It was a rough initiation; Denise had to choose between sex—which meant "I would have to allow anyone who wanted it to actually fuck me and I didn't want that"—and taking a beating. Without hesitation, she chose the beating. "I drank some 40s. They only punched me a couple of times and then it was over."

Here, Denise's story differs from many accounts of female initiation into gang life. In avoiding any sort of group sexual assault, Denise was lucky. Most women are not as fortunate. They're already traumatized, and many feel forced to endure a sexual initiation. On top of that, as the journalist Gini Sikes first recounted over twenty years ago in her book *8 Ball Chicks*, one of the biggest problems for gang-involved girls is their unwillingness to report rape, especially group rape—they don't even want to see it as a crime.[1] If anyone actually convinces them it *is* a crime, they still don't want to report a sexual assault because that might be viewed as snitching. For Denise, after avoiding sexual attack and humiliation, her initiation was a minor problem to endure. After that, she began "putting in work" for the gang, whatever illegal activities they might ask her to be involved in, and ended up getting arrested. "That was when I really felt like I was in the hood. I was really a home-girl—'China.' I'll never forget it." This is Denise's identity, her roots. She will never let that go.

Understanding the connection between trauma, gang membership, and incarceration is tricky. For the women I knew, their trauma led to their turning to men for protection, which ended up as a precursor to gang involvement. Gang research maintains that there is no single pathway into the hood—it results from a combination of multiple risk factors and the absence of any protective factors. These risk factors diverge in one area: when studies take gender into account. Gang-involved young women are survivors of physical and sexual abuse at a much higher rate than young men.[2] In their research, Karen Joe and Meda Chesney-Lind have found that 75 percent of the female gang members they interviewed experienced physical abuse, and 62 percent reported that they'd experienced sexual abuse.[3] For girls, early trauma is a major risk factor—perhaps *the* major risk factor—for gang membership and involvement.

This wasn't just an idea rolling around in my head. Beginning with the staff at the Homegirl Café and branching out from there, since 2008, I'd interviewed eighty women who'd been gang involved, had engaged in criminal activity and ultimately had been incarcerated. I never planned to conduct that many interviews; it wasn't a formal study. But the women I spent hours with at Homegirl kept telling me about someone else they thought I had to talk to. There was always a new name, a new story and a homegirl urging me, "You gotta talk to her, Little Mama." It was like some gigantic chain letter that I couldn't resist. I kept seeing how formerly incarcerated women were strong and resilient in the face of so many obstacles. The portrayal of these women as victims was a lie. I'd never understood this. On top of that, I'd never really grasped how many formerly incarcerated women lived in the communities I worked in, and I'd rarely spent time with them. Driven to learn as much as I could, I felt overwhelmed as they shared their stories. I got to know these women over long time periods, interviewing them and spending time with many of them from 2008 onward. They became part of my life, part of my chosen family, and I wanted to honor their pain and their resilience.

Probably one of the most stunning "findings" that emerged from this study that wasn't a study was that, with a few exceptions, almost all eighty women had experienced sexual abuse along with physical abuse and related trauma in their childhood. Only seven women had escaped molestation, telling me that while they'd witnessed and even experienced violence, they'd never been sexually abused. One woman, Adela, had been free of any childhood abuse but had witnessed her father abusing her mother over time and had felt responsible for shielding her younger siblings from the violence. Still, she was grateful, telling me, "For all the homegirls I've known, I'm the only one who wasn't beaten or raped when she was growing up." Adela had other wounds from violence and pain in adulthood. But, in the end, she was one of a small group of outliers in a group of women who'd been sexually traumatized from their childhoods onward.

Whatever their experience, once girls sought protection from the boys and men who ultimately led them into gang life, they were pretty much viewed in terms of their sexuality; all roles assigned to them smacked of sexual objectification. Gang terminology attested to that: the girls were baby mamas or whores; they were bitches or hood rats. There were exceptions—girls who were willing to be violent and women claiming to have moved high up the gang food chain. *Los Angeles* magazine had profiled Arlene Rodriguez, who was considered, "the queen of Florencia" and lived a Dr. Jekyll–Mr. Hyde life as a real estate agent and shot caller for Florencia 13.[4] But such women were few and far between.

Instead, virtually all of the homegirls were desperate to escape the trauma of their homes, their feelings of aloneness and fear. They deeply believed a man would take care of them, and if that man was part of a gang, they would have even more protection. So, despite the sexual assault associated with initiation and their resulting objectification, most of the girls and women I talked with believed that their man and his gang provided a safe haven—including Denise, who took to gangbanging with particular fervor. "I had a boyfriend and I had the hood," she says. "I was really off the chain—no one could talk to me."

Denise is clear: no matter what anyone said or how they tried to intervene, the hood was everything to her. Even now, she still feels an attachment to the gang, telling me, "I can't ever leave it behind. When I think about that period of my life, now—at this age—I remember my hood with love. They've got my loyalty. Forever. You know what I mean?"

I'd like to tell her I know exactly what she means. I can't. I don't feel anything close to the deep ties of loyalty Denise describes. There is no specific group I feel connected to. The number of people I can't leave behind is small: my husband, my daughter, my brothers, and a handful of friends—my chosen family. There is no hood in my life. But there was never any molestation or trauma either.

Denise believes the hood was there for her and will always be. She explains to me that her past is something an outsider just can't understand—she *felt* safe when she was with her man and other gang members. She doesn't say a lot about women; there's no sense of the role they played in hood life. Men were the ones who shielded her from danger. What matters to Denise is how the hood's code of respect and the consequences for disrespect helped to protect her from outside harm. Still, the protection she sought in the hood and the relationships she encountered with men as a result were much more complicated.

For as long as Denise could remember, men were attracted to her, and once in the hood, she jumped right into a series of relationships. Sitting in my office, talking with me, Denise's lively attractiveness is in full flower. I'm certain she was beautiful as a young woman, an object of desire. Yet from the beginning, Denise's encounters with men invariably involved abuse as well as sex. In the hood, love and violence were intertwined, and Denise accepted that abuse was just a side effect of being involved with a man; her trauma had laid the foundation for that belief. "It is what it is," Denise tells me. But that façade of cynical detachment changes when Denise describes how she found herself in love for the first time.

"Eric was different," Denise says, sighing. "He'd been in the pen. He'd been involved in some serious crimes in the past—I knew he was violent. But I felt safe with him—so, so safe. It was crazy, right?" From the beginning, Denise was attracted to Eric's sensitivity, how he was able to tune in to her feelings and understand what she was going through. Yet while the attraction grew, she was failing to recognize the control Eric subtly exerted. She recalls, "I didn't realize, he was isolating me from everyone." This isolation is a hallmark of an abusive relationship and is one of the key signs that a woman may be in danger.[5] Denise knew nothing about the warning signs and danger assessment that Rachel Snyder later detailed so powerfully in *No Visible Bruises*; all she knew was that she was deeply in love for the first time in her life.[6] She slowly pulled away from the hood and stopped seeing her friends. She worked at entry-level jobs for low wages while Eric started up a business as a tattoo artist. "I wanted to have a normal life, with a boyfriend, work hard, have fun, the two of us together, but Eric . . ." Denise's voice trails off for a moment, then she continues. "He was so crazy. He wanted to control me. He started beating me up. I was part of the LA County probation system when I was a teenager. I was never *off* probation—until I met Eric. I was nineteen and free for the first time. So . . . instead of probation, I got into an abusive relationship."

Denise was with Eric for five years. "It was a chunk of time that I was away from the system. And then after the relationship with Eric was over, I went back to the system. It's like I had to have someone or something abusing me."

Her words are echoed in the stories told by many others. Formerly incarcerated women all too often experience abuse that is both violent and humiliating. They enter into relationships listening to men who re-assure them that, whatever happens, they'll be protected. "Eric kept tell-ing me he'd take care of me," Denise recalled. "When he started abusing me, I couldn't believe it." She was like so many others, believing in the promises of men who offered them safety and a place to belong. These women ultimately feel betrayed and ashamed because they are battered or assaulted by someone they believe they love.[7] When family or friends question what's going on in their relationships, women hide the truth and make excuses, telling themselves they've got no choice. If they have children, they're terrified the child welfare system will step in and take their babies away. On top of that, Black women and women of color are caught between their humiliation and their mistrust of the criminal jus-tice system, which for decades has responded with harsh treatment and the brutalization of their men and their communities. This all results in the under-reporting of domestic abuse and violence. In a reversal of the safety they sought from men, now-traumatized women have to protect their men, their families. And they're not going to say a word against them.

Instead, women internalize feelings of guilt surrounding the assault and abuse they suffer. In blaming themselves, many women are at risk for something I've begun to think of as "abuse recidivism," which occurs when the violence they experience is repeated and almost normalized. Often the abuse isn't consistent, and women convince themselves that the bad times won't last. This cycle—in and out of abusive relationships—is something other researchers refer to as *relationship churning*.[8] From youth onward, women may know the physical and emotional abuse is damaging at many levels, but they continue, supported by the belief that their partner will change or that the relationship is the only constant in their lives—living out Denise's shopworn credo "It is what it is."

"You gotta understand about Eric. He was abusive in so many ways. The trouble is, it wasn't all the time." Denise describes a familiar pat-tern: things would be peacefully happy, and she'd believe the worst was over. But the abuse would always start again, with increasing force. She would call the police and press charges, then renege after Eric begged for forgiveness. "I was so damn stupid. I kept telling myself he was taking care of me, that I couldn't be without him—I needed him."

Ironically, Eric was the one who needed Denise: his tattoo business wasn't working out and he became increasingly disturbed. "He got so crazy, he said he was going to kill me and then kill himself—murder-suicide. I just kept thinking if I just loved him enough, supported him enough, it would be okay." Every once in a while, she would catch a glimpse of the old Eric, kind and sensitive, and that fueled her hope. But in reality, Eric was deteriorating. He insisted Denise quit work and collect welfare, and abused her repeatedly. "He would hit me, I would run away, and then I would always go back. I thought he was the one who would always be there. I thought he would protect me."

I thought he would protect me.

In their childhood and youth, women weren't safe in their homes, within their families. Their fathers or stepfathers or brothers or cousins molested them, and they wanted someone—anyone—to protect them. In return for protection from these childhood predators, they paid the price of abuse over and over again, believing this was simply the way life was. And many women were fearful that no one else besides their boyfriend would desire them, no one else would take care of them. They depended on their boyfriends or husbands or partners emotionally and economically. Many of them hadn't completed high school and most weren't legally employed. Because of the abuse they suffered throughout their lives, they felt unattractive, unlovable, that only this man would want them. They were drowning in a tsunami of trauma and powerlessness. Denise, Rosa, and so many others believed they had no alternative—even with the abuse. If they lost their man, *where would they go?*

This was exactly what had happened to both Janeth and Ivy. When Janeth was abandoned by her mother, she immediately turned to her boyfriend, Luis. This was also the solution Ivy sought, but for both women it brought something they didn't anticipate, intimate-partner violence. Luis cheated on Janeth. When she confronted him, he often beat her up. Still, when she became pregnant with Angelina, Luis pledged he'd never hit her again, that he'd be a good father.

Ivy was not so lucky. At seventeen, she became involved in an abusive relationship with Julio, an older gang member she lived with for eight years. There were drugs and violent fights, and often Ivy was afraid for her life. But she was equally fearful that she had nowhere to go. She was totally dependent on Julio, emotionally and economically. She'd seen what happened to her mother, and she didn't want to wind up on the streets. Throughout this period, she worked, mainly part-time, at jobs that never paid enough to set her free. Finally, after finding a full-time job that paid a living wage, Ivy managed to leave the relationship. Six months later, Julio was killed in a gang shootout. In a morass of guilt and fear, Ivy sank into depression, finding solace in drugs and gangbanging.

It was then that she met Carlos and they began seeing each other; eventually they moved in together. Ivy wanted a peaceful life, a good job—and she then discovered she was pregnant. Neither Carlos nor she was ready for a baby, yet neither one of them would consider abortion. They both felt overwhelmed, and their anxiety translated into domestic violence. Carlos had already hit her a few times before; now the abuse escalated. The pregnancy was difficult: Ivy was often sick, but much of the time she'd miss doctor's appointments. She wouldn't even talk to her friends. Her face and body were so bruised and battered that she was ashamed for anyone to see what was happening to her. More than anything, she couldn't believe that she was in the same situation again, with the same type of man. Only this time it was much worse. She'd believed that Carlos was different, she had believed she'd learned her lesson, she'd believed Carlos would take care of her. She thought she was safe with a new boyfriend. Instead, she was afraid for her life and didn't know where to turn. Just like Janeth, she felt she had nowhere else to go, so she focused on her pregnancy, accepting that being battered was the price she had to pay.

Over and over again, my work exposed the prevalence of this dangerous belief. In recounting the experiences leading up to their incarceration, more than four out of five women, sixty-six in all, described domestic violence that ranged from hitting, whipping, and burning to torture, literal imprisonment and beatings that were so vicious it's difficult to describe, let alone fathom. Yet, they stayed and endured the abuse because, as Ivy, Janeth, Rosa, and so many others had asked, "Who else would want me or would want to take care of me?"

What was the link between childhood trauma and violent adult relationships? As early as 1996, researchers found that sexual abuse in childhood was strongly linked to physical abuse by a partner and sexual assault in adulthood.[9] Since then, this connection has been confirmed in over two decades of research. One study bluntly concluded that victims of childhood sexual assault were more likely to be assaulted after they turned sixteen years old than women who had not been sexually abused as children.[10] Additionally, being sexually abused as a child increased the risk for mental health problems in adulthood, including anxiety disorders, depression, suicidality, and substance abuse along with greater risk of physical assault in adult relationships.[11] All these studies confirmed what so many formerly incarcerated women already knew: that their untreated trauma and the thoughts and feelings that surrounded it led women into desperate and violent relationships.

Despite the research, it's difficult to adequately portray the relationship between formerly incarcerated women and ongoing trauma. It reminds me of the legal cases I've worked on that involved "gang enhancements": individuals who'd been found guilty of charges received even harsher penalties added to their sentences if they were gang members. For these women, it's as if there is a "trauma enhancement" in their lives—an added emotional penalty that can be traced back to what they experienced in childhood. Along the way, incarceration turbocharges the trauma women are already living through. This process is consistent, but the symptoms women exhibit are not. Some women act out violently, some become deeply depressed, some suffer with physical illness, and some experience a combination of physical, emotional, and mental struggles. This connection is clearly borne out by studies showing that women who experience multiple traumas suffer from even more severe symptoms.[12] Beyond this, the greater the severity and frequency of trauma and violence, the more intense the resulting symptoms.[13]

Rosa Lucero's story followed this familiar, tragic pathway. After she fled being sex-trafficked by her mother with the man who enmeshed her in the cycle of gang life and crime, Rosa felt trapped in their relationship and left him. She wanted to try to be on her own and she wanted to get her son, Arturo, back. Instead, she was soon entangled in the juvenile justice system, sent away to a probation camp. After her release, she fell into another abusive relationship with the man who fathered her second child, her daughter, Pahola. They broke up, and she started yet another abusive relationship with the man with whom she would have a third child, Daniel. All of these relationships were filled with rage, violence, and cruelty. "We would fight and hit each other and stab each other, then sleep with each other and forget about it the next day." Always, Rosa was acting out her pain. Neighbors awakened at night by the violence called the police, and her two children were removed by the Department of Children and Family Services. With all three of her children in foster homes, Rosa was beset with sorrow; she medicated her pain. "I just didn't know how to stay sober," Rosa explains, describing how she descended further into drug abuse and relationships with men who physically abused her and fed her addictions.

"Now I try not to think about it. I just want to live my life," she tells me. But that's a desire not easily fulfilled. To this day, the smallest thing, even a scent, triggers her memories. "One day I smelled Old Spice, and I really thought I was going to throw up. It reminded me of one of the men who abused me." Rosa is courageously open about the multiple ways she has tried to deal with the emotional impact of trauma over the years, from substance misuse and self-medication to eating disorders in the form of bulimia. "I used to make myself throw up because I felt so dirty inside," she tells me. "I just wanted to cleanse myself—that went on for a lot of years."

Rosa's insights, while heartbreaking, are actually a sign of her deep internal strength. Over the years, she never lied to herself and she never told herself that anything she was experiencing was normal. And now she is very clear that she was wrong to believe that a man would be the answer. "I kept thinking," she remembers, "how could anyone love me when my mother didn't love me? When she just turned me out? She didn't take care of me. And, so, I kept going to men who really didn't love me either, thinking they'd take care of me. I should have known: the only person who could take care of me was myself. I had to learn that. And I did. And I know that's what helped me get my kids back."

When I hear Rosa describe her realization that she had to take care of herself, my thoughts drift to Denise. An hour later, I get a text. "G-ma-it's def. Dr. says am pregnant."

SIX

BABY PRISON

I went into the system when my mom had caught a case of child neglect. Once you get into the system, the next step is going to juvenile, and then the next step is going to prison. Everybody knows that, it's almost common sense. You never hear it being any other way.

—SERENA LOCKHART

I'm back at Homegirl, and the café is buzzing with excitement. Two tables away, Jim Carrey is eating lunch with Father Greg. Carrey is a delight, submitting to endless selfies with the homies, joking, and asking Greg thoughtful questions. The waitresses, all homegirls, ask Carrey to pose with them, and as I watch the joyful antics, their stories keep running through my mind. Probably because I'm getting ready for my monthly lunch with the woman who funds my research at Homegirl. Dr. Beatriz Solis, one of the leading lights at the California Endowment, is committed to creating pathways for women in leadership, lifting up their intelligence and resilience. Because she's a leader herself as well as the sister of the then secretary of labor, Hilda Solis, Bea is focused on how women overcome the trauma they experience to survive and ultimately thrive.

Once she joins me—after taking her own selfie with Jim Carrey—we immediately start talking about what my research is revealing. Most important, the trap young women find themselves in—experiencing trauma, turning to men, and then, all too often, finding themselves enmeshed in the juvenile justice system. When our waitress finally arrives, she listens to our conversation for a moment, puts her hands on her hips, then blurts out, "You wanna help women? I'll tell you what you've gotta do. Help the girls, before they get in more trouble. And that means, you gotta do something about the camps. I couldn't believe it when I was in there. It really was prison. I got locked up and no one was there to help me. They treated us like we were boys—they even gave us boys' clothes to wear. The girls got nothing we needed, not even Tampax! And there weren't any programs for us. We really need people to help the girls." Bea and I both instinctively reach out to comfort her, but she shakes her head. "I'm okay. But you gotta do something!"

For a long time, little attention was paid to young women involved in the juvenile justice system. It was the identical twin of the situation with adult women: in the juvenile system as well, boys were front and center in studies of delinquency, youth gangs, and criminal behavior. Girls were pretty much an afterthought, and only a handful of researchers, mainly women, looked at female delinquency and gangs. Trauma wasn't even on the radar. Male concerns dominated juvenile justice, and its facilities were designed for and populated primarily by boys. These juvenile facilities mirrored their adult counterparts: similar to jails, the halls, like the camps, were for temporary "detention" with youth held in these settings for a limited number of days, until juvenile court judges decided whether they should go on to probation camp or back into the community. In the network of camps—prisons for juveniles—youth served long-term sentences ranging from six months to two years in low- to high-security settings. Once again, girls weren't treated any differently than boys—it was the one-size-fits-all approach all over again—only this time it involved the system of incarceration reaching down into the lives of preteens and adolescents.[1] And beyond that, what happened to young women after involvement in the juvenile justice system also, tragically, mimicked the hopeless responses of the adult criminal justice system. Very few reentry programs or community-based supports addressed the specific needs of young women. Once they were released from the halls or from longer stays in camp, traumatized young women went right back to the situations—men, gangs, violence—that had led them into the system in the first place.

The shadow of the juvenile justice system was everywhere I looked. Rosa had been in the system, Denise had been in the system, Ivy and Janeth had been in the system—for God's sake, Susan Burton had been in the system. Over and over again, I heard women talk about going to the halls, going to camp. Almost every woman's pathway into the criminal justice system actually began when they were girls—long before their eighteenth birthday. And because they'd been part of the system from such an early age, their involvement felt almost predetermined. Much of this could be chalked up to a nonsensical gender-based double standard that had devastating consequences.

Research shows that both boys and girls involved with the juvenile justice system are most often charged with "status offenses," legal violations involving youth under eighteen that include such crimes as "running away" and "incorrigibility." However, when it comes to the legal consequences for status offenses, there is a dramatic split: more young women than young men are actually locked up for such offenses with the glib justification that it is "for their own protection." It's anything but protection. Instead, it is punishment disguised as placement. These girls don't need detention so much as counseling and an honest assessment of their living situations. It's also apparent that controlling budding sexuality is the subtext in these and many other offenses. Still, instead of examining whether a girl is running around because she is being abused or is sexually acting out because of a deeper underlying issue, she may instead be characterized as "immoral" or "deviant" and requiring the intervention of law enforcement to control her behavior.[2] It's the juvenile justice equivalent of "Lock up your daughters," with the added unspoken admonition "And stop them from sexually acting out." No one with any power is connecting the dots to see how trauma may have led to acting out that took the form of sexual activity and gang involvement.

This was very much the case with Rosa, although to simply say she was acting out is like saying the hydrogen bomb might have caused some property damage. Her gang involvement, delinquent behavior, and substance abuse expanded as the emotional impact of her untreated trauma grew. By the time she turned fifteen, Rosa had already lived through enough for three lifetimes, including giving up her first child, Arturo, to the Department of Children and Family Services. It was when she was arrested for gang activity and carrying a firearm that she first entered the juvenile justice system, courtesy of the Los Angeles County Probation Department. A juvenile court judge decided that Rosa should be sent to a probation camp. This euphemism, "camp," conjuring up visions of cabins and pine trees, was about as far from the truth as the actual location of the camp itself, forty miles from the streets Rosa knew.

I was already familiar with what went on in probation facilities: their camps and halls had been part of my work for the past ten years, and I was heavily invested, both personally and professionally, in juvenile justice reform. One of my best friends, Carol Biondi, had an almost encyclopedic knowledge of the system and its offenses—and she didn't hesitate to share these with me whenever I needed some information. I'd also heard plenty of horror stories from youth who'd been detained in the probation system; tales of solitary confinement, use of pepper spray to control boys and girls, even "fight clubs" spurred on by abusive corrections officers. All these tortuous practices and more figured in the narratives of young men and women who described the trauma they endured in facilities that were more punitive than rehabilitative. One gang member told me, "The halls were where I learned about pain."

But not for Rosa. Paradoxically, for her, camp was "paradise." It was the first place she found peace in her life. She had her own bed, her own room, and time to herself. The fact that probation camp represented nirvana speaks volumes about her earlier experiences. *Rosa loved probation camp. She didn't want to leave. She finally felt safe.* Unlike most system-involved youth, initially she felt at home while she was incarcerated—or, as the courts euphemistically referred to it "detained"—in juvenile probation facilities. However, while the local halls and camps may have given her a bed of her own, they made no effort to address her psychological or practical needs. She was released after six months with nothing awaiting her but the gangs and violence she'd left behind. As her illegal activities on the streets accelerated, Rosa was repeatedly arrested and eventually labeled too serious a criminal for local detention. Instead, she was remanded to the state juvenile justice system, which meant she was "detained" by the California Youth Authority, YA. This was when everything changed.

YA—commonly known at that time as "baby prison"—was a brutal place, full of violence, with youth allowed to freely intimidate and attack one another. As one former detainee, a woman, told me, "It was fight club, 24–7. We all slept with knives or forks so we'd be ready to stab someone if they came at us while we were sleeping." YA mirrored everything Rosa had experienced on the street. She emerged broken from her year-long detention there. Her mental health issues grew more pronounced, her rage more extreme, and her despair more intense, until her physical and mental survival were at stake. And she was only sixteen years old.

After a few weeks back on the street, Rosa was arrested again. Then, her luck changed. Instead of YA, the judge sent her to Dorothy Kirby Residential Treatment and Placement Center. It was still juvenile detention, but this time was different. At Dorothy Kirby, four separate Los Angeles County agencies worked together to provide a therapeutic environment for the boys and girls "in the system" who needed help. There were psychological assessments, medical tests and treatment, counseling, and group therapy. Mental health practitioners worked with probation officers to address the problems these youth had suffered in their homes and in their communities. Finally, Rosa felt she was in the right place.

It was here that she met Tommie Baines.

To this day, Tommie is known as one of the most gifted professionals in LA County Probation, intelligent and deeply compassionate. Those traits along with the warmth of his personality combine to invite the trust of the children—and make no mistake, these are children—he has responsibility for helping. Eighteen years later Rosa remembers him vividly and is overjoyed to learn that I know him. Her voice rises an octave.

"Tommie Baines! You know him! Tommie Baines *knew I was different.* He affected my life. You know, if you ever hear human-trafficking survivors, they say there's this one person that plants that seed of hope in you. He was that seed for me."

Other women talked about the one probation officer who stood out in their lives, who encouraged them to grow, told them they could succeed. Denise had similar memories, telling me, "My PO is one of the big reasons I wanted to become a social worker—he really helped me. I saw what a person could do to change your life. I want to be that person for the girls today who are like I was then. I want to go back and help them." Denise's goals weren't unusual. Most women I've met who've been detained in the probation camps and halls express a wish to help girls currently in the system. But not every woman found someone who planted that seed of hope. Denise was one of the lucky ones. So was Rosa, who recalled her days at Dorothy Kirby with genuine affection. "I thought I was in the right place. I thought the system was gonna work for me."

For the first time, Rosa felt trust and began opening up to Tommie Baines. "I told him about the men and what had happened to me." He became her champion. He helped her obtain the counseling she needed. He encouraged her efforts to obtain a high school diploma or a GED. When she was slated for release, Tommie accompanied Rosa to her disposition hearing, telling the judge she should remain at Dorothy Kirby. He pleaded her case, explaining that she was protected there, that she was flourishing in school and needed the structure of the treatment center to recover from the experiences of trafficking and living on the street. The judge denied his request, instead releasing Rosa *to her mother's custody.* "That broke him. He was so upset. I think he wanted to choke the judge. Can you imagine? They released me to her. *They released me to her.*"

Being sent home to her mother—who had trafficked her—was the final breaking point for Rosa. "It all changed when they sent me home to my mother. My life was never the same after that. I think of it—even nowadays—I think of it as 'before and after.'"

This decision destroyed what was left of Rosa's trust in life and faith in the system. She immediately ran away from her mother, back to the gang, and took up where she left off, with a vengeance. Only now she was getting arrested on more serious charges—attempted murders, DUIs, batteries—all signs of her boundless rage that had nowhere to go but out, into behavior that was criminalized. Rosa's response was not unusual. I was finding that in the lives of formerly incarcerated women, rage looms large, and research confirms this.[3]

In Kimberly Flemke's work on women's trauma, she explains how "triggers of past abuse and violation, whether physical and/or emotional, create an intergenerational legacy of not only violence but also rage."[4] In a qualitative study of thirty-six incarcerated women, 90 percent cited at least one childhood experience that triggered them to feel rage as adults—including physical abuse, sexual abuse, and observing domestic violence. Most significantly, these triggered feelings end up causing women to feel "helpless and vulnerable all over again."[5] When I talked with her about what happened after Dorothy Kirby, Rosa told me that all she felt was "the rage, the rage, the incredible rage."

"I've picked up so many charges throughout the years because I was enraged. I was enraged at my mother; I was enraged at the system. And I wanted people to feel the rage I had in me. It was like I was thinking, '*I need you to feel this pain that I was feeling.*' And I took it out on the wrong people. I was in this rage where I just wanted something to relieve me. Send me away, out of this world—just take all this pain away. I didn't want to feel it anymore. And if I have to feel it, I'ma let you feel it."

Rosa's words show how rage can play a significant role in women's journey from trauma to relationships with violent men and criminal activity to detention and incarceration. It is crucial to see that rage merges with gender in different ways. Plenty of young men are enraged as well, but the roots of their rage and the consequences of that rage differ vastly from those of young women. What so many people—including young women—don't realize is that their gender as well as their rage aren't just part of their criminal activities; they also affect their reaction to being powerless. Denise once asked me, "Why didn't they give me therapy? Why did they put me in a probation camp? It didn't help with what I'd gone through at home."

It's also clear that anger management classes aren't going to do the job. Rage was, and is, distinct from anger in profound ways. While anger is in fact manageable and doesn't cloud a woman's judgment, rage as a force overtakes judgment and causes women to feel they cannot control their feelings. For girls, trauma and rage interact, often leading to what is labeled criminal behavior and its consequence: involvement in the juvenile justice system. But the problem is, these young women aren't criminals; they are most often adolescents acting out against a troubled or even abusive environment.

Researchers have been interested in how the connection between a violent childhood at home and later criminal behavior play out in different ways depending on gender. Meda Chesney-Lind was among those who pointed out that childhood victimization ultimately leads to the criminal justice system, and for girls, this usually starts with the status offense of running away. In declaring this a juvenile "crime," what the system fails to recognize is that girls often run away to survive, fleeing a violent home and child abuse.[6] So why is a survival mechanism labeled a crime? And how does such labeling affect young women who are actually looking for some sort of protection? Do they turn to men because the system only offers punishment, not support? These are key questions. Researchers haven't been the only ones trying to answer them and understand the relationship between young women's trauma and criminal behavior. As other voices have weighed in, the issue has grown much more complicated and, worse yet, confused.

It all began in the mid-1990s, with the mythology surrounding the youth "super-predator" and the political scientist John Dilulio Jr.'s now-discredited predictions of an explosion of young men committing violent crimes.[7] At the time, reports also warned that young women, too, were becoming more violent. This histrionic prediction didn't come close to portraying what was really going on, which had less to do with violence and more to do with labels. Between 1989 and 1993, the juvenile arrest rate escalated, but the relative rate of juvenile arrests for girls went up more than it did for boys—in fact it was more than double the number. Girls' arrest rates rose 23 percent compared with boys' arrest rates, which went up 11 percent.[8] Beginning in the 2000s, boys' arrest rates began to drop while girls' arrest rates continued to rise. This was the era when Rosa, Denise, and so many other teenage girls were locked up.

Researchers in the Girls Study Group, a project of the US Department of Justice's Office for Juvenile Justice and Delinquency Prevention, set out to understand the increase in girls' arrests.[9] No single factor emerged to explain what was happening. Instead, these researchers pointed to several issues, including how parental or caretaker behavioral expectations and standards for obedience differed according to gender; they also zeroed in on girls' tendency to act out at home rather than at school or in other public settings. Chesney-Lind argued that changes in public policy, particularly the redefinition of domestic violence to include issues beyond partner violence, ultimately led to an increase in girls' arrests.[10] This was traced to a strange bend in logic that occurred when police responded to reports of parents and daughters physically fighting. Rather than settling the situation or questioning the parent, who often was caring for multiple children, police wound up arresting the daughter, claiming this was done to protect her. But that wasn't the only thing going on, because police perceived that if the parent were to be questioned and eventually detained, there might not be anyone at home to take care of the other children. So, they came down hard on the daughter. All of this pointed to the larger issue of how law enforcement was brought into situations they were not properly trained or even qualified to assess, creating a situation that just didn't make sense: girls were criminalized because of stress and conflict within their homes, including conflict that was due to family violence.

To make matters even more confusing, young women were more likely to be arrested in these situations because, as the Girls Study Group had found, girls acted out at home while boys acted out at school. At school, neither policies nor arrest rates had changed over time. But all kinds of things had changed in the home, or in the way events in the home were interpreted and acted on. This was the fallout from new domestic violence laws first passed by Congress in 1994, then reauthorized in 2000. These laws had unintended consequences, which experts, including the national juvenile justice expert Barry Krisberg, called "upcriming." In general, upcriming occurs when a new law or policy ends up "widening the net," ultimately embroiling more individuals—in this case, girls—in the justice system. Suddenly, the acting out of girls, often due to trauma and abuse, was criminalized. Additionally, as more schools adopted "zero-tolerance" policies, law enforcement started being called in for any and every type of misbehavior, no matter how minor (including, once again, incidents that would have been handled informally in the past). Ironically, zero-tolerance policies did not drastically increase the number of boys in the system—they were already being criminalized for acting out at school—but they affected girls. On top of this, researchers tallied up the most serious crimes that led to youth being detained in the juvenile justice system.[11] Overall, girls were locked up for much less serious charges than boys. Together, these factors went a long way to explain the rising arrest rates of girls compared with those of boys.

I was now seeing women who as girls had been part of "upcriming" and "zero tolerance" and had ended up wrongfully detained in the juvenile justice system. The impact of this detention was mixed, with women describing very different experiences in the probation system. A handful of these women were like Rosa, who actually reported flourishing at a probation facility. Along with building a relationship with Tommie Baines, for the first time she began to feel a sense of comradeship with other young women who had, she said, "been through bad experiences. Maybe they hadn't been trafficked, but they'd been abused, and they knew what it felt like to be afraid." Rosa also felt relieved that she didn't have to rely on a man or suffer abuse because she was afraid to be without a boyfriend. "I felt protected for the first time in my life, really protected," she told me. "I thought that everyone in the system cared for me and about me. No one was abusing me, no one was hurting me.

I could go to sleep and not worry someone was going to wake me up and beat me up." But Rosa's experience wasn't the norm. What many girls, among them Denise, encountered was not so positive.

Denise was part of the fallout from upcriming. She ultimately got sent to camp for fighting with her aunt while staying at her home. But this wasn't just a simple domestic violence case. Her aunt was a county sheriff, so Denise was charged with assault on a state peace officer. To this day, Denise believes that her aunt didn't want to press charges, explaining that "she probably felt me being off the street was the best thing for me." In court, Denise was offered the option of detention or returning to her mother's supervision. She chose detention.

"I did *not* want to go to my mom. She was an alcoholic and she just let things happen to my sister and me. It wasn't on purpose; it still happened. So, I was, like, 'Just give me the time and I'll just go to camp.' To this day, I don't regret that decision. It wasn't that camp was so great; it was terrible, but it was better than my mother."

Denise felt she'd been part of the system "my whole life—it was always there. It was like going to school. You saw your PO and you spent time at camp and you met up with people from the halls. It was just what we did. We never thought about whether it did us any good." She cycled in and out of the juvenile justice system through her adolescence. Unlike Rosa, Denise didn't go to Dorothy Kirby. Instead, she was detained at Challenger Memorial Youth Center in the 1990s, when young women were still placed there. This facility honored the ill-fated space shuttle, with each of its six different camps named for an astronaut along with a high school named for "NASA Teacher-in-Space" Christa McAuliffe. It was the closest to secular heresy that I could imagine; from the day it was opened, Challenger was a hellhole. It was located next to a state prison, and if a visitor missed that subtle hint, once inside its walls, it was clear that punishment, not rehabilitation, formed the culture of Challenger. The "dorms"—if they could be called that—had floors and walls of concrete; all that was missing to make this a prison were bars. Toilets and showers were open to public view at all times. Wild birds bearing germs flew in and out of the windows day and night.

There was no kitchen at Challenger. "Food" sent in on steam tables was stomach-turning in its appearance. And this was what passed for a detention facility to "rehabilitate young men and young women" under the age of eighteen. My distress over this wasn't personal. In 2010, the ACLU sued Los Angeles County over the conditions at Challenger, which it described as a "broken" system. The lawsuit was settled in 2011 and led to a series of reforms in the facility's educational system.[12]

None of these reforms arrived in time for Denise. She'd gone to camp when she was fifteen years old and stayed for nine months. Her detention often felt unbearable, and she made it through in a state of numb denial. When she marked her sixteenth birthday at Challenger, "I didn't even know how I felt. I was blank. All the time."

She wasn't like Rosa. Having her own bed wasn't enough to make Denise happy. She had to adjust to sleeping in a dorm with four rows of twelve beds each watched over by probation officers 24–7. Over two decades later, Denise recalled it all vividly: "There was this teacher, her name was Ms. Lacey—she was a little bitty Black lady. Instead of school, we were forced to sit in a classroom sewing and listening to oldies." Along with learning to sew, a skill she never used again, Denise tried out to be a cheerleader for the Mustangs football team at Camp Kilpatrick (immortalized in the movie *Gridiron Gang*). "I wanted it to be like a normal high school," she recalled. Instead, the twenty-four-foot-high fence topped with concertina wire was always there to remind her that this wasn't a normal high school. And to drive home that point, Denise couldn't be a cheerleader because her "high risk" classification prohibited her from being transported to away games. There were other problems, mainly because she kept getting in trouble for her rage. But instead of receiving therapy or any mental health intervention, Denise was sent to solitary confinement several times after acting out. "They kept saying it was rehabilitation. In my mind, it felt like punishment. I was only in solitary for a day or two. One time it was a week. It was scary."[13]

These painful recollections are leavened with Denise's memories of friendships that grew among the young women. On the streets, girls were rivals, both for men and for protection. In camp, however, there was no danger of abuse or violence. For so many girls, these were the first "safe" relationships with women they'd ever experienced. But the temporary nature of their friendships and the fear of losing these attachments drove many to act out. One of her friends grew upset when she learned that Denise was scheduled to leave camp in two weeks. "She thought if we got in a fight I would get more time and have to stay. I wouldn't fight her. Then, she tried to hang herself. After that, she ended up going to YA. That was one place I didn't want to end up: YA. It was bad."

Denise knew YA—the California Youth Authority—was baby prison, the point of no return. Despite abuse from POs, the tedium of sewing class, and problems with bedbugs in their sheets, probation camp, even Challenger, was a lark compared to YA. Denise was luckier than Rosa and so many others; she avoided being sent to YA because she was never charged with a major violent crime. Although she was on community-based probation until she was nineteen years old, once she left Challenger, Denise didn't clock another long-term stay in probation camp. After that, "I only had to go to one of the halls," she recounted. "I got caught at school with some weed and I'd have a nice vacation. I never went to camp again. But I was still in the system."

The system. It's important to understand that juvenile justice is a system beyond camps and halls. It is a complicated labyrinth of suitable placements and probation. Community-based probation officers follow juveniles once they leave the camps and halls, making sure that they are attending "probation schools" and staying out of trouble. Just like staff in the camps and halls, there is no consistency among community-based POs: some are caring and some are abusive.

This was where Denise lucked out: at a probation school in Watts, she was assigned to Chester Leonard, a combination teacher, probation officer, and academic counselor. "He was an older Black man, down to earth but stern, and he let you know that he didn't play." Len, as the kids called him, was flexible, possessing a realistic view of adolescent development. Denise recalled how she "breezed through school, doing everyone's homework for them." Len recognized both her activities and her intelligence, naming her valedictorian of her probation class. More than that, she says, "he kept telling me I was smart." After graduation, she worked full-time at a state college cafeteria. Still, Denise didn't want to just work at a college—*she wanted to go to college.* Her wish fit with what the research shows: girls detained in the juvenile justice system have a much greater desire to obtain advanced education than boys.[14] She knew college was a long shot; still she tucked the idea away in her mind, determined to fulfill her plans for the future.

There was another positive outcome to Denise's involvement with the juvenile probation system: in camp she made a true friend, Clara Vasquez. Their attachment and love for one another remains strong to this day. Despite the fact that as a Latina, Clara might be Denise's enemy on the street, their stories were eerily parallel—she too had landed in the juvenile justice system after running away from a foster home. Here was the experience of the young women who research studies showed weren't super-predators. Instead, Denise, Rosa, and Clara were and are typical of girls who enter the juvenile justice system because they'd been abandoned or abused by parents and had become part of the child welfare and foster-care system.[15] They were all part of a group often labeled as "crossover youth," boys and girls who moved between the child welfare and juvenile justice systems. And that was only the start of their similarities.

Girls like Clara, Denise, and Rosa, who'd been detained in juvenile justice facilities for various lengths of time, all struggled with the same problems that women experienced in the adult jail and prison system: growing mental health issues, the beginnings of substance abuse, twice as many reports of physical abuse as boys, four times as many reports of sexual abuse as boys, and twice as many suicide attempts. And that's just what's reported.

Their experience mirrors that of women in another way: for most of these girls, there were no services in the community. "You go to a school and that's it," Denise ruefully observed. "You got a probation officer out in the community. I don't remember even interacting with my last PO. I was assigned one—I don't remember anything else about him. Not the way I remember Len. There was no one like Len. After school, there was no one helping me. I wish someone or something had been there to help me."

Denise's words are emblematic of what so many young women encounter once they are released from the juvenile justice system. There is nothing awaiting them when they return to the homes and streets that have been a source of violence and pain. After detention in the camps and halls, most young women try to create relationships, they try to find supports—but they are completely on their own. Often there is no one to turn to except the men who have led them into criminal activity in the first place.

"Why do they go back to their boyfriends, why do they go back to the streets? Why don't they change?" an elected official in Washington, DC, asked me after I appeared before a House of Representatives subcommittee. I couldn't get the words out fast enough. *Because there is nothing else for them.* It was hard for me to believe he didn't understand, that he couldn't see what was so obvious. He wasn't alone in this. In the end, the public systems that are supposed to support girls are hamstrung by gendered public policies. There is no sustained understanding of trauma and no community-based support to meet these young women's needs. Still, the juvenile justice system is not alone in failing these young women and pushing them further down the path of incarceration and despair. There is one other system that touches so many of these women's lives, an institution they fear and find themselves enmeshed with from the time they are girls. And while the juvenile justice system ultimately betrays the young women it is supposed to help rehabilitate, its failures are overshadowed by what happens within the structure that is established to shield them from harm: the child welfare system.

INTERLUDE

I n late February, Elie goes to see Pedro, Ivy, and Janeth get arraigned
and formally charged with the murder of the church deacon. The
charges are expanded to include gang enhancements. Afterward, Elie
goes to see Ivy, who cries throughout their entire visit. Ivy tells Elie
she relapsed while the couple was on the run. She can't believe what's
happened and she worries she'll spend the rest of her life in jail. While
Elie agrees that she'll probably be going to prison, she also reassures Ivy
that no one knows what will happen.

In the weeks that follow, as their lawyers prepare for trial, everyone
remains locked up; despite some feeble attempts at raising money, neither Ivy nor Janeth can make bail. Still, bail is not what either woman
thinks about. Because she is undocumented, Janeth has a pair of intertwined fears: Her daughter, Angelina, is just a toddler, and she worries
what will happen to her if she is deported. At the same time, Ivy is
focused on the fate of her son, Jessie. She's the only parent he has—
Carlos, his father, is going to be in prison for a long time. Ivy and Jessie
have been living with a couple she calls her in-laws, but their family tree
is actually much more complicated. Ivy and Carlos aren't married, and
Jessie's grandfather (Carlos's father) lives with Sonja Vallejo, his girlfriend. Despite the unusual relationships, everything was working out
until the deacon's murder. Now, Ivy is terrified that because she and
Carlos are both locked up, four-year-old Jessie will be swept into the

child welfare system and adopted by a stranger. She's pretty sure that his "grandparents" won't want to take care of Jessie now, with all the trouble the case has stirred up. They're furious because their house was raided the Tuesday after the shooting when the police came searching for Ivy. Ivy believes they might want to cut ties with her and her child altogether. They'd been supportive of Ivy for so many years, promising her they'd never give up on her and they'd always take care of Jessie.

Janeth isn't as worried about her daughter, Angelina, going into the system. She knows that Luis, her baby's daddy, is immature, yet she also knows he loves his daughter. They're both dependent on Myra, Luis's mother, who's already told them she'll always take care of their little girl. She wishes she had a real mother she could have depended on—not the woman who raised her, dead and buried in some anonymous grave in Mexico. Now Janeth knows she has no choice: she's got to rely on Luis and his family.

The homegirls make sure there is a steady stream of visitors who see Ivy and Janeth and offer them emotional support. They all worry about the trial and carefully watch both women's attorneys. Everyone likes Janeth's public defender. She's working hard on Janeth's defense and talks to her every day. Because they are both petite, the attorney says she will bring some of her own clothes for Janeth to wear when they go to trial.

But Ivy's lawyer is another matter. From the outset, everyone quickly sees he's completely incompetent. Unfortunately, Ivy doesn't have much of a choice in who represents her. None of the three can afford a private attorney, and each need their own counsel. Janeth was assigned a public defender because she was apprehended first. Pedro, because technically he was apprehended second, was assigned a lawyer from the alternate public defender's office. Just as the name implies, an alternate public defender steps in when there is a conflict of interest—in criminal hearings, only one individual can be represented by a public defender. Since Ivy was arrested last, she was assigned what's known as a panel attorney, from the lowest rung of public defense. Panel attorneys are obtained through the Office of the Indigent Criminal Defense Attorney. Any lawyer from "the panel" is paid a flat fee to defend cases, no matter how many hours they put in, and the fee, even for homicide cases, is small. Their incentive to work many hours on any case is very low—most try to negotiate deals as quickly as possible. Everyone is worried about the panel attorney's abilities except Ivy. She keeps telling the women from the café who visit that things will work out and says she believes that Pedro will honor the hood and take responsibility for the crime. "I trust him," she reassures the women. "He said he would take care of me."

But the women from Homegirl are full of anxiety—they don't trust Pedro, and they've seen Ivy's attorney fall asleep in court during two of the preliminary hearings. Adela is furious, "I told Ivy, you better throw some water at this fool. Your attorney's no good. Fire him. Get rid of him!" At the café, she tells Erika, "We should take some eggs to throw at him. Wake his ass up—he's terrible."

Ivy doesn't listen. Her attorney reassures her that he's going to get her case dismissed in the preliminary hearing. She hopes he's right, and she's preoccupied with Jessie. Unlike Janeth, she can't depend on her baby daddy's family if she's sent to prison. The homegirls keep asking Elie what will happen to Ivy's little boy. "He's really a cute kid," Elie tells me. "I think someone will want to adopt him." But for once, the worst doesn't happen. Jessie's paternal grandfather and his girlfriend file for guardianship—they are dead set against their grandchild going into the system. Ivy doesn't like the fact that they're planning to ask for custody and she fears losing her parental rights, but at least Jessie isn't in foster care.

For now, both Ivy and Janeth start to concentrate on the case. Pedro will be tried first, and the women wonder what he's going to do. Is he going to stand up for them? Is he going to explain that he pushed them, that they didn't want to kill anyone? Ivy and Janeth still don't know how things got out of control, they still don't understand what Pedro was thinking or doing. It all happened so fast. They are both frightened about what will happen when they go to court.

SEVEN

CROSSOVER KIDS

*When I went into foster care, it was the worst day of my life.
It was worse than being abused. I swore I'd never let that
happen to my kids. Then it happened.*

—MELODY DAWSON

I'm listening to the familiar disembodied message—computer generated—informing me that an "inmate at Los Angeles County jail" is calling. After accepting the collect-call charges, which will be exorbitant, I'm on the phone with Melody Dawson, a woman I know from Jordan Downs, a public housing development in Watts. She's crying, and all I can make out between her sobs is that the Department of Children and Family Services (DCFS) paid a visit to her neighbor, Ginger, who's been taking care of her two daughters while Melody's been locked up. Ginger had told the girls their mama would be back soon, but the DCFS social worker disagreed, insisting there was no way of knowing how long Melody would be locked up. Ginger said she would keep the girls with her as long as it took; then the social worker announced that the girls would be "removed for evaluation" the next day. Melody knows, as I do, that this is code for placement in foster care.

None of this is unusual. For incarcerated women, the child welfare system most often becomes involved at the point of arrest, justifying their presence as being "in the best interests of the child." But research has shown how a system that is supposed to be protective is actually punitive, for mothers as well as their children. In reality, across the US, corrections officials and child welfare workers rarely inquire or even think about how incarceration will negatively impact the parent-child relationship during the possible phases of trial, sentencing, and prison intake.[1] And here, as parents facing incarceration, the consequences for women differ radically from those experienced by men. Although all mothers and fathers have to cope with separation from their children, for men, there's usually a woman on the outside—mothers, wives, girl-friends—to care for their offspring. In fact, when men are incarcerated, whether it's in a state or federal prison, 90 percent of the time the children they have together are taken care of by their mother. But women don't have the same backup. Few men—somewhere between 22 and 28 percent—assume responsibility for childrearing if their female spouses or partners are incarcerated.[2] Instead, when women are locked up, families are splintered, and the upheaval affects communities as well. Children all too often lose any sense of permanence and feel they don't belong anywhere. They stop attending school, feeling unmoored and uncertain, emotions they share with their mothers. And despite all the upheaval, there is simply no support and no reentry planning for women and their children once mothers are incarcerated. Instead, there is a void that, all too often, children's protective services rush in to fill.

I reassure Melody that I will call Elie as she's pleading, "I just want my kids back. I don't want them to go through what I had to go through." Her words sting, even though they're all too familiar to me. I've heard those two phrases over and over because Melody's experience is tragically common among incarcerated women. The reason for this is sadly straightforward; throughout their lives, in different forms and different ways, one force is a constant: the child welfare system. Most of these women have been entangled with DCFS for as long as they can remember—first as children, then as mothers.

So many previously incarcerated women possess painful memories of being separated from their own families as girls, of the miseries and abuses that occurred in foster care. They will do anything to save their children from the same fate but are often powerless to do so. Despite their devotion to their children, they usually experience a series of heartbreaking outcomes that cascade through their lives, once they are locked up, even if it is before a trial.

Overwhelmingly, women struggle to keep their children within their extended family system while they are incarcerated. Most often they reach out to grandparents, usually their own mothers or those of the father. But rarely does this represent the best of solutions, particularly when the parents are elderly or unable to care for their grandchildren. Many women also are reluctant to rely on their families if there's been a history of abuse or neglect involving them. This represents a "Sophie's choice" for many incarcerated women: if they can't rely on their families because that's where they were abused, their own children—like Melody's—may be placed in foster care.

This then brings on the threat of adoption. Once children are placed in foster care, the clock begins to tick. Then the parents or—in many cases—single parent will have a specific period of time—in California, it's eighteen months—to comply with whatever conditions are set up before the family can be reunified. For so many women, either during or after incarceration, such "family reunification" represents an impossibility. If family reunification fails, time's up and the children are eligible for adoption. Sometimes, extended-family members adopt the children; sometimes complete strangers become the new parents for the sons and daughters whose mothers are locked away in jail or prison. For children who are "too old" to be adopted, usually adolescents, there may be placement in a "group home," which is just what the name implies: a setting where groups of older foster kids reside together under the care of an adult, with little in common except their lack of a permanent home.

These outcomes are not just a matter of public policy. Over the past ten years, the number of women I'd interviewed who'd been involved in the child welfare system as children was stunning. Among the eighty women who shared their histories with me, sixty-one had been entangled with the child welfare system when they were girls. They'd been in foster care or extended-family or kinship care or in group homes or in some combination of all three. And most of them had vowed their own children would be free of such pain. "I was determined that no child of mine was gonna get mixed up in the system," one woman told me. "I didn't want them to suffer what I'd suffered. And I didn't want them to go into foster care or get adopted. No baby of mine was getting adopted."

What's unsettling about all this is that even as they struggled to avoid it, most women acknowledged, and even accepted, the ongoing presence of the child welfare system in their lives. Whether it was a part of their experience as girls or a threat to their own families as women, "the county" or "children's services" always seemed to be there in the background. And incarceration just made everything worse for each of these women. It meant that they were further behind and more disempowered than the other mothers who were involved with the system. It also meant they had more to fear, more to lose, and no one there to help them. Ivy and Janeth were practically the poster children for the problems that mothers encountered even before they went to trial, let alone after they were convicted.

The problems began once bail was set and grew from there. It's generally acknowledged that today, in America, money bail represents a major criminal justice issue. In particular, the cash bail system affects Black people, people of color, and the poor disproportionately, even when they are being held after arrest for nonviolent crimes.[3] Today, individuals await trial in overcrowded jails for unimaginable periods of time. I had seen this firsthand as an expert witness in a gang case, where the accused had already been in jail for five years and his trial date *still* had not been set. And this was before the Covid-19 pandemic, which ultimately set things back even further. The title of a recent book examining the inequities of bail tells the whole story in three words: *Incarceration Without Conviction.*[4]

On top of its disproportionate impacts on Blacks, people of color, and the poor, the effects of bail are gendered, with profound consequences for the children of women who are locked up. The long-term effects of the ill-fated War on Drugs started the incarceration ball rolling. Today, money bail is critical to understanding why the percentage of women America imprisons continues climbing: the number of women now incarcerated in jail is fourteen times as high as it was in the 1970s. Still, what is crucial in all of this is the fact that, as so many sources report, the majority of women are being held in jail on what is termed "pretrial" status, purely because they cannot post bail.[5] *They have not been found guilty of any crime. They have not even gone to court.* On top of that, most women are charged with low-level, nonviolent offenses, such as drug possession, shoplifting, and parole violations. The result of women's inability to make bail is that more than a quarter of a million children in the US have a mother in jail, awaiting trial.[6]

But the problem doesn't stop with bail. If a woman is ultimately found guilty of the crime she's been arrested for, she goes to jail or prison. At this point, there is further evaluation by and involvement of the child welfare system, with devastating consequences. The children of incarcerated mothers are five times as likely to wind up in foster care as those with incarcerated fathers. In certain states, such as Oklahoma, once a child is in foster care, the state can completely terminate parental rights in two years. As with bail, Black families and families of color are affected in greater numbers than any other group. The last year that national data was made available through the US Bureau of Justice was 2008. At that time, 62 percent of women in state prisons nationwide reported having a minor child, and 42 percent of these women reported being the single parent in the household. Incarcerated mothers were three times as likely as fathers to report they provided the daily care for their children. As of 2019, the Prison Policy Initiative estimated that nationwide 80 percent of incarcerated women in jails had children. Recent estimates also put the number of children in the US with an incarcerated parent at 2.7 million, or 1 of every 28 children. Broken down by race, the numbers are even more disproportionate and disturbing: 1 in 9 Black children, 1 in 28 Latino children, and 1 in 57 white children in the US have a parent who is incarcerated.[7] These women and their children don't have anyone to turn to for help. There are few services available for them, and very little effort is made to strengthen the relationship between mothers and children separated by incarceration. Because of all this, mothers who can't afford bail and want to get back to their children swiftly are motivated to plead guilty even when they haven't committed any crime.

What makes things worse for so many of these mothers was just what Melody cried over—their own involvement with the child welfare system as children. Their experiences had scarred them and had led them down the trajectory of bad relationships, trauma, addiction, and crime. They desperately wanted to raise their sons and daughters while avoiding any contact with the child welfare system and often trying to circumvent its authority. And yet they were often powerless to escape this fate. There was no one who embodied this double trauma more than a woman I first met through Denise, who had insisted, "You gotta talk to my friend. You gotta talk to Clara."

Clara Vasquez was born in Sonora, Mexico, where she lived with her great-grandmother until she was seven years old. Then, she traveled to the United States to reunite with the mother she'd never known. In Los Angeles, her mother's husband was the man Clara eventually considered her father. "Gilbert is the person who raised me, gave me his last name. He's not my biological father. But he put shoes on my feet, a roof over my head, so I'm grateful to him, even though he was very, very abusive." As she recalls her childhood Clara looks tired, yet there are traces of the girl she once was in the warmth of her eyes and her smile. Her round face is surrounded by a penumbra of light brown hair, and she speaks softly, almost liltingly. She looks like what she is today: a sweet, middle-aged mother, smiling as she checks her phone for texts from her daughter. "You have to understand," she tells me, "it's just the way life went on in those days. Everyone accepted that my dad would get angry and he'd beat us."

But, as things turned out, not everyone accepted the abuse. Clara's oldest sister, Maria, started getting into fights at school and running away from home—girls' most common response to trauma, as research has revealed. It was not until *her mother* lost control and beat Maria that she ran away—straight to the police. Shortly after that, officers arrived at the Vasquez household. In response, the family was fearfully cooperative. Clara's mother and stepfather were "legal," but the three girls were undocumented, and their polite responses masked anxiety. They needn't have worried. Unless the abuse was egregious, most cops weren't interested in a child welfare case. They wanted to chase bad guys and leave "domestics"—intrafamily issues—to social workers. Their attitude worked to the advantage of Clara's family and the case was referred to the Department of Children and Family Services. Now Clara's story took a strange twist: in follow-up visits with a social worker, her mother decided the children would be safer and have more opportunities if they were in foster care. Clara never forgot the day her life changed.

"My mom sat my sisters and me down and told us, 'You guys are going to go to a foster home; they're going to help you out.' So, my mom basically just gave us up to the foster system. She told us this would help us to get ahead in the world and—most important—we would get our papers." I'd never thought of foster care as a pathway to citizenship and upward mobility. I knew Clara was telling the truth—but the story just didn't make sense. Worst of all, her mother's unusual decision kicked off what became Clara's lifelong struggle with the child welfare system.

Clara is certain her mother is the reason she's now a citizen. But the price was high; the talk with her mother marked the last time she lived with her family. After that, she became a child of DCFS. Once she and her sisters were "placed," Clara moved through four different foster homes sprawled throughout Los Angeles County, in the working-class communities of Whittier, South Gate, and East Los Angeles. During this time, there was one social worker she always remembered, Deborah. "She talked to me," Clara says. "She tried to help me—all the time." Just as Tommie Baines had connected with Rosa, Deborah built a relationship with Clara, making sure that she went to school and that her foster home offered at least an accepting environment, if not a loving one. Then Deborah moved on from DCFS, worn out by the demands of a huge case load and limited resources. This often happens. Some of the most compassionate social workers leave child-welfare work behind because of the pain, the demands, the secondary trauma. I'd experienced this when I worked briefly as a children's social worker. It was why, I constantly explained to people, working with gang members was actually less painful than working with DCFS. In their families, gang members had frequently suffered child abuse and acted out their rage, sometimes with horrifying results. Still, they weren't denying what they'd experienced, and their rage was out in the open. Clara, thirteen, with her beloved social worker gone, encountered what many think of as the second abuse, at the hands of the child welfare system.

The foster homes were always pretty wretched, but one stands out in Clara's mind. "The foster kids used to stay in a little room, like a shack, in back of the house. It wasn't even attached to the house; it was next to the doghouse. There was no bathroom and we slept in there. We could go inside the house at certain times. The mother gave us food; there just wasn't enough. We were starving all the time. I never forgot that little shack." Eventually, Clara moved to another foster home, and there were more changes in store. She couldn't adjust, and then the social worker discovered that there were more foster children in the home than the law allowed. After that, when Clara was moved to her fourth foster home, she was done. She ran away when she was fourteen years old, and homelessness became her reality.

"Most nights, I didn't know where I was going to sleep. But it was still better than foster care. Once in a blue moon, I'd call my mom and be like 'Hey, Mom, I'm still alive.'" On the streets, the inevitable involvement with gangs, drugs, and violence began as Clara struggled to survive. At first, drugs weren't part of the picture; she focused on survival, and that meant being part of a gang. She didn't have time to get high; her fight to belong somewhere, to something, was all-consuming. In Central Los Angeles, Clara latched on to the West Side Rebels, or WSR13, a barrio well known throughout Hollywood.[8]

Unlike most of the women I was interviewing, Clara bypassed men, turning to the gang directly for protection. Her attraction to gangs "wasn't so much that I was looking for a boyfriend or a family," she says. "I was just looking for somebody to be there with me." The gang members squatted together in abandoned apartments. One homie would steal radios from cars and sell them to get money for food.

She ultimately wound up at one of her homeboy's houses after almost a year on the streets, where, in the barrio version of foster care, "the dad took me in, and I was his daughter." Just as with the other girls, men, not women, helped her. Women were rivals; ultimately only men could be trusted to take care of you. "He was a good man and that was where I lived for six months until I went to jail." Like most youth, Clara refused to accept the vocabulary of juvenile justice and its empty euphemisms: "halls and camps," "detention," and "placement." Her description of her crimes was equally straightforward. "I was about sixteen, and I got arrested because we were gangbanging and we were robbing people, and someone got hurt." She went to Central Juvenile Hall and then to Camp Resnick at Challenger Memorial Youth Center, where she met Denise and "we first ran together. We've been friends ever since." She shows me the photos Denise has been texting her with the caption, "Guess where I'm at?" We're both laughing at this point—Denise is on a UCLA field trip to Challenger. Holding her smartphone close to her face, Clara scrolls through her memories as well as the photographs.

Just like Denise, Clara was part of a group that researchers and policymakers refer to as "crossover youth." These are the boys and girls whose lives consist of overlapping risk factors that lead first to involvement with more than one system. Usually, they all begin in child welfare. However, because the risk factors include trauma, family dysfunction, abuse, neglect, substance abuse, and mental health issues, they act out or commit an offense, leading to involvement with a second system, juvenile justice. The term "crossover" tells the story—these youths literally "cross over," becoming engaged with multiple systems, with little attention paid to the intensity of their needs. Too often, young men and young women exit both systems without resolving past traumas and familial issues, seriously hindering their abilities to succeed in education, employment, or future relationships.[9] As crossover youths, both Clara and Denise experienced this, moving from supervision by DCFS to detention under the jurisdiction of the LA County Probation Department.

Clara was scared at first, but once she had her own bed, she realized that Camp Resnick actually was a solution to her homelessness. She was even back attending classes there—the camp had a school on site. As she talked about how relieved she felt, I thought of Rosa. And I remembered what Father Greg Boyle had told me: that for many kids—especially girls—camp represents the first time they truly feel taken care of and safe. It's not a punishment so much as a respite.

No one knew she was locked up. When Clara was arrested, there wasn't anyone to call; she was just a teenage runaway and she didn't want to risk a return to foster care. Out on the streets, she'd made up a name that followed her into Camp Resnick. Then, one Sunday, the front desk announced she had a visitor. "I kept saying, 'Are you sure, cuz it's my fake name,' and they're like 'Yeah, yeah.' So, I went over to the visiting area and it was my mom. We both started crying."

To this day, Clara doesn't know how her mother found her. Sadly, after their tearful reunion, her mother only visited once more over the year and a half Clara was locked up. "I never really know if she loves me," Clara said, sighing. "I wonder what it is about me that makes it so she doesn't care. I knew I couldn't count on anyone except for the barrio, the gang. They are the only ones who cared about me." She sounded like Denise talking about her hood. All I could think was that this pathway of trauma is also a pathway of abandonment.

Clara sometimes wondered why a social worker from the child welfare system hadn't found her. These thoughts invariably ended with a sense of resolution. Even though she'd been abandoned to the streets, she felt relieved that she'd escaped foster care. That relief would soon change. Having fulfilled her detention, Clara was discharged from Challenger Memorial, and just as with women exiting jail or prison, there were no support services for her, no reentry plan. The LA County Probation Department was notorious for banking all the state funds allocated for reentry services but failing to develop any meaningful aftercare programming. Instead, Clara was released to DCFS and sent right back into the foster-care system. Her involvement with this system had caused all the problems that she'd run away from. Now she had to return. And to make things worse, she was placed with the first family she'd lived with—the one that had put her in the room next to the dog-house before being forced to move her into a bedroom. Now she was assigned to the exact same bedroom.

It was full circle with a vengeance, and Clara exploded. Again, it was the rage, the same rage Rosa had experienced when the court returned her to her mother. Within days, Clara beat up her roommate, another foster child. The beating was so severe that the police were called, Clara was arrested, taken into custody and eventually placed at MacLaren Hall Children's Center, a huge child welfare facility routinely referred to as "the orphanage." Located in El Monte, east of Los Angeles, Mac-Laren was little more than a warehouse for children who had nowhere else to go. MacLaren was also the notorious emblem of the failure of both the child welfare and juvenile justice systems. It was overcrowded and under-resourced, and the staff violently abused the children in their care. In 2003, after years of horrifying rumors and reports, MacLaren finally closed permanently, but not before the ACLU and other groups had filed a lawsuit against Los Angeles County over the treatment there of children with emotional and behavioral problems. At the same time, a class-action lawsuit was filed that sought unspecified damages for more than a thousand children who'd been physically and/or emotion-ally abused at MacLaren. To this day, there is a website, Survivors of MacLaren, where survivors' accounts are collected.[10]

All this was ten years too late for Clara, who sized up the situation and knew there was more trauma in store for her. Within days, she ran away from MacLaren, and her "protection" by the child welfare system came to an unofficial end. It was 1993 and Clara was seventeen years old. She was on the streets at the height of the decade of death in Cali-fornia: the crack epidemic was in full swing and gangs were murdering people at a rapid rate, accounting for most of the 1,200 homicides re-corded that year in Los Angeles.

Clara developed the skill set of someone decades older, working her street networks and selling drugs. Within months she'd put enough money together to rent an apartment. She connected with her mother, who wove in and out of her life once Clara reassured her that she wouldn't ask for any money. It was not lost on Clara that she expressed an odd kind of satisfaction in her daughter's activities. "My mom lived the life that I lived—she'd been part of the gangs in Mexico. So, she'd say to me, 'Good, you're on the street working. Don't be a bum.'" Much of what Clara said reminded me of my much loved Joanna Carillo, whose parents actually reveled in her achievements as a drug dealer, often expressing their pride in her "success."

Clara got a job at Little Caesar's Pizza and sold drugs on the side. She was free and making enough money to enjoy herself. "I felt good," she said. This way of life lasted almost two years, until Clara met Javier. She sounds a lot like Denise and so many other women when she tells me, "I left behind everything for him. He told me I didn't need to work, he would take care of me." She gave up her apartment and they lived together happily until Clara discovered she was pregnant. Two weeks later, Javier left her for someone else. Again, she was homeless with no money, squatting in abandoned apartments. "Sometimes I'd fall asleep on a dirty couch on the street," Clara says. "I was so ashamed! When I got with Javier, I had my apartment, I had my furniture, I had my job, I had my money. When he left me, I was broke, pregnant, and in the streets. He took everything. I thought, I'll just sell some drugs and figure it out later." Temporary relief came when her sister Maria offered Clara room and board in return for watching her children. Between babysitting and drug dealing, Clara saved her money, began learning about benefits she could apply for, and—ready to give birth—moved out again.

"I got an apartment and had my daughter, Theresa, two days later." Javier came to see her at the hospital and, acknowledging the baby for the first time, promised he'd be a good father. When Clara got home to the apartment, he took both mother and daughter out, buying a car seat and a crib. Their relationship began anew.

At first, Javier visited daily and gave Clara money to buy whatever she needed. But soon his interest and his money began to flag. Then Clara discovered that the girl he'd left her for earlier was pregnant. Three months later, Javier had a second daughter. "After that baby was born, he stopped coming completely. So, there I was, on my own. I wanted someone to help me. Anyone."

Javier's abandonment traumatized her; it was her mother all over again. Lonely and frightened, she began depending on Eduardo Lopez, who she knew from the neighborhood. They moved in together, and this marked the time in Clara's life "when a lot of things went downhill. He was on drugs. I started using drugs with him, and then he started physically abusing me." Her drug use escalated—whatever was available, she used. It was always a way to run away from her pain, to deny the abuse she was experiencing. Still, she couldn't leave Eduardo. "What was I supposed to do, go back to the street? I thought he would take care of me." Those words. Again.

There were days Clara wanted to give up and end her life. But if she committed suicide, Theresa would go into the child welfare system—she couldn't let that happen. She was looking for a purpose, any purpose, and in the midst of her pain and confusion, she made her first attempt to go to school, enrolling in Los Angeles Community College. "I wanted an education. I didn't want to live in that abusive relationship. That's one thing I've always thought. I didn't want to be one of these statistics of a useless gangbanger. I didn't want to end up in the streets." This sounds unimaginable and meaningful all at once. Somehow, some way, Clara had both resilience and the seeds of self-esteem. And she had direction. A neighbor in her building knew both English and Spanish versions of American Sign Language and started to teach her interpretation. "I remember when I was in the foster system, my mom would go to the courts, and she always had to get an interpreter because she didn't speak English. That's when I knew, I want to help people like my mom, who can't speak for themselves."

At first, she was excited to be in school. She'd stopped using drugs and Eduardo was supportive. He told her they'd work it out. "School was like being a kid in Disneyland. You know you want to be there, but you don't know what to do; you don't know even where to start. I made so many mistakes." Clara hadn't been in any kind of school since Camp Resnick. Without knowing how to navigate the system, she floundered. "I was failing in my classes, so I dropped out." What she'd begun with so much hope quickly fell apart.

Clara descended into drug use, self-medicating her depression and her trauma. Her emotions mirrored what many young women caught up in the spiral of trauma, pain, and system involvement lived through each day. When Eduardo's abuse grew more violent, Clara knew that he wasn't protecting her, he was trying to destroy her. She kicked him out, and then discovered she was pregnant again. Overwhelmed with the thought of bringing a second child into all this chaos, she broke down. She'd stay in bed all day, dozing off from the drugs, then awakening in a panic that her daughter would make noise and "somebody would knock on the door, and we'd have to answer. They'd see me high and take my daughter to foster care. I didn't want that to happen to her."

Her emotional distress and her addiction crushed her spirit. Eduardo moved back in, promising to support her. Instead, they wound up spending their money on drugs and inching closer to homelessness. Disturbed at what they saw, Clara's mother and sister called the Department of Children and Family Services. The subsequent investigation led DCFS to recommend that custody of Theresa be awarded to Javier. Clara was frantic. "My daughter had no idea who Javier was, and now she was going to live with him!"

In a cascade of crises, she learned there was a warrant out for her arrest for witness intimidation in connection with a gang case, and a few days later, she was picked up by the police. Eight months pregnant, Clara was sentenced to jail; she gave birth to her second daughter while she was incarcerated. Clara only saw her for a few moments—long enough to hold her and name her Aracely—then the DCFS took charge. There was one piece of good news: Clara's sister was awarded temporary custody of both girls. But after a few days, her sister complained that it was too much work and called DCFS to come get both children. Theresa was given to Javier, and Eduardo's family were granted custody of Aracely. Locked up, Clara became even more upset when she learned that the Lopezes wanted to adopt Aracely. No matter who the girls were living with, she was *still* involved with the child welfare system.

This outcome, all too frequent in the lives of incarcerated women, can be traced to a piece of federal legislation signed into law by President Bill Clinton. At the time, the 1997 Adoption and Safe Families Act (ASFA) was heralded as a breakthrough that would ensure children's health and safety. Today, it's largely viewed as causing the shift toward a more punitive child welfare system. ASFA was supposed to be a fix for the problems and abuses that had riddled foster care, many of which resulted from earlier legislation, the Adoption Assistance and Child Welfare Act of 1980. In the end, ASFA turned out to be an overcorrection: by focusing more on what were thought to be children's best interests, there was less emphasis on families being kept together. Among its provisions, ASFA established set deadlines for terminating parental rights for children in foster care: if a child spends fifteen out of twenty-two months in foster care, time's up and they're ready to be adopted. Talking to any woman who's faced poverty, trauma, and incarceration, this rapid timeline feels impossible to beat. For so many mothers who are unable to pay cash bail and secure freedom with the clock ticking, the child welfare and criminal justice systems almost seem to conspire to sever a mother's ties to her children rapidly and permanently.

There are exceptions that can be granted: if the state determines that terminating parental rights isn't in the child's best interest, if the state hasn't provided services to ensure the safe return of the child home, or if the child is being cared for by a relative. But in many cases, even if relatives are involved or the mother is receiving services to facilitate reunification, there is still risk of her parental rights being terminated. The impact of ASFA has turned out to be both tragic and lethal for families. According to the Marshall Project, a criminal justice journalism organization, because of ASFA's strict provisions, "at least 32,000 parents since 2006 have had their children permanently taken from them without being accused of physical or sexual abuse, though other factors, often related to their poverty, may have been involved. *Of those, nearly 5,000 appear to have lost their parental rights because of their imprisonment alone.*[11]

After serving her sentence, Clara wasn't sure what would happen with her girls. It felt like public policy was literally structured to deny her custody of her daughters. She had no idea how she was going to fight the loss of her children, but she was determined to do it. In the meantime, as part of her probation, she was attending anger management and domestic violence classes, which were literally her only form of reentry support. Ignoring Eduardo's pleas to give him another chance, she focused on her two-hour supervised visits with Theresa. She'd arrive early to meet Javier at the LAPD Hollywood Station, though he was always late; her complaints to the social worker were ignored. "I felt like the social worker and the whole child welfare system were all just lined up against me."

In reality, Clara was living out what the research over the past decade has shown: the child welfare system routinely creates a series of obstacles that further separate formerly incarcerated women and their children. Despite the pretense of supervised visits and the empty words about progress, formerly incarcerated women believe they're outmatched in trying to maintain connections with their children. Clara and so many others saw the child welfare system as just another institution working against them, like juvenile probation and adult criminal justice. For women lacking a stable income and secure housing, it's extremely difficult if not impossible for a woman to meet the state's requirements that will allow her children to return to her.[12] Women are also haunted by the very real anxiety that they may lose custody of their children forever. The fear Clara experienced was compounded by her knowledge that "my sister and my mom were actually helping Javier get permanent custody of Theresa." Clara was reliving the nightmare of her childhood through the experiences of her daughters. She started crying as she remembered the trifecta of trauma she experienced: domestic violence, incarceration, and the loss of her children, all at the hands of her family. "I can't believe they helped Javier get custody, even though some of it was my fault as well because I wouldn't leave that abusive relationship, that's all I knew. *I thought he would take care of me.*"

Overwhelmed by what she was facing, Clara returned to Eduardo. The physical abuse had finally stopped, but in its place his verbal and emotional abuse now escalated. They were also beginning to "chip," using drugs on occasion. Clara kept all of this hidden—she had to complete probation and she wanted her daughters back. It was frightening: all this time it felt like DCFS was speeding things up and she was falling farther behind. As the Lopezes' adoption of Aracely moved forward, Clara tried to make her peace with the situation. "At least I knew where she was living—and she was with blood, not strangers. It was a stable home; Eduardo's parents had been married for over fifty years." She saw Aracely whenever she could.

Her supervised visits with Theresa at the LAPD Hollywood station continued to be humiliating. Then one day, even though she arrived early, the social worker was already waiting for her. She couldn't make eye contact with Clara as she told her that Javier and Theresa had disappeared; he'd severed all contact and had "failed to inform" DCFS where the family had moved. The system that was punishing her because it was supposedly "protecting" her children had now failed her daughter completely. It reminded Clara of her life after probation camp: how DCFS had sent her back to foster care at the same neglectful household she'd run away from before. It reminded her of all the times she'd tried to do her best as systems and forces bigger and stronger than she'd ever be just ran her over. Her drug use continued; it was the only way Clara could deal with the pain she was experiencing. She felt powerless and alone.

It's no wonder that women who struggled with trauma and incarceration felt like they couldn't stand up against the institutional strength of criminal justice and child welfare. It's no wonder they turned to self-medication. It wasn't substance abuse; it was a matter of survival. How else could they face the loss and the stress of their lives? I was tired of so many people—well intentioned and yet poorly informed—asking me why women would drink or use drugs when they were mothers. Didn't they care about their children? Didn't they care about themselves? The simple answer to both questions was "Yes, *and . . .*" Yes, and they were dealing with several pressures at the same time without any supports, without anyone to stand with them and help them through the pain of their lives. Clara and so many others self-medicated while they dealt with all these pressures, *and they kept going.*

For two years, Clara had no idea where Theresa was living or if she was even alive. She asked everyone who might know Javier or might have heard something about where he'd gone. She called the 800 number that helped parents search for missing children. Every time she got close to finding Theresa, all signs of Javier would vanish, again and again—he moved repeatedly. And then she found out she was pregnant.

EIGHT

SELF-MEDICATION

I never took drugs to have fun. I just took drugs to face life.

—ANIKA JOHNSON

Once she found out she was pregnant, Clara knew she had to get clean. But she didn't know how. It felt like drugs had always been part of her life, and the reasons she kept relapsing were always the same. She and other women who'd been locked up faced so many obstacles once they were released—children, money, housing, jobs, partners, family; the list was endless. And all that didn't account for what they didn't talk about—the background noise of deep pain that was a constant element of the trauma they'd experienced throughout their lives. Their bodies and their emotions were on red alert, but not because of a single crisis; they were dealing with a lifetime of multiple traumas that often began before they even had their first period.

Most women in jail and prison are victims of multiple abuses—sexual abuse in childhood, passage through the child welfare system with resulting abuses there, then intimate partner violence—a perfect storm resulting in mental health issues and self-medication through drugs. In most cases, drugs ultimately lead to criminal activity and incarceration. And once they leave jail or prison, drugs are what lead women right back in.

The research attests to this. Studies show that severe trauma is a major contributing factor in female incarceration. So is addiction. Eighty-six percent of jailed women have experienced sexual violence, and the majority have problems with substance abuse. There's often a feedback loop between the two: drugs can serve as an escape from trauma, and addiction can make a woman more vulnerable to further abuse.[1] Over nearly two decades, researchers have agreed that "the most common pathways to crime for women are based on their history of trauma and abuse, poverty and substance abuse."[2]

How did the substance abuse begin? From the time they were girls, most women developed treatment for their trauma "on the fly." They didn't go once a week to see a therapist; they didn't receive "trauma informed care." Instead, their default was self-medication. "It's hood therapy," a woman named Vonnie Johnson, who'd been incarcerated seventeen years for killing her abuser, told me with insight and accuracy. But if "hood therapy" was cheaper than appointments at a professional's office, the bill for self-medication soon came due: addiction and heightened criminal activity. Women sometimes talked about "getting high" or "partying" when they referred to drug use. But despite their using words that connoted fun and enjoyment, drug use was not about fun. It was about survival.

Drug use was also, always, about medicating the trauma. From the time she was thirteen years old, this was exactly what Ivy had done. She could never remember a time when there wasn't drug use and drug dealing going on in the house. And, so, it was no surprise that by the time she was thirteen Ivy was already using cocaine, a habit that only escalated by the time she dropped out of school at sixteen. Drugs were what got her through her first abusive relationship. When her ex-boyfriend and her mother died in the same year, drugs were what got her through the loss. Ivy knew without knowing that the trauma of these deaths, especially her mother's, was too much to bear. She'd been depressed before, but now she sank even deeper into hopelessness and despair, engaging in a cross between self-medication and slow-motion suicide. All she wanted to do was get high—it was important; no, it was a matter of survival—not to feel anything. Ivy did whatever she could do to avoid the pain: drugs, drinking, gangbanging. Even after she gave birth to her son, Jessie, the pain and self-medication continued.

It was not until she was arrested on drug charges and sentenced to two years in state prison that depression gave way to fear. The fear was not for her own life but for Jessie. She feared that he'd go into the child welfare system and would be lost to her forever. Finally, she knew, this was a loss and a trauma she could not survive. She vowed she'd never use again. I still didn't know what happened the day that Pedro shot the deacon. There were rumors Ivy had relapsed, that the emotional and physical pain of having fallen into yet another abusive relationship was too much for her to handle. No one could say for certain. Many of the women at the Homegirl Café faced the same losses, the same traumas, and the same struggles with using that Ivy had confronted, but they hadn't resorted to violence. We all shared our thoughts, but I was haunted by what one of the homegirls asked me: "It coulda been any of us. Why Ivy?"

Incarcerated women of every racial and ethnic group report high levels of substance abuse and addiction. And this kicks off a tragic chain of events: drug-related arrests and recidivism make up a large segment of the overall arrests of girls and women.[3] This all begins at a young age. Even in the juvenile system, research shows, girls are involved in more extensive drug use than boys, experimenting as well as showing the signs of addiction with a broader range of drugs. Their drug use also leads to a higher rate of resulting problems when compared with boys, and in what is a recurring problem, there are fewer drug treatment programs for girls than boys while they're in detention or in placement.[4]

This happened with Denise, who started smoking dope when she was part of the hood. She drank and smoked bud pretty steadily, worrying that she was suffering from substance abuse. Once she started working, Denise began limiting her drug use to weekends. Then, her drug use tapered off even more once she became involved with Eric. Falling in love made her far happier than any substance she might have used in the past. But things started to change as her relationship with Eric became more tumultuous and violent. Eric was alternately controlling, then adoring. Their living situation in LA worsened—Eric wasn't working, they couldn't afford their rent. The couple moved to San Diego, and he ended up going to jail there. "I still loved him," Denise says, "and I waited for him the whole year he was locked up." Once Eric was released, the two traveled back to Los Angeles, where they started working. Denise felt hope again, until she discovered that Eric was cheating on her with one of her friends. She told Eric she was done and left, moving in with her aunt. Almost immediately, Eric begged her to come back. "He kept saying, 'Please, please, I love you, I'm sorry,' and I kept saying, 'I'm so done.' He was trying to do things to show me he was being a better person. I just didn't believe him."

Eric kept hoping this was going to play out just like other breakups the couple had gone through, until the night everything changed. Denise's voice turned to a whisper as she talked about what happened. "It had been about two weeks and Eric came over with his friends. He was already drunk, and I sent him back home, to his godmother's. A few hours later he came back, and he had a gun. I wouldn't let him into my aunt's house. I stayed outside, talking to him, and he kept saying he was going to kill me and kill himself. I told him to go home. . . . Then he tried to shoot me, and I ran into my aunt's. I don't remember much. I swear, I didn't hear the gun shots. But I opened the door and I saw him lying there, in the front yard. I knew he shot himself. He was dead, and I don't remember anything . . . only his body, lying there. I remember screaming and hollering. Then I went blank."

Denise rarely cried in front of me, but now tears were running down her cheeks. She sat silent for a moment, then motioned for me to go ahead.

"How did you get through it?" I asked.

"I. Did. Not."

Denise looked down for several moments, then continued.

"I did not get through it. His sister was talking shit to me the next day—she said I was having an affair with another man. I stopped talking to her. Then I started talking to his godmother. I told her I wanted to die. She wanted me to go to the hospital—she said I needed help. I thought she was right, so I called my boss."

Denise's supervisor told her she'd be fired if she didn't return in two days, so she went back to work. In the meantime, Eric's mother told the police Denise had killed her son; they launched an investigation and quickly confirmed that Eric had killed himself. After that, Denise's aunt told her she had to move out; she'd traumatized her family. "I lived with my mom for a couple of months. Then she told me to leave, and I was on the street." Denise was twenty-two years old.

Soon after that, Denise met a new guy, Dino. She moved in with him because, she says, "I felt safe. He was taking care of me. He had money and he told me not worry." Dino was the first person who completely supported Denise. He was also the person who introduced her to crack cocaine. It was cheap, brought on an immediate high, and proved to be extremely addictive. Whatever pain Denise felt about Eric, about her life, became meaningless—with crack, it all went away.

The trouble started when Dino's money ran out and he started boosting merchandise from stores. Denise had no idea how much illegal activity was going on until Dino was arrested, pled guilty, and went to jail. His departure barely registered; she was still doing crack, and a month later, she was evicted from Dino's apartment. "After that, I went back to my mom's for a few months." But her mother wasn't prepared to provide long-term housing and told Denise to leave. Again.

"I was living on the street five maybe six years." Denise didn't "seek treatment" for her traumas. She was in survival mode. The only treatment available involved substances. These weren't prescription-based pharmaceuticals; she relied on street drugs for relief. I could only imagine her life and how she must have felt like she was being electroshocked—a melding of pain and unreality, with both past and future slipping away.

"I was on Western Avenue selling dope and whoring. I smoked crack because I was so fucking damaged. My life experience from when I was a girl had just hurt me so much. Having my boyfriend commit suicide and not being able to save him was like the catapult into drugs.

ENTRY LESSONS | 115

Whatever I could do, I *would* do to make it go away. I was in and out of jail. I got locked up and then I would get out. Over and over again—put me in jail, stay behind bars, then back on the street. It wasn't as bad for me as some of the women I was locked up with—they had kids. Kids. In that life—can you imagine?" Denise looks at me, wide-eyed. It's hard to reconcile this reality with the woman sitting in front of me, clad in knee-high boots, black pants, and a brightly colored turquoise sweater. She has a backpack full of books on public policy, race relations, and a guide to MSW programs in California.

It's a miracle that she never got pregnant, never had to have a baby or an abortion. She insists she faced fewer obstacles because she was alone—not a single mother with a child—but even so there was nothing out there to meet her needs, no one to help. "I didn't need reentry services, I needed *entry* services—like how do you enter into a normal life? Reentry is a lie; it's the wrong word. What we need is help on how to heal, how to live, how to enter this world."

When I ask Denise what enabled her to survive, she answers, "I honestly don't know." Listening to her story, I don't know either. She remembers "random acts of kindness. There was a guy named Charlie—he did heroin—and the two of us were doing drugs when the police rolled up on us. Charlie took the blame and went to jail that day." Denise never forgot what he did for her. "Every time I saw him, I'd always ask, 'What do you need?' I told people on the street, 'He's good; he took a motherfucking case for me.' Those random acts of kindness, they were genuine; they kept me going."

Despite this kindness, Denise knew she wasn't going to rely on anyone. She had to take care of herself. What helped her get through each day was crack or whatever other drugs were around. Addiction is the thread running through all of her memories. Addiction and incarceration.

Cycling in and out of jail was dehumanizing. "The police would pull up on me and say, 'What's up, China?' and I'd think, 'Here we go again.' It was ridiculous. I'd do three or four months and then I'd get out and start using again. If you got sick on the street, sick from the dope, you don't go to the hospital or rehab, you go to jail. If you go to jail, you get a place to sleep and maybe, just maybe, get the basic treatment that you needed."

Jail offered its own set of humiliations. But living on the street had fine-tuned her coping skills, and Denise adapted. "After going through it all so much, it got to the point that it was par for the course. You know that you're going to jail—you know what the process is like. You know what's going to happen. They're going to look up my ass with a flashlight. They're going to make me squat and cough, they're going to give me two minutes in a shower. Most of the guards are disrespectful motherfuckers—there are a few good ones who are kind, but they don't last long. And no matter how many times you get locked up and no matter how much you get used to it, you never forget. . . . It's always bad."

Eventually, Denise experienced a break in the cycle of street and jail with the passage of Proposition 36, the California State Substance Abuse and Crime Prevention Act of 2000. Because of Prop 36, anyone who was arrested for "simple drug possession"—meaning they were an addict, not a dealer—was supposed to be sentenced to treatment instead of incarceration. But treatment was never straightforward. Anyone who gets a Prop 36 sentence enters a twisting system of drug court and drug testing and 12-step groups and antidrug education that must be fulfilled. Still, all this was better than sending someone into the disastrously overcrowded county jails and state prisons. No one in the justice system, from cops to wardens, wanted to deal with people who were simply addicts, not criminals.

Whenever she qualified for a Prop 36 sentence, Denise would complete all the necessary steps in her treatment, then go right back to using. She had a spot in an alley where she lived. If she needed to shower or clean up, she would stop by the home of a friend or relative. No one offered her a place to stay permanently. There was no plan for the future—she simply existed day to day.

I'd never spent time with a woman whose experience on the streets was as extreme as Denise's. Some women faced temporary homelessness that lasted two or three months until they ultimately found some sort of housing. Very few had to resort to sex work for an extended period of time. No one matched Denise for the sheer number of years spent on the street. But whatever the women's experiences, there were still more similarities among the women than differences. And the biggest similarities always came down to the relationship between trauma, self-medication, and drug addiction. So many had encountered physical and sexual abuse within their families and then had fled into relationships with abusive men. With only two exceptions, every single woman I interviewed had struggled with addiction to drugs and drinking. And in every single case, substance abuse was never recreational; it was always to dull the pain.

This was achingly clear with Rosa and Denise, who despite their different ages and different colors were sisters under the skin. They both experienced cycles of unimaginable trauma which led to self-medication and substance abuse. When I asked Rosa what her drug of choice was, she laughingly told me, "*All* of them." But her laughter was hollow and underwrote a reality for every woman who'd been locked up for criminal activity: crime was not the issue. Crime was secondary to all of the related problems that drove women to substance abuse. Susan Burton understood this reality, which was why she talked about the "criminalization of trauma."

From the time I began studying gangs, I quickly learned that for both men and women, drugs represented the greatest risk to their survival, especially when they tried to go "mainstream" and leave gang life behind. When faced with anxiety, fear, rage, or any of the by-products of trauma, gangs, and incarceration, individuals often succumbed to the need, again, to self-medicate. In recent years, with the ready availability of medical marijuana, the picture of drug abuse and self-medication has grown even more ambiguous. Most of the women involved with the criminal justice system come from homes and communities where drugs were part of the wreckage of families and violence. I had seen firsthand how the crack-cocaine epidemic had a long-term impact on families already mired in poverty. What civil rights attorney Connie Rice often referred to as "the spiral of despair" was turbo-charged by the ill-fated War on Drugs, which filled jails and prisons, fragmented families, and never addressed the root causes of substance abuse. And these problems were not in the past. The women I interviewed described long-term struggles with addiction, and they lacked any resources to deal with it. Even if they made progress and moved toward mainstream life, the vulnerability to relapse was always there.

That vulnerability plagued Clara as she struggled with addiction, not knowing where to turn. She couldn't afford a rehab facility, and even if she could, she wasn't sure how to find the right one, especially one that treated pregnant women who'd been incarcerated. Desperate to start over, Clara moved with Eduardo to Kentucky, where his cousin helped them get settled. But Clara couldn't outrun her trauma, and her drug use continued until she received a long-distance phone call from a DCFS social worker telling her they'd found Theresa. Her relief at the news was short-lived: Javier had been arrested for child abuse, accused of sexually abusing his other daughter. Theresa was in foster care—Clara's worst nightmare. As quickly as she could arrange it, she flew back to California, and in this jumble of crises her third daughter, Veronica, was born. She was on overload. Still, Clara felt hopeful because "this time Javier was the bad guy. Maybe I could get Theresa back!"

Her hope didn't last long. The newest DCFS social worker warned her that she had to leave Eduardo or they'd take custody of Veronica. Clara wasn't about to let that happen. When Veronica was two weeks old, they moved into a domestic violence shelter managed by House of Ruth, an organization that helped women and children victimized by domestic violence. I knew about the House of Ruth—it had long been a resource for women at the Homegirl Café. Many of the homegirls had sought refuge there when they tried to leave abusive relationships. Although it didn't have a program specifically geared to formerly incarcerated women, it offered the services Clara desperately needed. It would turn out to offer even more. The agency had an emergency shelter program, where Clara received housing, food, and clothing along with counseling and help in dealing with DCFS. She told her case manager she wanted to stop using drugs and rebuild her life. Her desires fit her new environment; the shelter had a zero-tolerance policy toward drug use.

After a few days, Clara was relieved to learn she could stay for a longer time, moving from the House of Ruth Emergency Shelter to their Transitional Living Program. This program provided women with job placement, case management, counseling, the services they needed, and, most important, a place to live for up to two years. There were children's programs, child abuse treatment, and assistance in ensuring that school-age children would continue to go to their usual schools so their education wouldn't be disrupted. Equally significant, once residents of this program were working or receiving government assistance, they were required to save 30 percent of their income to eventually obtain housing, buy a car, or pursue educational goals. All of this was designed to help women work toward independent living in safe, nonviolent homes.

In this supportive environment, Clara finally stopped using drugs and began creating stability in her life, saving up money and focusing anew on her relationships with her children. Still, DCFS continued to derail her plans, failing to document or even see the progress she was making. Javier's mother was awarded temporary custody of Theresa. Again, Clara told herself this was better than foster care—and then she received more devastating news: Aracely had been legally adopted by Eduardo's parents.

She felt despair but kept going. Several months later, the bureaucratic inconsistency of the child welfare system finally worked in Clara's favor. DCFS awarded her custody of Theresa, who joined Clara and Veronica at House of Ruth. Eduardo's family was bringing Aracely for visits, encouraging her as she stayed off drugs. They'd always urged her to leave Eduardo. "Now, his mother told me, live your life. This is your chance; this is your opportunity."

Clara decided to try again to pursue her dream of getting an education, feeling excitement as well as fear, remembering her past failure. But now she wasn't completely alone. This is what made the difference as she tried to move forward—she had support.

Often, what causes women to fall back into a pattern of self-destructiveness is the sense of being alone as they face a tsunami of obstacles. Women who've been incarcerated struggle with addiction alongside the lack of an economic and emotional safety net. Both factors are critical in sustaining change.

For the first time in Clara's life, she had an entire system of support at the House of Ruth. Four years had passed since she'd last been enrolled in school. Now, things felt more positive. She met Rowena Smith, a coordinator at the Los Angeles City College Extended Opportunity Programs and Services (EOPS) office. Rowena was a recovering drug addict who'd been in an abusive relationship. "I don't even remember how I ran into her. All I know is, she guided me, she helped me, and that's how I started school." Clara was still in the shelter, required to attend parenting classes, domestic violence classes, and other learning skills classes. With so many commitments, Clara worried that she might not be smart enough. "School was hard . . . I'm not the brightest star in the sky." The EOPS office helped, offering financial assistance with books and school supplies; they also provided counseling.

Even as she struggled with school, Clara drew upon depths of encouragement as well as services that every formerly incarcerated woman needs. "I'm very, very grateful for House of Ruth. They gave me a home. They really helped me. They would give me bus tokens for me to get to class. They would take care of the baby. But I didn't want to take advantage. I knew I had to get ready to be on my own."

It was time to get out into the real world.

After eighteen months she left the shelter. She believed she was ready for the next step in finally changing.

Then she went back to Eduardo.

To so many people it's unthinkable that Clara would do this. But I understood. It's part of being in the club. Anyone who's been in an abusive relationship knows how both psychological and economic dependence can drive you back into a relationship that you know is abusive, and nevertheless you believe you need to survive. I wasn't formerly incarcerated; I didn't have struggles with trauma or drug addiction. I was white and I had a graduate degree, yet it took years for me to end a relationship that had been emotionally abusive. I could have walked out at any moment. But I stayed.

The experience of domestic violence lives inside many women's narratives, intertwined with substance abuse. Relapse is a theme in both of these struggles. In 2014, the *Journal of the American Medical Association* reported that 40 to 60 percent of the men and women who've been treated for addiction or alcoholism relapse within a year.[5] In the same way, women "relapse" into abusive relationships, and research shows that it takes multiple attempts to escape. Most victims of domestic abuse make an average of seven attempts before successfully exiting the relationship. And a real risk undergirds these efforts: 75 percent of the homicides linked to domestic violence occur when the woman tries to end and/or leave an abusive relationship. And the authorities—instead of understanding the women's lives and the ways trauma leads to substance abuse and criminal activity—frequently criminalize survivors of domestic violence.[6]

In criminalizing these women, what so many fail to understand is how Clara and others like her face ongoing pressure—economic, social, and psychological—all at the same time. The pressure is constant, and it comes from every direction. Leaving the shelter, trying to make a life on her own, Clara felt overwhelmed. Eduardo was familiar, he was what she knew. "He was the father of my children, and he was there for me," she tells me, "but the abuse still continued." Eduardo was using drugs, only now Clara refused to use with him. She was no longer self-medicating, yet her dependence on Eduardo was another form of addiction and she knew she had to get away. She would take hold of whatever might be offered to her *if she could just get away.*

Her sister Maria was living in Arizona and urged her to come and start a new life. Listening to her sister talk about the warmth and affordability of Arizona, Clara saw the way to finally leave Eduardo. She couldn't let him know her plans; instead she told him she was going back to the shelter.

When she arrived in Arizona, she found an apartment, happily discovering that rents were much cheaper than in Los Angeles. But her happiness was leavened with loneliness and economic need. "I'm alone in a state, in a place where I don't know anyone, I don't know anything. So, I started selling drugs again, because that's what I knew."

Clara's sister introduced her to a drug connection. Only this time, it wasn't just nickel and dime bags of marijuana, she says. "This time it was bundles." Inexperienced at dealing with larger quantities of drugs, Clara got caught. She was convicted of transporting drugs across state lines and sentenced to six months in federal prison. Still, there was a sliver of light in the darkness. Because she was a new resident, children's services never showed up. "The judge on my case said because I was clean and didn't have a record in Arizona, he would let me out for two weeks . . . to get things in order." Clara scrambled to find someone to take care of her daughters. She reached out so the girls could stay with family, then her sister turned her down. In the end, she split the girls up. Theresa was fifteen and stayed with a friend in Arizona. Veronica, still a toddler, went to join Aracely with Eduardo's parents.

In the lonely months of incarceration, no one came to see her. Clara didn't want Theresa to visit, and Veronica was settled in LA with the Lopezes along with Aracely. She felt despair, but her daughters were all that mattered; she'd endure prison. Clara's experience lines up with research that shows how incarcerated parents struggle more adapting to prison as they face separation from their children; women are particularly hard hit when they lose their identity as mothers.[7] However, there's another, more positive side to this struggle. Research has also shown that women who are able to see themselves as good mothers, even while incarcerated, actually use this belief as a coping mechanism. This process helps women to look beyond their status as inmates and to concentrate on what they need to achieve once they leave jail or prison. It also helps ease women into reentry after incarceration.[8]

Thinking about her children, planning for their futures, turned out to be the healthiest, most positive thing Clara could do. It was the only thing she could do. She also knew, once she was released, she had to change. The only question was how. She had to rebuild her life and her family. This meant dealing with her trauma, loss, and substance abuse, which had all led her into prison. She never wanted anything to do with drugs again, whether selling them or using them. But she also knew she needed help. It wasn't a matter of simply promising herself or her children that things would change. Where was the place that would help her to change? Where could she go?

Clara was not the only one asking these questions. A world away, Denise continued to endure the cycle of arrest, lockup, and release, using drugs to ease the pain. Where would this all end for her? Would there ever be any help?

Rosa, Anika, Vonnie, and other women all faced the same struggle: Was there a place anywhere that could help them to heal? Was there a place that understood what they had gone through when they were incarcerated? A place that offered support and shelter to build on their strengths and make sure they never used, they never relapsed, they never were incarcerated again?

PART TWO

THE JOURNEY OUT

NINE

HALFWAY IS JUST THAT

Every time I reached out, every time I tried to get some help,
all I got were some phone numbers of halfway houses and
men's programs that might let women in. I really didn't
want to go to a halfway house—I'd only heard bad things.
And then—it was worse than I expected.

—SHERI WARREN

The experience and trauma of incarceration doesn't end once a
woman finishes serving time. When Clara walked out of federal
prison, she didn't feel relieved or happy. She was terrified. She didn't
know what she was going to do. And she wasn't alone in feeling that
way. More than anything, after incarceration, women experience a
sense of dislocation. Several women told me about suddenly becoming dizzy once they were outside the gate; more than one remembered
throwing up once she exited jail or prison. "I almost felt seasick," Angela Washington told me. What's clear is that few women experience
feelings of joy or freedom. And if they do feel any sort of happiness, it is
fleeting. The pain of memory is matched by the obstacles these women
face in the immediate future.

All the statistics pointed to the reality that after incarceration,
most women confront a huge gap between what they need and what is

available to them. In one study of incarcerated women who were scheduled for release within two weeks to a month, mental health treatment, healthcare, and social services were listed as their primary reentry needs. Using qualitative methods, researchers wanted to know what barriers women—in this case, 309 of them—experienced in finding services to match these critical needs. The study participants overwhelmingly suffered with complex mental health problems related to trauma. This meant they needed but couldn't find gender-specific assessment and treatment programs to meet even their most basic requirements.[1] Another study showed that when reentry services were provided, "program participants were convicted on new charges at lower rates than non-participants."[2] Still another study of women's lives after incarceration reported how jobs that offer financial security, vocational training, and education all helped reduce the chances that the women would return to the criminal justice system.[3]

While it's tempting to sarcastically ask "Really?" these research studies are desperately needed to prove what anyone with common sense already knows: women, as well as men, are much less likely to engage in criminal activity if they have work and can earn a living wage. This reality guided Father Greg Boyle's earliest mission statement at Homeboy Industries, "Jobs Not Jails."

But G would now also be quick to add, "And paying attention to trauma." Father Greg Boyle wasn't the only one to realize the long-term impacts of trauma. Over time, researchers have consistently found that along with housing and jobs, mental health counseling and substance abuse treatment are crucial to successful reentry. They have concluded that these services represent the deepest hope for ending women's lawbreaking behavior.[4] Yet, as Barry Krisberg observes, "These services are often too scarce, a situation exaggerated even more by the explosive growth of the number of women in prison."[5] It is maddening that, despite this "explosive growth," there has been no real reentry system to provide women what they need. And what they need is a place where it is understood that the cycle of trauma is the story of reentry. That they have been traumatized and re-traumatized, trapped in a cycle of pain and incarceration. Where is the place that understands this? Where is the program that truly grasps how women's reentry into mainstream life is plagued with false starts and unfulfilled dreams?

Formerly incarcerated women need a place to live—ideally with their children—that recognizes the *nonlinear nature* of their recovery and reentry. Programs for women who've encountered intimate partner violence, like the House of Ruth, provide space and programming for women *and* their children. These programs also understand that it might take a woman several tries to finally separate from her abusive partner and gradually become strong enough to start a new life. In the same way, formerly incarcerated women don't follow a direct reentry pathway; obstacles and setbacks are part of the process of transformation. What they need to find after incarceration is programs that understand that reality.

Instead, what they find awaiting them can best be understood from examining the language used to describe jails, prisons, and life after incarceration: *Corrections. Offenders. Ex-offenders. Probation. Parole. Halfway houses.* It's that last term that offers a sign of things to come. Very little of what awaits women is positive or empowering. The halfway house, the first place a recently released woman often lives, is just that: a partial solution, an incomplete return to life. There are very few options available to a formerly incarcerated population whose size is increasing at a rapid rate. There's a huge need and simply not enough reentry programs up and running, working for women. There aren't even enough halfway houses to serve women after incarceration. But despite their limited availability and their problematic philosophy, halfway houses remain the default reentry option, while the number of women exiting prison keeps getting bigger every year.

This isn't an abstract idea. One look at a map drawn up by the Prison Policy Initiative (PPI) shows just how big those numbers are.[6] According to the PPI, there are 81,000 women released from state prisons each year and 1.8 million women released from jails. However, these statistics are misleading for several reasons, having mainly to do with the number of women released from jail.

First, although the Bureau of Justice Statistics' most recent census of jails was completed in 2019, the "latest data available" used by the PPI actually dates to 2013.[7] Since that time, as I kept seeing and reading, the numbers of incarcerated women have been rising. Second, the number of women released from jail each year is actually probably larger because not all states collect data on jail releases. Worse yet, even among the states that do collect this information, "a significant portion" don't include what turns out to be missing data on gender.[8] Even research was gendered! Barry Krisberg confirmed this when he wrote, "Women have typically been excluded from criminology research, being unspecified and undifferentiated in the collection and analysis of data. The BJS collects a vast amount of data each year . . . but very little of its reporting specifies women and men as distinct groups. Even less of it breaks the gender categories down further by other variables, such as race, ethnicity or socioeconomic class."[9] It's very clear in all of this that women's reentry isn't a priority for the Bureau of Justice Statistics.

Even when one looks at the dated and incomplete 2013 data available from the Bureau of Justice Statistics, a deeply troubling picture emerges. Nationally, one out every eight individuals released from state prisons and more than one out of every six people released from jail is a woman. What's more, in twenty states, at least one out of five individuals released from any sort of incarceration is a woman. When things are broken down state by state, the numbers are even more revealing. Half of the states in the US release at least 1,000 women from prison each year, and among these Texas is the heaviest hitter of all, releasing over 12,000 women a year. Arkansas is a distant second, releasing 4,456. However, the statistics become much more startling when these numbers are combined with the number of women released from local jails. In that case, Texas, with a total of 157,883 women released from both prisons and jails, comes in second to California. The Golden State clocks in with a total of 189,066 women released annually from prisons and jails combined, a staggering figure when it's compared with the rest of the country. And most of them have nowhere to go.

So just what happened to all these women? Where women ended up was partially determined by their crime, their sentence, and *where* they served their time—in prison or in jail. Women were more likely than men to wind up in jails instead of prisons, where there are few if any reentry planning programs and literally no opportunities to prepare for what would happen after they were released. That meant if a woman was sentenced to jail for lower-level crimes, such as drug possession and prostitution, no one paid any attention to the issue of reentry. After jail, women were released and, in effect, kicked to the curb. Nothing was required of a woman except that she serve her time and not get in trouble again.

In California, the one exception to this practice was the Proposition 36 sentence, which replaced jail with drug court and community-based programs. A voter-approved initiative passed in 2000, Prop 36 allowed individuals charged with low-level crimes to remain in their community. This was the same Prop 36 that had enabled Denise to reduce at least some of her time in jail. For mothers, this was a godsend—they could stay at home with their children instead of being incarcerated. But, as Denise discovered when she received community-based sentencing courtesy of Prop 36, there was no wiggle room: individuals were required to attend classes and group therapy at approved agencies, check in with probation officers, account for their movements, and never miss a class or meeting. Despite all these requirements, Prop 36 sentences offered a structure for recovery and represented at least a step in the right direction, inadvertently assisting mothers in avoiding further separation from their children. But not every woman qualified for a Prop 36 sentence, which leaves the question still unanswered: Where are the post-incarceration, reentry programs that specially address women's struggles?

The answer to that question is alarming. Susan Burton's organization, A New Way of Life, accurately reports that the vast majority of states do not have any sort of gender-responsive programs at a scale to serve even half of women released from prison every year. On top of that, twelve states have absolutely no "women-only" program or can serve less than 10 percent of the women leaving state prison after incarceration. Only five states—Colorado, Connecticut, Maine, Massachusetts, and Rhode Island—provide services to women released from prison each year, and not all of these programs provide housing.[10] The situation is dire for women emerging into mainstream life after incarceration.[11]

In what seems like yet another statement of the obvious, research has repeatedly demonstrated the deep need for better links between detention facilities and community-based service providers, along with additional funding for reentry planning and actual transition.[12] Still, despite these findings, throughout California in particular and the US in general, there really is no systematic reentry planning for women. Most women go right back to where they got into trouble in the first place and, without any social supports, immediately reoffend. And if women have been in jail pretrial, waiting for long periods of time to go to court, the innocent face the same obstacles as the guilty. Some women have sat in jail for up to a year only to be found innocent and released. These women fell into the abyss with no options except to continue on the pathway they had started down, a pathway that led back to jail.

More than once I sat outside LA County's jail for women in Lynwood waiting to pick up someone after release. I watched the flow of women just leaving lockup and getting picked up by their mothers, their boyfriends, their friends, or, as one woman told me, "I'm just waiting for my pimp." I wondered what would happen to each of them and who'd be returning to jail, not because they wanted to but because no one had even asked if they had a reentry plan, no one had given them a phone number to call or the name of someone who could help.

Once you move beyond the jail system, there are glimmerings of preparation for women facing life after incarceration, particularly in state and federal prisons. Often, more serious crimes often lead to longer sentences in these settings and—ironically—actual reentry planning. Yet even after serving their sentences in state prison, women face no set pathway and have access to very limited resources. Often, the attention each woman receives depends on the type of crime she's been convicted of and how much time she's served. In most cases, women were headed for "community correctional facilities" or—as they were better known—halfway houses.

There are certain prison systems that allow women to serve the final months of their sentence in halfway houses. In California, both of the women's prisons offer something called the Alternative Custody Program (ACP), which was established in 2011. Women who qualify for ACP are released to a private residence, transitional care facility, or residential drug or other treatment program, and are required to wear an ankle monitor.[13] However, few women are eligible for this "opportunity." Those who don't are still required to spend a certain amount of time in a halfway house even after they've served their sentences as a condition of their parole. And still others are released from prison with nothing but "gate money," a small amount of cash given to men and women as they exit the prison gates. Others receive nothing.[14] I was confused about who might have to go to a halfway house and who was left to make their own reentry arrangements.

As always, the homie lawyer Elie Miller explained things to me. "Because of prison overcrowding, they're offering certain women— maybe the ones who've had a first offense and don't have a criminal history—the ACP program. They're not trying to be kind. They're dealing with the fact there're too many women sentenced to incarceration and not enough beds for them in the facilities. And, for most women, if you get a life sentence or you're doing a chunk of time or you're in federal prison, corrections is going to require that you show where you're going to live once you've finish serving your sentence. They require you live in that halfway house for three to six months, and of course, there's going to be a parole or probation officer following you. They also require that a halfway house or transitional care facility indicate that they've accepted you."

So, a woman who's been found guilty of killing her abusive spouse and has served twenty-four years in a state prison is required to find an acceptable placement, then present letters from residential reentry programs licensed and certified by the state stating that she has secured placement with their program and verifying how long she will live there and what program services she'll receive. There are case managers who assist women scheduled for release, helping them identify suitable sites and prepare their paperwork. But more often, while incarcerated, women turn to one another for information and recommendations for where they should go, what they should avoid, and how to gain admission to an acceptable site.

Beyond getting to the right place, there is little discussion about what really happens inside these transitional living facilities, although no one uses that official terminology. Everyone from judges to lawyers to formerly incarcerated women—even officials in the facilities themselves—invariably refers to such places as halfway houses. Ideally, halfway houses are supposed to help women transition from incarceration to the community. In reality, the word "halfway" turned out to more accurately describe their overall ineffectiveness. "'Half-assed' is more like it," Angela Washington told me when she described her reentry experiences.

In general, very little is known about halfway houses—there's barely any data available, and there's not even much clarity about what defines a halfway house. According to the Prison Policy Initiative, it's an umbrella term that can refer to anything from a sober-living home to a community-based correctional facility.[15] Some of these places serve more than one function, although the vast majority are, in fact, just another form of incarceration, and many women live there because it's required. But other women wind up in halfway houses because they simply have no other place to go—they're desperate, and often halfway house operators take advantage of that. There's no oversight and no accountability for anyone who sets up a halfway house.

According to PPI, "Conditions in halfway houses often involve violence, abuse and neglect." Far too often, women find themselves in settings that actually *continue* what they experienced in jails and prisons, with rules and regulations that mirror those in institutional facilities. There are curfews and check-ins, and parole and probation officers are on speed-dial to intervene if a woman acts out. Several women at the Homegirl Café, as well as other women I've interviewed, described the identical experience. Halfway houses were like being locked up, with one exception: the women are able to leave the residence during specific hours to go to work. This isn't true for every single halfway house in Los Angeles County; some sites offer supportive services. Still, the truth is that many function as work-release sites.

What reinforces the institutional aspect of these homes is the fact that most of them are partially or totally funded by federal parole, state corrections, or local probation departments. Any public money that a halfway house receives has strings attached: they have to fulfill specific requirements and report any and all misdeeds to probation or parole. The specific requirements are punitive. Women are required to be home by a certain time for "the count." They are then restricted to staying on-site, *locked in*, until the next day. After obtaining jobs, they are required to give 20 to 30 percent of their gross earnings to the halfway house. Any woman who fails to abide by the rules and restrictions is reported to her PO, who can then declare that she violated probation, inevitably sending her back to jail or prison for three months to one year or longer. And forget about any sort of gender-specific programming. The majority of halfway houses are co-ed, with some (not all) including residents who have served time for violent crimes *against* women. Women don't choose to go to halfway houses because they want to; they choose halfway houses because there are no alternatives.

"You have to understand how bad the halfway houses are," Adela Juarez told me. "Near the end of my sentence, they told me I could serve the last three months in a halfway house. I gave my sister's address as the place I would be living when I got out. So, I had to go to the halfway house that was close to her home. It wasn't what I wanted. But I didn't have any other choice."

I've known Adela for over a decade and have always admired her strength and stability, raising a son and daughter alone while their two fathers were serving twenty-five years to life as semipermanent guests of the California state prison system. When we first started talking, she was a calm, dignified staff member and "lead" at the Homegirl Café. She always came to work early and was neatly dressed and immaculately groomed. Adela was physically beautiful; the symmetry of her facial features reminded me of Jennifer Lopez. She wore slacks and blouses that were pressed and complemented her small, compact body. Her carefully maintained appearance was completed by softly wavy hair, often swept up in a bun. Throughout our conversations, her language was gentle and her voice soft. I kept trying to figure out how she fit in, what her story was. I assumed she'd experienced substance abuse issues, like so many of the women at Homegirl. I knew she'd been locked up in federal prison. But I didn't know a lot beyond that. Still, there was something about Adela and the way she carried herself. The other women in the café respected her and depended on her. She was just . . . different.

I gradually learned her story, and it was nothing like what I'd expected. What she'd experienced was a book unto itself, which I promised to help her write when she was ready. She'd grown up gang-involved and had always liked organizing, whether it was coordinating "ditch days" and skipping school or helping her father with his illegal drug distribution business. From early on, she knew she was smart; she graduated high school with a strong GPA and trained to be a dental assistant. Years later, as a single mother raising two children and working in a dentist's office, she began supplementing her meager salary with some minor drug deals. As time passed, she became more deeply involved in criminal activity, which matched what was going on within her extended family. Her father had always lived "off the books," and some of his children followed in his footsteps. Not all of Adela's siblings were involved in illegal activities—oddly enough, one of her sisters was a corrections officer. Still, there were other family members who couldn't resist the lure of easy money. Almost everyone was cautious not to attract attention to their "enterprises." Then, one of Adela's brothers went too far, was accused of multiple homicides, and wound up as one of the FBI's Ten Most Wanted fugitives. This brought Adela to the attention of the US Department of Justice. The feds followed her for over a year, and when she was finally arrested, she faced charges that numbered in the double digits and involved cross-border drug trafficking and weapons distribution, among other things. But what the feds really wanted were her brother's whereabouts. "After I bailed out, I hired a lawyer," she told me, "and I told him I had no information for the cops."

Even that brief account shows why Adela was different. No public defender for her—she had enough money for bail *and* a private attorney. While the charges against her were serious they also represented— at the age of thirty-five—her first offense. Her lawyer dug in, and there were extensive negotiations. The feds said she would walk if she told them where her brother was. She insisted she didn't know where he was living. In the end, they offered a plea bargain of two to five years in federal prison. Adela and her lawyer asked for probation and presented the court with literally hundreds of letters from people she'd known throughout her life. The judge ultimately told her, "I've read everything. You know you already have a history of getting caught at the border more than ten times—"

Adela was taken aback and blurted out, "Damn, ten times? I guess you think I did a lot of business." The judge laughed, then continued, "I'm sure by all the letters that I received from your family and the community, that you're a good person. But I feel if you don't get a sentence, you won't change." Adela remembers, "I went mute; I just went blank. All I heard was 'federal penitentiary.' . . . I didn't even hear the rest. My attorney bumped me to accept the deal." Afterward, she had to ask her attorney what had happened.

Adela was sentenced to two years in federal prison and five years' probation. Because of this, she was subject to the rules and regulations of the Federal Bureau of Prisons, which has the authority to allow "good inmates" to end their sentences in halfway houses. Or, as the BOP refers to them, "residential reentry centers." Once again, the name change is purely cosmetic. These federally subsidized halfway houses are supposed to support the individual's transition back to mainstream life, enabling them to look for work and housing and to rebuild their family and community ties. Adela qualified for this early release, only to discover it was no blessing. She actually preferred being locked up. "In some ways, the halfway houses were worse than being locked up. In prison, you had programs, you had education, and you got a job—you could make money. I worked in the call center; I was an information operator—I *did* something. Not here. Before I even got to the halfway house, they told me if I was late, they'd consider it a violation and I could go back to prison. So right from the start, you knew it was gonna be bad."

The residents are required to look for work, but they never receive any referrals. "You had to find the jobs by yourself—maybe look at ads," Adela said. "And if you did work, you had to be back before count at four o'clock. On top of that, they took thirty percent of your paycheck." As part of her sentence, Adela had to pay restitution for her crimes. She was outraged that the halfway house could take part of the money she earned, money she needed to pay down her restitution debt. "There was no way you could ever climb out of the trap of debt they put you in." In the end, she pretended to look for jobs. She never went to work. "I had my family, I had support, so I knew I would be okay," she told me. "The other women there, they were just lost, and the halfway house wasn't doing anything to help them. They had so many other problems—they should have had therapy; they should have had help. Instead, all they got was more punishment."

Adela resigned herself to doing what was expected of her—yet there were problems. "I tried to do everything they asked me. How come they wouldn't do what they were supposed to?" The people running the halfway house threatened her, she said, and told her, "'If you don't get a job by next month, we're going to send you back to Dublin [prison].' I told them, 'So send me back to Dublin—I would rather finish my time there, than pay you guys money.' Then I found out they were making money both ways—they got funding from the state and they took the residents' pay. That's when I decided I wasn't getting a job until after I got out. They couldn't keep me there after my sentence was over. I wasn't afraid. They were mad because I left without paying them anything—without getting a job." To this day, Adela remembers her experience at the halfway house as *worse than prison*. "At least in prison, you knew what they were doing. At the halfway house, they promised to help but they set you up to fail."

What Adela had faced wasn't unusual. Lydia Sherman, a woman I'd met through one of the men at Project Fatherhood, described what she encountered after being released from prison on ACP. She was required to spend the remaining six months of her five-year sentence in a halfway house. "You'd think I was gonna be happy, getting out of prison. It was better in prison! I hated that place, that halfway house—it was a halfway prison. It was all confined. You're treated like an animal. They literally close the gate on you. Having my grandchildren visit me there—they had to get 'buzzed in'—was the worst thing in my life. I even told them to their faces that they were abusive. You have chore day, you have double scrub day—it's insane. It wasn't a program; it was a slave house. You feel like an inmate, not a resident. The food was horrible. They had us cooking things in lard; it wasn't healthy. And they were getting a lot of funding from the state and the federal government. They weren't spending the money on the women—they were spending the money on themselves. I just barely held on. No one should have to go through that."

What was their alternative? Some women told me the only person they could turn to for help was a parole or probation officer. After Ivy served two years in prison, her parole officer was actually the person who steered her toward living at a rehabilitation center, approving it as a place she could stay after she was released. While she was living at the rehab center and searching for work, another resident recommended going to Homeboy Industries. For once, Ivy was lucky; her PO was "one of the good ones." POs responsible for women might help with housing or job placement. Or they might not. It depends on the mindset of the PO—it's all random, and once again, there is no accountability. There are women like Ivy whose probation or parole officers have truly helped them, both during juvenile detention and in adulthood, after incarceration. Others described to me POs who were negative and cynical. Once Angela moved out of the halfway house, her PO sadistically announced, "I'm gonna test you. Let's see if you can just stay out of trouble for a few months. I won't call you or bother you—I'll just check the inmate locator at county jail. I need a break from you." The man showed up at her house two days later saying, "I just wanted to see what you'd do if you thought I wasn't around." She laughed when she recalled his duplicity. "I knew he was trying to trick me. And I wasn't gonna let him win."

These problems weren't unique to the women I knew. In a study of sixty formerly incarcerated women living in a southern state, the women clearly recognized that parole was a way for them to be held accountable for their daily decisions and choices; they were told their parole officers would serve as a resource. After incarceration, the women faced multiple obstacles involving housing, transportation, paying monthly fees for restitution and supervision, random drug testing, staying clean, and keeping up a positive rapport with their parole officers. Instead of serving as case managers, their POs created another obstacle, waiting for them to fail instead of helping them navigate the thicket of expectations. These women felt overwhelmed. In frustration and panic, they violated parole or engaged in more criminal behavior.[16]

It was all too clear that this patchwork of "supervision" and halfway houses wasn't going to address women's needs in reentry. Instead of helping them to heal, what women encountered reinforced the trauma they'd already experienced. Women needed something more than "halfway." Whatever their race, age, or state, most women *needed* housing, financial support, case management, and services when they exited prison or jail—this was the key to starting anew and succeeding. But they weren't getting this from the current system.

These needs are easily prioritized. First, research continues to show that for women, housing is consistently listed as a primary need, along with child custody assistance and childcare services.[17] Housing and family reunification are strongly intertwined: anything women face in relation to their children becomes even harder to handle when housing is uncertain. One study specifically pinpointed affordable housing for women and their children as critical to prevent both homelessness and recidivism.[18] But how many times must researchers point out the need for stable housing that would allow women to live in a safe, drug-free environment where they can focus on reuniting with their children and finding a job? When were philanthropists and public policymakers going to listen to what women like Angela, Rosa, Adela, Clara, and Denise had told me?

This need for a secure home didn't just pop up unexpectedly in adulthood. Rosa, Clara, and Denise had all needed and wanted a safe place to live since they were girls. I kept thinking about the work of Laura Abrams and Diane Fields, who'd written about the need to provide housing assistance for juveniles. In 2013 these two researchers had observed, "Given the potential instability in their home environments it may be important for policy makers and practitioners to design services for young female offenders aimed at preparing them to live on their own, such as independent living skills classes and transitional housing."[19] It was now a decade later, and little had changed. How much could housing like this have helped Denise when she was young and alone on the streets? Or Rosa, trying to escape a life of being trafficked? Housing and support services could help keep women—whether juvenile or adult—from falling back into the cycle of suffering and incarceration so many were stuck in for too many years. I was seeing this firsthand, and research was reinforcing everything I was learning from the women themselves.

It is clear that the halfway-house model isn't going to serve the needs of formerly incarcerated women, not even in the most basic ways. With rigidly enforced requirements and benchmarks, this model is frequently designed more to punish than to help; there is no category for healing in its operating instructions. All around me, there was ongoing attention to the #MeToo movement and the issue of sexual harassment and abuse. The brutal death of George Floyd had brought about a national outcry for the end of systemic racism and the need for anti-racist reforms in all mainstream institutions and personal behaviors. Even then, a telephone call from Denise was haunting me. "I'm a Black woman and I care about George Floyd and Breonna Taylor. What about me? Who's gonna help someone like me? I need racism to end. But I need a home and I need money. Where do I fit in?"

TEN

THE HOPE
OF REENTRY

*Oftentimes, people view the homegirls as garbage
or disposable members of society. This is the space
where we eliminate those walls. There is no us
and them. It's just us.*

—ERIKA CUELLAR

In 2011, Ivy Navarrete was released after spending two years in state prison on drug distribution charges. After staying a few months in a halfway house, she didn't have any real plans for the future. Her little boy, Jessie, who'd been a baby when she was locked up, was living with his grandparents—her boyfriend's father and his girlfriend. They'd reassured Ivy she could come live with them; they'd be a family. Ivy was grateful to them. They'd taken care of Jessie and had never contacted DCFS about gaining permanent custody, but she also worried about leaning on them too much. She felt it was important to be on her own. Other women at the halfway house kept telling her she was lucky—she would have a roof over her head and childcare. None of them knew about any places where women could live with their kids or get the help they needed to restart their lives. Ivy decided she *was* lucky to have a place to go. Her own mother had died over five years before, and she had no idea where her father was. This was the closest to family she'd ever have.

Ivy knew that living with the people she thought of as her in-laws involved lots of problems, many stemming from the fact that Carlos, their son and Jessie's father, was locked up, for a long time. But they took Ivy in anyway, and she felt grateful for their love and attention. She wanted to reward them for everything they'd done for her, and she didn't want to mess up. How would they react if she wanted to go out with friends or with a man? Ivy figured she'd work things out as they came up. Right now she had to stay clean and sober and get a job. Raising Jessie right and staying out of trouble were her priorities. Despite her uncertainty, she decided to say yes to their offer.

Once Ivy got settled in, she reached out to people who'd known her when she was with Carlos and wound up connecting with Janeth Lopez, who was working at the Homegirl Café. Ivy didn't know her that well but remembered that Janeth had hung around Carlos and his homies. Janeth was young, a cute little homegirl with tattoos wreathing her neck. She had a baby girl, Angelina, and told Ivy that she was living with the baby's father, Luis, and his family. She also admitted that Luis cheated on her and even beat her sometimes, but she would always take him back. She reminded Ivy of herself—including being in an abusive relationship. As the two women talked, Janeth grew excited, telling Ivy she should apply to work at Homegirl.

Janeth's endorsement was sincere. She loved working at the Homegirl Café and had grown close to Adela Juarez, who felt protective of her. "I think I saw her as a daughter. She just didn't know what she wanted," Adela explained. "I think her having a baby so young was hard. All Janeth ever had was her neighborhood and her baby daddy. And her only family, her baby daddy, was her abuser. There was so much violence around Janeth, all the time. I don't think she ever realized how traumatized she was."

Adela and Janeth talked constantly. They drove to work together and had the same shifts. One day, Janeth told Adela about Ivy—that she was just out of prison and needed a job. Adela told her she'd check with Father Greg and ask if they could hire her.

A few weeks later, Janeth brought Ivy to meet Father Greg, who hugged her and, thanks to Adela's efforts, told her she was hired immediately. She worked hard, and the café directors, Erika Cuellar, Shannon Smith, and Pati Zarate, took to her right away. Erika and Ivy grew especially close, and Erika was drawn to Ivy's work ethic. "She had *chispa*— that spark that made me want to learn more about her. I saw that and I always knew that my responsibilities at Homegirl required me to have someone shadow behind me. It just became a natural role for her."

As they spent more time together, Erika began to realize that Ivy had many talents. "I remember I was in the Homegirl office, sitting at the end of the day at that desk, counting out the money. Ivy approached me and said, 'I used to be a paralegal. Let me know if you need help.' That was it. I saw that she had administrative skill, and she started doing the report. It wasn't hard, but you had to be focused and you had to be someone I could trust—that was when that *chispa* would be revealed."

Adela watched out for her as well. "Ivy was good, she was responsible. I did a couple of caterings with her at the café. But it's never easy when you've been locked up so long. She was traumatized and she was institutionalized. She wanted to get over being in prison. She wanted to change. It was gonna be hard, she'd gone through so much." Adela told Ivy that she'd been in prison, too, but now she was beginning to deal with what had happened when she was locked up. Ivy reached out to her for support almost every day, and Adela reassured her that just like other women in the café who'd been in prison, she'd get the support at Homegirl to deal with her trauma and adjust to how life had changed at home, in her family.

Ivy tried hard, but the years of untreated trauma that had started with her childhood clearly affected her. As the women at the café learned, her parents had been addicts, her mother had been a sex worker, and her first boyfriend had abused her for years and then died. For a long time, the gang was her only constant. Adela understood how "Ivy was still drawn into hanging out with the homeboys and the lifestyle. She was so abused and so traumatized, she really thought it was all she deserved. I think that's how she ended up with Pedro. She had such low self-esteem, she thought no one else would love her. And he was brutal." Most of the women in the café worried about her relationship with Pedro from the start.

"Ivy could see a better life for herself—I think she really wanted it," Erika remembered. As she talked about how promising Ivy's life was, Erika's voice started to shake.

"She worked so hard, but temptation came around . . . Temptation . . . ," she said. "Homegirl got six tickets to the live filming of Jamie Oliver's cooking show. Somewhere there's a photo that was taken, and she was there with this dude. A lot of us were confused—we were like, 'Ivy, who's this dude? You haven't told us about him.' He was this rough-around-the-edges guy; he had just gotten out of prison. It was only a few weeks from that day to when the incident happened—the killing of the deacon. She was still working with us then. I remember she had just not shown up for a few days. It was so unlike her not to be there. Then when the details started coming in, word in the café quickly spread, and it all had to do with Pedro, that somehow that guy had been involved. For a long time, I had wished she had not met that guy."

Erika was heartbroken. When she first found out that Ivy was on the run, she was in denial, hoping the rumors weren't true. "I remember reaching out to Ivy and of course not getting through to her. I just didn't understand what happened."

Adela understood much more than Erika. "Ivy really didn't know where to go, what to do," Adele said sadly. "She just didn't know where she belonged. She wanted to try to change, but that old life was just so familiar . . ."

Ivy's uncertainty and her attraction to her old life isn't unusual. As they work through reentry, many women feel the pull of the past and the need for some sort of network of friendships and a sense of belonging. A handful, like Adela, have family to turn to who can help them. But Adela was an exception: many women come from families struggling with poverty, fear, and marginalization; their families want to help but they're already overburdened and worn down. Then there are women who don't seek any family support because, like Rosa, their family is where they experienced trauma or they were involved in criminal activity. Some women think about returning to abusive partners or their last relationship, though unhealthy. They might be tempted because this is all they've known—yet, they can't go back or they'll be doomed.

———————

Denise's journey into mainstream life was DOA, devoid of any reentry services. For years, she seemed destined to revolve in and out of jail in a familiar pattern. "It was drugs, jail, rinse, repeat," she told me, and this continued until she was arrested with enough drugs on her to sell, not simply use. "When I caught the last case, it was bad. I didn't qualify for Prop 36. I was really in trouble." Denise went straight to jail, and once she got there, she was unprepared for what happened, beginning with the fact that for the first time, bail was set. It didn't matter that it was a "low-level" bail of $10,000—it could have been a million dollars—Denise didn't have any money. So, she was locked up in October of 2006 with no trial date set. As time passed, Denise worried. "All that time, I was waiting—and I didn't have a good feeling. It wasn't like all the other times I was locked up. It felt different this time. And I had no idea what the judge was gonna decide."

What happened next paints a striking picture of the justice system's ineptitude. Over the days, then weeks, then months, then *more than a year* that Denise was locked up, she kept appearing in court. She started the case with a court-appointed attorney who barely knew her. But surprisingly, at her first court appearance there was another person who knew her well, who stood alongside Denise and her lawyer facing the judge: her mother, Celeste. As her case unfolded, Celeste was in court for the entire fifteen months of Denise's court appearances and even developed what looked like a relationship with the judge, another woman, around the same age. "I love my mother for being there," Denise told me. "I think she was really trying to make up for what happened when I was younger."

Ultimately, her mother was more reliable than her attorney, who "fell off," Denise said. "I didn't have a consistent lawyer the whole time. Every time I showed up in court, I had a new lawyer." One day, no lawyer showed up for her hearing, and the judge recognized that the unreliable representation was costing both the court and Denise too much time. It would soon be sixteen months that she'd been locked up, pretrial, unable to make bail and unable to resolve her case. The judge offered her the opportunity to speak on her own behalf rather than wait for yet another lawyer. Denise quickly agreed. Speaking directly to the court, Denise asked that she be released for time served or at least that her time be reduced. The judge turned her down but asked Celeste what she wanted for her daughter. "My mom asked my judge for a drug treatment program, and I managed to bargain my sentence down to two and a half years, which could be fulfilled by being in drug rehab and then on probation," said Denise.

I wasn't surprised—Denise could negotiate tirelessly. I'd seen her in action: on campus, she was always arguing about something, primarily systemic racism or the need for more Black students to be admitted. And she often accompanied other students who came to see me, coaching them in how to argue with me for a higher grade. I'm sure she was just as convincing in front of the judge. But her brain was not the problem—her addiction was.

While the judge had been more than fair, she also warned Denise that if she didn't comply, she would go to prison for five years. "That was our deal," Denise said. "If you don't complete this program now that your mom has advocated for you—if you fuck this up—I'm going to give you *all* your time back. Although she said it in a nice way."

Whatever the terms used, the judge's meaning was clear: she would show no mercy if Denise didn't stick to rehab. And this really was Denise's first rodeo—she'd never been to a residential rehab program before. The body of research on addiction points to the idea that she might not have been a promising candidate for a permanent recovery.

Beyond the statistics, there is a deeper problem that drug rehab doesn't address: trauma. Fourteen years ago, when Denise went into rehab, the idea of trauma-informed care had not entered into mainstream discussion. Residential and outpatient rehab programs both had their hands full just treating the intertwined problems of addiction and dependence. This meant the chances of it all working for Denise this first time out were slim. Nevertheless, at the end of 2007, Denise checked into a residential treatment program at the Alcoholism Center for Women in LA.

ACW has been in operation since 1974 with a mission "to provide a safe and supportive sober environment in which women and youth can repair, restore and reclaim their lives, strengthen families and communities by making new choices for positive futures." The words sounded great, but there's no real record of its effectiveness. However, by the time Denise went there, ACW was well known in Los Angeles as the first place that offered a residential program *only* for women.

Located at Eleventh and Alvarado, "kinda, sorta downtown," as Denise described it, to this day ACW provides both residential and outpatient programs for women. It definitely isn't Betty Ford or Promises Malibu or the CLARE Foundation, where Susan Burton's recovery began. Instead, ACW works directly with LA County Health Services to provide substance abuse programs to women who don't have private insurance and need public support for their treatment. Women in their residential program live in a thirty-two-bed facility consisting of two large, reconfigured frame houses. These are euphemistically described as "historic homes," but in LA, anything older than fifty years is historic. "Ha! Historic? More like rundown, honey," a woman who'd been treated at ACW told me.

Denise was assigned to their residential program, which would house and treat her for at least six months. After that, the court would decide if she needed to stay longer or go to prison. Right after she was admitted, Denise told staff she was determined to change. She was allowed to go out after two weeks, once she detoxed and adjusted to living on-site. Things went well. Her forays into the world were uneventful, and she would return at the end of each day out, safe and sober.

"It was all going along fine. I really thought I was on my way. I was in the program three months and I got my usual day pass. I'd been going out before then and it had been all good. But on this particular day, I'd gone out and ended up taking a hit. I relapsed. I came back to the program that night and I told them what I'd done." The immediate reaction to her relapse was well intentioned and based on teaching Denise the consequences of her actions. There was no discussion of trauma or triggers. Instead, staff told Denise to "take the opportunity" to go in front of a judge the next day. That was the bottom line: she could spend the night at ACW; then in the morning, she had to report to the court that she'd violated the agreement.

She didn't appear in front of her original judge, who wasn't hearing cases. This was where bureaucratic confusion came into play. The new judge told Denise to report back to the drug and alcohol rehab program *in thirty days.* When she first told me the story, I asked Denise to repeat that little piece of judicial decision-making two more times, just to make sure I'd heard it right. The judge also set a new court date for her: three months from those thirty days. So basically, Denise didn't have to report back to court for four months, because she had an additional month allowing her to take her time before returning to a rehab program. I asked Denise if I had this right, and she laughed. "Yes, ma'am. I felt like I had a pass—I would have a little fun and then go back to rehab *at the end of the first month.* By the time the thirty days had passed, I was homeless and I was using everything—there was nothing you could hand me that I wasn't gonna smoke."

Denise's downward spiral began with ACW's initial response to her relapse. This wasn't unusual. The consequences for drug use have always been severe, including programs that clearly state their mission to support formerly incarcerated women and treat their problems. Most programs like ACW maintain a "zero tolerance" policy in which anyone using drugs is asked to leave the program; in residential programs like Denise's that also means they must give up their housing. And no one was asking about trauma; no one was asking about the wounds of jail and incarceration. Instead, the focus was on consequences—and that was it.

Treatment programs weren't the only ones to respond to relapse with extreme consequences. Women trying to reunite with their children also faced drug testing mandated by DCFS. Any sign of drug use derailed their attempts to regain custody of their children and reunify their families. In the end, relapsing into drug abuse represented the greatest threat to their successfully reentering and living in mainstream society, even greater than the threat of returning to criminal activity. The women I knew and others like them were *not* at high risk of recidivism. What they were at risk of was relapsing; it was their drug-related behaviors and activities that got them back in trouble with the criminal justice system. In her memoir, *Becoming Ms. Burton*, Susan Burton recounted the cycle of drug use, incarceration, release, and drug use that arose from the pain of loss in her own life; this same cycle capsizes the lives of many other women. It was, as Susan so aptly describes, the criminalization of trauma and, by association, the drug abuse that stems from it.

But just as Susan Burton was intent on naming the problem, she was also intent on changing it. Even after meeting her at the philanthropists' field trip to visit the women's jail, I still didn't understand this. What I did understand was that the women I was spending time with, particularly those at the Homegirl Café and others in the community, all talked about how *after* they exited jail or prison it was difficult if not impossible to find a place that addressed their needs and struggles. Denise and Adela had to make do while they were meeting criminal justice system requirements, entering a substance abuse program or a halfway house. For Clara, on her own and faced with homelessness, it was a battered women's shelter. And their choices were not unusual. It is clear that often the only places where women can find rehabilitative programs that at least touch on their issues of trauma, pain, and self-medication are in alcohol and drug treatment programs or in programs for battered women.

Most of the women I know ultimately found that their needs were at least partially met in substance abuse treatment programs. Yet those settings, while well intentioned and filled with thoughtful staff, aren't always the best option for women trying to get used to life "on the outs." So many women suffer with more than substance abuse; they also face "co-occurring disorders" or "dual diagnoses," often resulting from trauma, which requires intense and sensitive treatment.

This leads to a conundrum: substance abuse programs traditionally try to stay away from uncovering trauma, the rationale being that individuals need to be sober and in recovery first. In turn, mental health programs don't want to treat women who are dealing with substance abuse issues.[1] Over the past decade, there's been a gradual increase in programs that treat both, but there's still not a well-developed model for how to actually do this.

Denise ran into that void head-on in her experience at ACW. The program wasn't dealing with the trauma she'd experienced as a girl nor with the ongoing trauma of multiple incarcerations. What was out there for the women who'd been locked up? I knew there were places outside of LA where such help existed: Crossroads in Claremont and A Place for Us in San Bernardino. What was working for women in the city of Los Angeles?

In the midst of all these interviews and the issues they raised, I received a call that would help answer my questions and also deeply impact my life. There was a name on my cell-phone screen: Susan Burton.

It may as well have said "God calling," because I felt compelled to immediately drop whatever I was doing and talk to Susan. A year later, at the annual fundraiser for A New Way of Life, LA County Supervisor Mark Ridley-Thomas said, "Even if I didn't want to answer the call from Susan, I knew I had to answer the call from Susan." The audience laughed in appreciation, and many of us, in recognition. Dr. Bob Ross, the president and CEO of the California Endowment, confirmed this when he later told me, "Whenever Susan calls, I know I have to answer the phone and I know I have to say yes."

That reassurance didn't come until later. I didn't know if anyone else reacted the way I did the first time Susan called. When I heard her voice on the phone, I was scared. She was tough and she was direct. She'd found out that the California Endowment was funding me to conduct a case study of A New Way of Life, whose study design was to follow the lives of the program's participants and describe how it worked. She wanted to meet and find out just what this was going to be about because—and my heart dropped—she wasn't sure she wanted me to do that.

What I learned when I showed up at the offices of A New Way of Life in Watts a week later was that Susan's priority was the women who'd come to heal and succeed, drawing upon the services and support of ANWOL. She didn't want research that was going to be intrusive; she didn't want anyone poking around, "mining the data," or entering these women's lives in ways that would be exploitive or hurtful. "They've been through enough," she told me. What she didn't know at the time was that we shared identical values. I'd seen too much research going on in the name of science that didn't take its "subjects" into consideration. This wasn't what I wanted to do. What I wanted was to help Susan document her model, show how it worked, and strengthen her case to obtain the funding that she needed.

I had no desire to publish any research studies. There was already enough research that examined the issue of what women needed; too little had actually been done to actually address those needs. On top of that, by that time, I had managed to thrive for twenty-eight years as an adjunct professor at UCLA, a position that meant I had no job security but also no expectations of publication of my work in peer-reviewed journals. But I was lucky. UCLA had provided a home for me where I could teach and conduct community-based, deeply participatory research. Once we realized how strongly we were aligned around the meaning and conduct of research, Susan was ready to collaborate. "All right, missy," she said with a laugh. "Let's get to work."

With the promised funding from the California Endowment, along with the support and help of two women I worked with, Karrah Lompa and Stephanie Benson, I spent over a year at A New Way of Life, talking with Susan and her staff, listening to the stories of pain, strength, and redemption that characterized every woman who lived in one of the program houses. I was also learning the nuts and bolts of ANWOL. Susan had steered clear of the research process, and she was gratified with the case study we produced, having it bound and printed for distribution at the ANWOL fundraiser. She also asked me to assist her as she moved forward with creating a strategic plan for her organization.[2] The research was fascinating, and I was committed to doing whatever I could to help. But more than that, I was learning even more about what a compassionate reentry program consisted of and how it could fulfill women's needs, contributing to their recovery as well as building their leadership skills and advocacy efforts.

What was immediately apparent to me was that everything Adela and so many others had told me was true: the people running the halfway houses had absolutely no idea what an effective reentry program should look like. A halfway house should foster healing from trauma, help build identity, and move women toward success instead of ignoring their needs and adding to their trauma. Whether this happened depended on understanding the experience of incarceration. Susan Burton knew it. She had lived it. Her trauma, incarceration, and recovery were part of the DNA of the organization whose mission statement could be found in its name: creating a new way of life. By emphasizing housing and healing while offering mental health and substance use treatment, job placement, legal services, and organizing and advocacy-skill building, ANWOL helped women find individual empowerment and add their efforts to systemic change.

By 2018, Susan Burton's organization was overseeing seven homes with fifty-five beds for women returning from jail or prison. Once they were ready to live more independently, there was transitional housing to further ease women into the mainstream. ANWOL placed no time limit on how long a woman stayed in residence—a marked difference from most basic community services, which often had expiration dates. No one at ANWOL was told, "You have six counseling sessions and you're done" or "You must move on after three months." Instead, any woman who became part of ANWOL received a huge range of supportive services to nurture and develop personal growth through every aspect of the reentry process, with no expiration date.

The women who participated in the case study described how important their experience of acceptance and support was. And they all talked about how they now felt in charge of their own lives, many for the first time. ANWOL homes were not run like halfway houses. Instead, women moved freely. They set their own hours. There was no count, and no one was going to report them to their probation officer. The houses *did* have requirements, but these all had to do with women determining the course of their recovery, including a personal commitment to complying with the conditions of their probation. No one was going to do it for them—they were in control. They were also expected to participate in the services offered, look for work, and engage in the community of women in the household.

Working on the case study, I found that the key to ANWOL's deep impact was that it gave these women more than the structure of the household. It provided each woman a sense of community with other women who *knew* what it was like to be released from prison with only the clothes on their back and $200 in gate money. It offered each woman leadership and mentorship that inspired them. Lee, a Black woman who'd been incarcerated for many years and exuded energy and beauty in our every interaction, told me, "Whenever I look at Susan, I feel like I can do it too. She went through terrible things. She lost her little boy—can you imagine that? Then she recovered and she helped people. I can recover and help people." Seeing this—and receiving treatment that was trauma informed and community-based—helped these women to heal.

One of the other factors that really made ANWOL successful was that Susan Burton didn't twist any part of her program to meet funding requirements. She rejected the limits that would have been imposed by some of the grants dangled in front of her. Despite the attraction of multiyear awards from government agencies, she was courageous enough to sometimes refuse funding, even when it was needed to help the houses function. "There's always funding out there," she told me. "We've just got to find it." She turned down money from the LA County Probation Department because "there were just too many strings." Instead, she continued to insist that any woman at ANWOL make her own decisions; self-determination was not a concept, it was a guiding reality. "I don't want to have to lock them up at six at night," she told me. "They know what they've got to do." Susan also addressed the problem of substance abuse and relapse on a case-by-case basis—there was no rigidity in her approach. From the beginning of my research, it was clear that there were rules at ANWOL, but they were not arbitrarily imposed; instead, they were designed to foster women's growth.

Women's development was always paramount for ANWOL. One day, as I sat in her office discussing the next phase of research, Susan warned me not to call her between January 4 and 11, explaining that she'd be on silent retreat. I was shocked but also impressed that she took the time to be mindful, intentional, thoughtful—all the adjectives fit.

These same practices inform everything that occurs at the ANWOL houses. Before they can come to ANWOL, women are asked to first write a letter from jail or prison in which they share their stories and their desire to come to one of the houses. Susan is determined to never turn down any request and always tries to find space for any woman who contacts her. Once they arrive, for the first thirty days they're in residence, women aren't allowed to schedule any outside visits unless there's a specific reason: for medical care, to obtain a social security card or an identification card, to file for an entitlement. There's no requirement that they work, no demand that they see family or friends. Instead, they are asked to focus on beginning to adjust to life after incarceration.

Beyond their emphasis on healing, ANWOL and Susan Burton are engaged in something crucial that is not readily noted in any of the research on women's reentry: the relationships that are built between the women who live there. Halfway houses and even other well-intentioned facilities often overlook what women need, individually and collectively: trusting relationships. They all place various emphases on having a place to live, a job to earn a living wage, and a way to reunite with their children and families. Still, weaving through this is a less recognized need, one that has to do with the attachments, the connections women make.

I would hear about these attachments over and over again. It came out during the interviews I completed at ANWOL that were part of the case study. But ANWOL wasn't the only place where I heard women talking about attachment. I also heard it when I sat in their kitchens or living rooms, when we worked side by side at the Homegirl Café, when we played with their children in parks or at neighborhood gardens; women who'd been incarcerated talked endlessly about their personal relationships. It dominated most of our discussions. And what emerged so clearly was that what women needed, when they exited incarceration, were relationships with other women who understood what they'd been through *because they have been through it themselves.* They need a place to belong and the knowledge that they belong to one another.

As part of their life after incarceration, women need to replace one community—of gangs, of drugs, of crime, of trauma—that has so deeply impacted their lives with a positive community. Their need is not geographic; it isn't based on moving away to a different location. Every one of the women I talked with described how when they were exiting jail or prison, the only people who really understood what they'd experienced were other women who'd been through the system. As they struggled to survive and to reenter, many women intuitively sought a network of women who knew how they felt. "You don't want to be a member of this club," said Shayna Welcher, a lively Black woman, born and raised in South LA, whom I'd known for ten years. "We all know what it took for us to get here. We all know who belongs." It was in these communities of women that I learned about and began to understand the daily realities of the reentry process.

The Homegirl Café stood out as a place where women who'd been locked up could find a community. "I love Homegirl; it's such an important part of my life," Shayna explained. "You need to understand what we all loved about Homegirl. As women, we come from all parts of LA. Then, when we get to the Homegirl Café, we become one person, one bond." Long before the term "safe space" crept into popular usage, that was what Homegirl offered up, along with the dishes on the menu all named after its waitresses. Within the larger structure of Homeboy Industries, the Homegirl Café was a sanctuary for women. It was housed in Homeboy headquarters, but it was a separate and authentically safe space. That had always been the vision of the woman who created it, Pati Zarate, and the two women who helped her run it, Erika Cuellar and Shannon Smith.[3] The women at Homegirl shared resources, took care of one another's children, and counseled each other whether they were dealing with relationships, money, or court appearances. Homeboy Industries and Father Greg Boyle were so deeply embedded in the public's mind as the place where there is "no us and them, just us," that it was hard to remember the unique mission of the Homegirl Café. When it first quietly began operating a few doors away from the original Homeboy headquarters in Boyle Heights, the café represented a ground-breaking idea: that girls and women who'd been gang involved and incarcerated needed a place of their own. Slowly and intentionally, the Homegirl Café grew into an innovative program dedicated to addressing women's needs after incarceration, creating a beloved community where they could not simply work but also help one another to heal the traumas they'd encountered.

Both Ivy and Janeth flourished at Homegirl. Janeth responded to Adela's love and caring, trying hard to grow up. She didn't have a car or a driver's license, so Adela would pick her up to make sure she got to the café on time. Ivy didn't need a mother figure, relating more to the women her own age. These were the sisters she'd needed and never had growing up. She grew close with Shayna, appearing in a TED talk with her. Both women talked about their fight to overcome trauma, drugs, and incarceration. Homegirl had changed their lives—they'd found somewhere they felt safe and other women who understood exactly what they'd experienced. They helped one another negotiate life after being locked up. "We have each other's backs," Ivy enthused.

I heard the same words at A New Way of Life. The women who lived in the houses or sought services at the main office all told me the same thing, that this was the first place they felt they really "belonged to one another." I witnessed firsthand how these women looked out for and took care of one another, comforting each other about relationships with their children, sharing their clothes and their resources. One staff member even gave a resident her car when she needed it. It was inspiring but also troubling, because it gave rise to the question that had no answer: Why was A New Way of Life unusual? Why wasn't there a program like this on every corner? The same questions haunted me at Homegirl. Why weren't there enough reentry programs across the country that addressed the specific issues formerly incarcerated women faced? And why did so much that was actually offered turn out to be just the opposite of what was required?

I didn't have answers to these questions, but A New Way of Life was giving me hope. I was thinking about all of this as I got ready to leave ANWOL one afternoon. It was pouring rain and I stood in the reception area looking out helplessly—I had forgotten my umbrella and my jacket. Susan's right hand and the organization's co-director, Pamela Marshall, sprang up from her desk and quickly fashioned a poncho for me out of a plastic garbage bag. Laughing, she solved the problem in the most immediate, practical way. The gesture represented the essence of ANWOL, a place where everyone focused on helping women and resolving their issues as swiftly and pragmatically as possible. But I also knew another element was at work here: no one wanted to destroy another person's dignity. That was the intangible in the air: respect. While Pamela was creating my poncho, I overheard a woman waiting to see Susan say, "I came here because Susan Burton cares about us—she gives us respect and hope. And your poncho looks great."

INTERLUDE

Pedro Martinez's trial for first-degree murder is scheduled to go first. Ivy and Janeth's trial will follow, with the two women being tried together. Janeth's attorney is deeply invested in her case and spends time preparing with her; Ivy's attorney is, as usual, MIA. Ivy's trauma has resulted in her ignoring everything that is going on; she is in complete denial.

But Janeth isn't. From the time she was arrested, Janeth began making plans for her baby girl, Angelina, just in case things went the wrong way and she was found guilty. Through the years of abuse and abandonment Janeth has experienced, Angelina has been her true north. Her daughter is her primary concern, and she openly admits, "I shoulda been home with my little girl. I shouldn't have been out. I've been acting just like my mother. Not all the way—my mother didn't take care of me. I'm gonna take care of Angelina, even if I get locked up for a long time. I'm not leaving her all alone—the way my mother left me." Before the trial starts, she asks Adela to adopt her daughter if things don't go well. She wants Angelina to have a good life. "I trust you," she tells Adela, "because I see how you're raising your own daughter."

Adela reassures her that she'd take the baby in a heartbeat, but Myra, the paternal grandmother, also wants Angelina. Janeth feels overwhelmed, crying, "I just know my mother-in-law is gonna keep me

away from her. I've been calling over there and she won't take my calls."
When another woman from the café reaches out to Myra, Myra hangs
up on her after saying, "I don't wanna talk to any gang members." Myra
thinks she will retain custody of Angelina even though DCFS is carefully investigating whether she can provide a "good enough" home for
Angelina. Both of her sons are in prison, locked up for committing violent crimes. "I've had enough things happen to me," Janeth tells Adela.
"You don't know what my mother did to me. I don't want anything like
that to happen to Angelina. Ever."

Pedro's trial is over in three days. The jury spends very little time
deliberating. The verdict comes down swiftly: guilty on all counts. He
is sentenced to "100 years to life in prison"—the equivalent of life without the possibility of parole. No one is surprised. Sadly, everyone at
Homeboy, at the Homegirl Café, and in the community, all agree that
Pedro was guilty of more than murder. He abused Ivy, adding to the
trauma she'd experienced in her life. In so many ways, he'd failed to
protect Ivy; he'd failed to be a man.

"At the trial," Adela remembers, "Pedro took no responsibility—he
was just sitting there, just quiet, staring into space. He didn't look at Ivy
or Janeth; he didn't talk to his lawyer. He sat there with no remorse, no
nothing. I think if he would have said, 'I did it and I'll carry the weight;
let's make a deal,' then those girls would have got off or gotten a lighter
sentence. But he wasn't a man. The girls wouldn't snitch and say what
he'd done. Ivy wouldn't talk about what he'd done to her. It was bad all
around."

This is all especially painful for Ivy. This is exactly what happened
when she went to prison the first time, for drug distribution. Her boyfriend wouldn't take the weight; he wouldn't say Ivy had nothing to do
with it. In reality, she'd had nothing to do with the crime she was sentenced for; she'd only been along for the ride. Ivy can't believe the same
thing is happening to her again.

Two weeks later, Ivy and Janeth's trial begins. Ivy's lawyer dozes off
while Janeth's alternate public defender does a remarkable job, arguing

that Janeth was in the kill zone, that she didn't want to shoot anyone and was actually in danger herself when Pedro started shooting. After a month, both sides rest their cases. The jury deliberates for a week and can't reach a verdict. The judge announces a hung jury. There will be another trial.

ELEVEN

THE STRUGGLES OF LIFE

You know what's hard about getting out of jail or getting out of prison? You're poor. You're even poorer than you were before you got locked up. And you got nowhere to go.

—SONIA ESTEVEZ

The July 2019 briefing released by the Prison Policy Initiative made public two equally compelling pieces of information: the growing number of women released from prison and jail in the United States each year, and the long list of unmet needs that sabotaged their successful reentry. This all led up to its most meaningful finding that, as early as 2004, researchers had established that *the strongest predictor of whether or not a woman would recidivate—or relapse into crime—was poverty.*[1] In turn, if their basic needs are fulfilled, even in the short term, the odds of recidivism are reduced by 83 percent for poor women on probation and parole.

The reality is that women leaving prison and jail are set up for economic failure. Women who've been incarcerated, especially if they are Black, Indigenous, or women of color, "have much higher rates of unemployment and homelessness, and are less likely to have a high school education when compared with formerly incarcerated men."[2] In addition, many states require women to pay restitution or victim compensation fines, which often rise into the thousands of dollars. In certain states, like Hawaii, women are asked to repay the state for welfare payments made to their children while they were locked up.[3] All this while dealing with trauma and, in far too many cases, substance abuse.

The stories of the women I'd listened to for the past decade matched up with the examples offered in the PPI briefing. In one setting, the PPI "identified homelessness and the lack of stable housing as the biggest problem facing women in the New York City Justice System," reporting that 80 percent of the women locked up in Rikers Island said they needed help finding housing once they were out of jail. But this wasn't news. Over a decade earlier, in 2006, researchers in California had reported that "75% of formerly incarcerated women surveyed had experienced homelessness at some point, and 41% were currently homeless."[4] And when it came to public housing, formerly incarcerated women were once again out of luck. The Housing Opportunity Program Extension Act of 1996 mandated that anyone with a drug or violent crime conviction couldn't receive assistance with public housing, whether it was living in a development or receiving a Section 8 certificate or voucher to help subsidize housing. It wasn't their weakness or their lack of resilience that drove women back to abusive partners or dysfunctional family situations. It was their need for housing and economic survival. Relationships and a lack of money were all tangled up together.

This entanglement was exactly what had happened with Clara and what had driven her back to Eduardo in the past. Locked up in federal prison, she promised herself those days were over. She was determined to change. When she was released, Clara didn't even think about the help she might need. She immediately took custody of Theresa, who'd been living with friends. The Lopezes sent Aracely and Veronica back from LA. All of this was easy—they weren't being monitored by children's services. Still, Clara didn't know what to do. No one had hooked her up with any services; she'd served her time and she wasn't required to live in a halfway house. There'd been no reentry planning while she was in prison. Once she was out, Arizona proved to be a wasteland in terms of women's reentry services.

Unsure of her next move, Clara stayed put in Arizona. Eduardo was still around, making empty promises that he was going to change. But he was using and came over at all hours, keeping her awake at night. "Finally, I told him that if he didn't leave, I was going to call immigration because he was illegal. I was fed up with him and I meant it." He got scared and went home to Los Angeles. After that, she was free. "I was away from drugs, away from emotional abuse. I was done. I finally felt at peace." She began looking for work and took on temporary employment—nothing illegal. Even if it meant confronting poverty, she was committed to change.

A few months after Eduardo returned to LA, he was arrested on drug charges and deported to Mexico. He called Clara for help, and, despite feeling guilty because "he was the father of my children," she refused, feeling relieved. She needed to think about the future; so much time had passed—she'd been in Arizona almost ten years. She wanted to go back to school but couldn't once she discovered that the state's cheap rents were balanced by its lack of financial assistance for college. Her relationship with her daughters was loving, yet unsettled; maybe they needed a fresh start, to live somewhere new. But when she brought up the idea of moving, Theresa, now a teenager, made it clear she was staying in Arizona. As if to solidify her intentions, right after she turned sixteen, Theresa got pregnant, had a baby, and moved out on her own.

By then it was summer, and Eduardo's parents arrived to pick up Veronica en route to Mexico with Aracely to see their son. Clara knew what she had to do. "I asked the grandparents if they could take care of Veronica along with Aracely because I wasn't making it in Arizona anymore. I had a record and I couldn't find a stable job. I knew I couldn't stay there anymore, otherwise I was going to go back to my life of selling drugs to support my family. I had to get out."

The grandparents stayed in Mexico with the girls after the summer, enrolling them in school there. Clara ended up back in California with very few options. She had no money, no support, and was once again homeless. "In LA, I was in the streets for a while, back to the gang and everything that was part of that life. It was like going backwards. I'm so lucky they were there for me. I stayed at one guy's house and he helped me out so I could start getting money." This didn't surprise me—I had found that gangs act as de facto social service agencies. There is a system of mutual aid among gang members and those who are no longer actively involved. I didn't ask for details, and Clara didn't volunteer any. Her resilience and her connections meant that she survived. Not every woman who's been incarcerated has the ability to claw her way back. Clara's strength was unique to her. But her lonely struggle was not. Confronted with economic obstacles, emotional trauma, and separation from her children, with no supports, she turned to what she knew—the network of gangs and the streets. This narrative is far too typical of women after they have been locked up, particularly those caught in the cycle of drugs and incarceration.

Clara's lack of options was emblematic of what formerly incarcerated mothers face. Many of these women have been on public assistance before getting locked up. After they're released, they have a criminal history and no longer qualify for public support. Like Clara, they find it impossible to attain the financial stability they need.[5] The odds are stacked against women trying to find a job who know that every application asks them to "check the box" and answer the question "Have you ever been convicted of a felony?" This narrows the chances of being hired in a wildly competitive employment market. Mothers who manage to get hired after incarceration most often find themselves with earnings that fall far below the poverty line.[6] One study demonstrates this with heartbreaking clarity: less than 1 percent of released mothers have the financial resources to move into private housing with their children.[7]

Clara hustled for several months, then rented an apartment. She tried to find legitimate work and enrolled in school. But after a few months she ran out of money. She knew one thing for certain: she didn't want to go back to the streets. She was afraid she'd get arrested and she'd promised herself that would never happen again. Despite shame and a sense of failure, she turned once more to the House of Ruth for support, and they welcomed her with open arms. "It felt good. They didn't judge me; they helped me." The shelter provided housing until she'd saved up enough to get an apartment.

At the House of Ruth, Clara started believing things were finally changing for the better. She felt safe in Los Angeles; Eduardo would never return. Just as importantly, she began pursuing her education more seriously, learning about programs that supported students. She returned to Los Angeles Community College (LACC) where she'd already accumulated some credits and reconnected with Rowena Smith, the Extended Opportunity Programs and Services coordinator she'd gotten to know before. Rowena told her she'd qualify to work at the EOPS office once she completed her first semester. After applying for financial aid, she enrolled in classes.

In the meantime, Theresa called Clara and told her she wanted to come live with her in Los Angeles. Then, the Lopezes returned from Mexico. Although they insisted on keeping Aracely with them, they were happy to see Clara reunited with her youngest daughter, Veronica. All these changes shaped Clara's plans for her future. She wanted to heal the problems that incarceration and being separated from her daughters had caused. She was glad she was in California, even though it was more expensive, because at LACC there was financial and emotional support for a student facing her challenges.

She was concerned about the impact on her health from her long-term drug use and all the blows to the head she'd endured as a result of domestic violence. She was frightened that she'd fail as a student. But her determination was greater than her fear. "I always wanted an education, not only so I can feel proud of myself; I want my kids to feel proud of me. To teach them, no matter what, to look at all that I've gone through—I've been to jail, I've been through domestic violence, I've been through drugs, I've been in the streets, I've been through everything, and I know, you can still come out ahead. You can make something out of yourself. You don't have to put up with abuse just because you don't have an education or because you have children! Educate yourself."

Clara and I sit across from each other at Jack's Burgers, a Boyle Heights landmark, as she tells me this. She is getting ready to graduate from community college and move on to finish her BA at a four-year university. Her eyes sparkle with anxiety as well as excitement. She's waiting to hear back from the three schools in the state university system. "It's been a long trek," she says, sighing. "It's actually taken me seven years and three attempts to finish school and I'm proud of myself because it's been me, all alone. I haven't had support of my family, but I had the support of the school and the shelter. That's what made the difference."

Clara's family betrayed her, repeatedly. Her mother handed her fate to DCFS twice—once in childhood, then again as an adult. Yet Clara kept going, telling me, "I survived child abuse. I survived domestic abuse. And I survived drugs. Now I have a new identity. I'm a mother and I'm a student." She has stayed off drugs, although she explains, "So far, it's a day-by-day thing that never ends." School is difficult; surviving economically is difficult. Still, for her, there is no other pathway now. She has a new boyfriend who works and contributes to the household, even though he doesn't stay there all the time; she is very careful with her money and her independence.

In her life now, rebuilding her relationship with her daughters has remained her highest priority. The House of Ruth staff helped her obtain Section 8 subsidized housing, and Clara found a small house where she could live with her oldest and youngest daughters. Some of her uncertainty and anxiety have been soothed now that she is living independently with Theresa and Veronica. She talks happily about having a home that is hers, that she doesn't share with an abusive partner. "It's peace. And I haven't felt that for a long time."

Still, the wounds of incarceration endure. Her eldest, Theresa, angrily pointed out that she attended nine different schools over the years that she lived with Clara, then with Eduardo, then in the foster-care system. But Clara's response was pragmatic: "We're not going to solve these problems overnight. I'm still working on my own problems—so we had to get help."

She's also clear that she doesn't want her kids to live the life she lived. Because of her inability to qualify for anything beyond a minimum-wage job, she sold drugs to support her family. It was a forced choice and not a desire—a by-product of how formerly incarcerated women are set up for failure. Today, Clara believes that higher education is a promising way to escape the past—otherwise, "even to work at McDonalds, they check your record." What she experienced still haunts her. "I never want my daughters, or any women, to go through what I went through," she tells me. "It's bad for any woman who's been locked up; it's really bad if you're Mexican, and it's worse if you're Black."

A week later, sitting in my UCLA office with Denise, I bring up what happens to Black women and women of color in what Susan Burton calls "the criminal injustice system." "You need to understand the reality, G-ma," she says with a sigh. As she dives into her subject, her voice takes on an angry edge. "When I was locked up and after I got out, what really kept me down was my color *and* poverty. I'm on the lowest rung because I'm a Black woman. Lower than anyone. You know, one of my closest friends is Mexican, and she had more hope than I did. She went to the penitentiary, she lost her baby, she'd already relapsed a couple of times, and *she had more hope than I did.*" Denise's voice shakes as she says this, and I know she's talking about Clara. "And you know there are more Black women in prison than any other group."

Her observation is backed up by the ACLU, which reports that Black women and women of color are overrepresented—substantially—in jails and prisons. Black women make up 30 percent of the population of incarcerated women in the US, even though they are only 13 percent of the female population. The ACLU's findings track with Denise's observation, that Latinas are overrepresented but not as drastically as Black women, who make up 16 percent of the incarcerated population while being only 11 percent of all women in the US.[8]

Denise is convinced—and her belief is borne out by statistics—that any Black formerly incarcerated woman is saddled with the lowest of statuses and the greatest of obstacles. There is the stigma of being formerly incarcerated—a diminished status for any individual. She notes, "A woman is always lower than a man. Then, in terms of color, it's the biggest difference. No matter how educated you are, you will never get the same options. Anyone else—they'll still have a better shot than you."

I had no counterargument for Denise—she was right. Race figured deeply in the lives of women after incarceration. It was always there, too often unacknowledged and adding even more pressure to what Black women already encountered in terms of poverty and trauma. The economic realities women faced and the trauma they attempted to relieve through self-medication were so tangled up, it felt impossible to know how to start to deal with them. How could you confront substance abuse issues without acknowledging that women were too poor to seek treatment? Denise's own story was a testament to this problem. This became brutally apparent as she described her battles with poverty, substance abuse, and a looming court date.

"When I think back on my life, I felt I had agency on the streets. I think that's why I had so much trouble at rehab—I didn't have control. Crazy as it sounds, on the streets, I made money. No one told me what to do. It didn't matter what color I was; I could take care of myself."

Denise laughs ruefully. "When I left rehab, it was like the party had started again . . ." Her voice trails off. The next four months passed in a blur. Because of the temporary judge's bizarre ruling that postponed Denise's new sentencing once she'd relapsed, she'd had four months without any supervision. The time passed swiftly, and her now delayed court date loomed. "Usually, my thing is running. But something happened inside of me—I finally knew I was done. I couldn't go on the way I was—no home, no money, no nothing. I was always poor; I was always high. And I was tired. It's like drugs and homelessness were gonna force me into rehab."

Still, up until the last minute, Denise felt ambivalent. When she got to court, "there was still a little pushback in me—I thought if I could just finagle it, if I could just convince them to let me walk out that day, I would do it. Right there I was loaded; I had drugs in my system. The clerk told me to wait." As she sat through both the morning and afternoon sessions of court, she realized that her case wasn't going to get heard. The day ended and she spent the night in jail.

The next morning, she stood before her original judge, who took one look at Denise and announced she was going to impose her original sentence. Denise pleaded to go back to the program and promised to stay. The judge relented, cautioning Denise that she'd give her one more chance *only* if ACW agreed to take her back. If she failed, she was going to prison. "Prison, prison, prison—she kept saying it." Denise had thirty days to make this happen. In the meantime, she'd have to stay locked up.

Getting back into ACW wasn't a slam dunk. Denise was in jail the whole thirty days waiting to see if they'd take her back. Her doubts increased, and she knew, she said, that if she had to go to prison, "that was it. I would serve my time and then I was going back to do my thing—drinking, drugs, whatever. I was gonna do it till I died." A supervisor, Anna, intervened on her behalf. She told the judge that ACW was willing to give Denise another shot, and if the court allowed her to come back, Anna would make sure Denise succeeded. The judge ruled that Denise would have to stay at ACW one year, followed by four years on probation.

This sounded like an eternity to Denise. "A year! I didn't wanna go into recovery for a year! Even once I was there, I wasn't sure I wanted to stay." Anna worked with her, and Denise decided that she'd only think about the first goal she had to fulfill: a year at ACW. After that, she'd deal with getting some money, living without drugs, and being on probation.

When her year's residence at ACW was complete, Denise tried to plan what she'd do once she was released. She didn't know about A New Way of Life because, in 2010, it was still operating pretty much under the radar. "I wish I'd found out about it. I could've used it," she told me. Denise couldn't work because she was still struggling with trauma, dealing with anxiety and PTSD—the laundry list of diagnoses was long. While at ACW, Anna had documented her mental health challenges, and she began receiving a small monthly disability payment. This would continue once she left; she also applied for food stamps and any other public support available. There wasn't enough money for an apartment, so with her limited funds, she rented a room in a single-room-occupancy hotel downtown. SROs are used by individuals with extremely low incomes, serving as a form of "affordable housing" for those whose only alternative is homelessness. In most SROs, men and women share bathrooms and kitchens. Still, for Denise, despite the minimal conditions, the SRO was more of a home than the streets. She could live there because she didn't have children. She'd always wanted a baby, but right now, she felt lucky to be alone.

While she looked every day, she couldn't find work. Every time she filled in an application and checked the "previous felony" box, prospective employers told her the position was filled. At night, unable to sleep, she'd wonder what she was going to do with her life. She'd always loved school, and just like Clara, she saw the promise of higher education. If she checked the box saying she had a college degree that might balance checking the box for being a felon. In the fall of 2010, she enrolled in LA Community College, taking night classes, because those seemed easier to her. Like Clara had, Denise told me, "I was self-conscious about my ability to learn and retain information because of all the drugs I had taken and everything I'd been through."

School proved difficult until a sociology professor, Anthony Clark, took an interest in her, steering her toward on-campus resources. Eventually, Clark and another professor both wrote letters recommending that Denise be released from probation, which ultimately worked. Along with going to classes, Denise checked in with her sponsor daily and attended 12-step groups; it was there she met Leroy. After several months focusing on her recovery, she began seeing him. She still felt unsure; Leroy was older and had been involved with the criminal justice system for decades. But they had a great deal in common. They'd both grown up in South Central LA; their families had been troubled. Leroy was committed to his recovery. He'd suffered with heroin addiction for over a decade. Denise felt safe with him: he understood what she'd been through and didn't judge her. After several months, they pooled their money and began living together. Denise moved their few possessions into an apartment, while Leroy found a temporary job as a long-distance truck driver. This was the start of a new pattern in their lives: Leroy was gone whenever he could find work and Denise would stay home alone, studying and going to meetings. Six months after moving in together, they got married. Despite this, Denise still felt anxious about money and long-term security.

She learned about a UCLA program that included a summer education intensive offering classes, mentoring, and help with transferring from a community college. She signed up, participated enthusiastically, and then submitted her application to the bachelor's program. She was overwhelmed when she received the acceptance letter that admitted her to UCLA as an undergraduate in African American studies. Once she started taking classes, she added a minor in disabilities studies. She thought about getting an MSW and enrolled in a new class, Social Welfare Policy and Practices. Which brought her to my door.

Right now, despite her success in school, worries about money are constant. Often, Denise can't sleep at night and her anxiety makes it difficult for her to sit still and concentrate. "I know I gotta deal with my trauma," she admits, "but where am I gonna get therapy? I went to the student counseling center—they didn't understand me—no one there has been locked up. Hell! No one there has even worked in a prison or a jail! I'm worried about how I'm gonna pay for graduate school. And with the baby coming, I really need money now."

Limited financial assistance represents a huge part of the lack of support for formerly incarcerated women. And over the past decade I've spent interviewing women, I've become a de facto job placement service for many of them. When they share their stories, it is the least I can do for them, along with paying them for their time. So I'm happy to find Denise a part-time job on campus. But that is one person and one job. And the need is huge. My small successes underscore the depth of the struggles these women face, the lack of available options to help them fulfill their lives and dreams.

There really is no systemic response to the needs of formerly incarcerated women. Instead, places like ANWOL, Hour Children, and

House of Ruth are "one-offs" on the West and East Coasts. That's why their work and all the initiatives they engage in represent fresh approaches that should serve as models for the entire nation to address a growing problem. But there are too many gaps, too many deficits, in terms of help for women. There are no recognized best practices—a method or a strategy generally viewed as the best of all options because research has shown it to be effective. The Prison Policy Initiative has recognized this, while offering some optimism about women's reentry programs serving as examples of success. The last section of the latest PPI briefing enthused, "Notably, A New Way of Life Reentry Project operates eight houses and is working toward expanding its model nationally." ANWOL was the first program among a handful of those described, and its approach was described in detail. I smiled after I read this, knowing I would be with Susan the next day to actually work on this expansion.

Twenty-four hours later, when I walk into the ANWOL conference room, Susan is eating lunch with several women on her staff; she tells me to sit down and have some food. Her dark, coiled hair frames her face as she announces, "All right! We know what we're doing is working and we've got the outcomes to show it. It's time to move on this national model." The creation of a national model—a written blueprint to guide the development of women's housing and reentry programs across the country—is critical. Susan's new plan represents—again those words— something new and completely different. I also know that Susan needs to justify her model, to show that it is working and can be expanded on a national scale. Her "proof" this should happen is that ANWOL is effective. But no one is going to take this on her say-so alone. As a researcher, no matter how participatory and community-based my work is, I also have to look at and report on the data. And what I discover, based on data ANWOL has collected, is that their success rate is 96 percent. Only 4 percent of the women in their program "recidivate."

"Recidivism" is an odd term—it smacks of the criminal justice system. I've never liked it, and particularly in the case of women, it's more useful to think of women relapsing. There are other issues surrounding the concept of recidivism. Some believe the term should be used whenever an individual experiences any sort of re-incarceration, including probation violations. So, if a PO decides to record a probation violation because a woman is out past curfew, this is the same term used to describe a woman who gets caught after going out, buying a gun illegally and stealing a car. Both constitute "recidivism." It sounds ludicrous, yet that's how statistics are often constructed. I've never believed in it, and in the language of community-based participatory research, recidivism is counted only when an individual commits a brand-new crime. Probation violations are *not* recidivism. On top of that, it's essential to consider whether the crime committed represents a less harmful crime than what's occurred in the past. If a woman has been locked up for assault with a deadly weapon and the new crime she committed during a relapse is shoplifting eye makeup, it's important to make a distinction between the two. So far, this idea has not been reflected in recidivism statistics, but there is hope of changing this.

In the meantime, at ANWOL, I'd checked and rechecked the data, and it showed that the clear majority of women were neither relapsing nor "recidivating." Their results matched the outcomes that Hour Children, a well-known New York program that served formerly incarcerated women and their families, was reporting. It was hard to know what this really meant. There aren't many programs for women and even fewer were collecting data. How could they? Women's reentry programs are barely funded as it is, and there is little money for evaluation. Women's reentry homes aren't focused on collecting data; they are focused on survival.

Lunch is over, staff have gone back to their offices, and it's time to talk about the nuts and bolts of the model. I ask Susan some questions about what she wants to do moving forward and then tell her I'm worried about the complexities of creating a national model. This is something no one has ever attempted. There are best practices—which are held out as examples of how reentry programs (again usually geared toward men) should operate—but there's no national model. What she's determined to implement is new and different and feels a bit overwhelming. Can she really do this? I can't control myself and blurt out, "Have you thought about what you're doing?"

Susan looks at me carefully and doesn't respond right away. I worry I've outworn her patience, or maybe I've got salad in my teeth. As if reading my mind, she gently begins, "Don't worry, you're not the only one asking that question. And . . . I wonder if you know how many obstacles I faced even starting up and then running this organization? I'm a Black woman who didn't graduate Yale or any Ivy League school, who was formerly incarcerated." I nod and think about how she's faced even more obstacles creating a program for *women.* Despite the ongoing lip service paid to "gender-specific programs," very few people in the criminal justice system talk about what women faced.

I could list all the obstacles women face. Still, nothing I wrote would be as eloquent as the words of Edith Robinson, a Black single mother with three children I met in San Diego early on while conducting my research. I'll never forget her description of what she faced after incarceration, while she was on probation. She was deeply grateful to have gotten a job at a warehouse, moving merchandise, updating inventory. But the systems that were supposed to support her all seemed to be more invested in creating stumbling blocks for her to overcome. "My PO always made appointments for me during work hours. I'd have to go to the boss and ask for time off. He was cool; he knew I had to see my PO. After he got promoted, my next boss wasn't so great about it and would make fun of me in front of the other workers, 'Edith's gotta go check in with her PO,' he'd yell out. He made me clock out and then come back and clock in and make up my hours. Sometimes that meant staying at the warehouse late, and I had to find someone to watch my kids—they're not really old enough to watch themselves; the oldest is twelve. I couldn't always find someone, and I'd have to leave them at home alone for an hour or two. I was scared what would happen to them. I was scared children's services would find them home alone.

"Then I had to find a bus that would get me to the PO on time, and sometimes the buses ran late or I didn't have the right change for the bus fare. And then I had the PO coming by my house and saying he needed me to do some random drug testing. I'd been through recovery, and I was never gonna use again—but there he was, this big white guy holding a little plastic cup. Then my children's social worker was showing up at my house all hours of the day and night to 'check' on me. I knew what all of them were doing—they wanted to know if I was home, if I was high, if I had a man over, if my kids were all right. I was worried I'd lose my job; I was worried I'd lose my kids. When the social worker asked me if I was experiencing any stress, I told her 'no' even though I wanted to say, 'Are you fucking kidding me?'"

Edith's "to-do" list is all too familiar. The requirements women confront after incarceration grow rather than diminish as the weeks go by. New dilemmas and requirements quickly spring up. And it feels as if it will never end.

No one knew this better and worked harder to address it than Susan Burton. Because of her unstoppable devotion to this issue, she'd been lauded by *New York Times* columnist Nicholas Kristof and the brilliant academic Michelle Alexander, both of whom called her a modern-day Harriet Tubman. Instead of letting all the attention inflate her ego, the woman in front of me had doubled down on her commitment to this mission. "Let's go over our survey and talk about how we're going to use it to reinforce the national model"—what Susan called the Sisterhood Alliance for Freedom and Equality (SAFE) Housing Network. "And let's talk about the replication training—how we'll get people together and teach them about the model so they can put it into action, in whatever state they're in."

Over a year before, Susan had overseen new research to help shed more light on the experiences of formerly incarcerated women. There had been pockets of academic research into the lives of formerly incarcerated women, but Susan was the first executive director of a nonprofit who wanted to serve as an active research partner. This was community-based participatory research playing out in a way I'd rarely heard about and only experienced one time before—at Homeboy Industries. We worked together for three months, designing a questionnaire that would capture the depth and breadth of women's needs and, just as significantly, the contents of their dreams and desires. ANWOL—not UCLA—sent out the survey in an email to states and organizations across the country and it was slow going—we weren't having an overwhelming response to our email.

In June of 2018, Susan called to tell me that in September we were going to Orlando, Florida, for a meeting of the National Network of Formerly Incarcerated Men and Women. She wanted to administer the survey there. This was going to be a heavy lift, though at this point, I also knew better than to object. In the humidity of late-summer Florida, we passed out and collected hundreds of surveys, winding up with a sample of more than four hundred respondents from across the country. The women who answered our questions described reentry experiences filled with fear, trauma, and a complete lack of support. And—no surprise here—their needs were familiar yet still important to record: housing, employment, education, access to financial safety nets, mental health treatment, and connection to their children and families. But what was different about this survey was how women gave voice to their dreams and plans. They were not only interested in themselves; the majority of the women who responded described their desire to give back to others, their hope to create a better life and more opportunities for their children, their drive to engage with their community, and, most significantly, their wish to lead systems-level change for women and families affected by mass incarceration.[9]

In her study of women at a Chicago-based halfway house, the sociologist Andrea Leverentz described how "in all relationships, the women carefully attempted to balance humility with 'carrying the message forward' about the possibility of change and serving as a role model for others in similar situations."[10] This desire to give back, to serve as role models—to truly help the community of women who have been incarcerated—would power the SAFE Housing Network, an interconnected system of reentry homes that would operate and collaborate across the country.

After we returned from Orlando, with the survey results collected and analyzed, Susan was moving toward training the folks from states across the country who wanted to be members of the SAFE network. She was putting the survey results into action, and I documented the systematic and intentional effort she was leading, refining the model's key components and building on the earlier work to create a national model. Susan was clear that the SAFE model was about much more than offering women a place to stay after incarceration. Most significantly, it was about building a national network of homes offering women the empowerment, opportunity, and freedom that could grow alongside secure housing.

I'd already seen the power of this idea as I watched the Global Homeboy Network evolve since it was founded in 2014. Originally the vision of Father Greg Boyle, the GHN worked with more than four hundred organizations all over the world to help create therapeutic communities, sharing tools and strategies to support marginalized men, women, and youth in a commitment to kinship and programmatic support. What Susan was developing was similar to Homeboy, but it focused specifically on women and the ways their overlooked needs affected families and communities. It also offered a specific model that could be put into practice across the country. Susan explained it eloquently to me: "The SAFE housing model and the network centers women, LGBTQIA people, children, and family in the movement to end mass incarceration and its mission to bring people back home."

Over several days, as we talked together, Susan outlined the program's guiding concepts, including personal agency and autonomy, multidimensional and holistic services, gender-specific support, and social transformation. It was also important to communicate in a way that anyone could understand how the work of the SAFE Housing Network was organized around three concepts: (1) basic human needs must be met; (2) reentry should address trauma and not further traumatize individuals; and (3) all barriers to accessing personal identification, housing, medical care, mental health, and public assistance should be removed.

Once we created and fine-tuned the model and posted it on the ANWOL website, I was looking forward to a brief respite, but that wasn't in the cards.[11] Instead, Susan wanted to get the network going—now. Christin Runkle, the ANWOL communications manager, and I worked to assist her in designing and presenting a two-day training on the SAFE house model (after a shakedown tryout it turned into a three-day training). Through the Ford Foundation, Susan obtained a grant to pay for participants' airfare and expenses so she could bring people together from across the country for three days, to instruct them in the SAFE house model and strengthen the network of SAFE houses that existed. I was training alongside her, and from day one, it was both an overwhelming responsibility and a joy. The participants in one room—straight, gay, lesbian, queer, trans, Black, people of color, and white—all came together to learn about this new model and to prepare to implement it in states from Minnesota to Arkansas.

Susan was the unifying figure. The people gathered responded to her with a combination of love, deep respect, and awe. While she appreciated their reverence, she was more interested in action and change. For six hours, we presented information, throwing concepts back and forth and posing examples to the group. Our training in using the model was followed and reinforced by guest speakers and field visits to the ANWOL houses. In the months that followed the second training, eleven states and fifteen cities participated in the SAFE Housing Network. A third training was on the books with eighty participants and a waiting list while ANWOL provided technical assistance to whoever desired it.

The SAFE Housing Network was a much-needed systemic answer to the needs of reentry women. It was designed to create spaces for formerly incarcerated women to be healed and lifted up. But it was also part of an effort to ensure that people who'd been incarcerated could now be empowered as the experts in a movement to ensure that civil rights as well as social and economic justice were restored and sustained for all formerly incarcerated individuals. This finally represented the chance for a strong and systemic response to the checklist of needs women faced after incarceration: help with housing, trauma, poverty, children, and the demands of probation or parole.

Yet, there was one facet of their lives that proved more difficult to address, that women struggled and needed ongoing help with: the problem of love and personal attachments. Weaving through all the obstacles they faced was the dilemma of how women dealt with the personal relationships in their lives before—and after—incarceration.

INTERLUDE

Janeth and Ivy are awaiting their retrial. The DA doesn't want to go through a second trial and puts a plea bargain on the table, an arrangement that increases the tension already growing between the two women. Ivy is offered twenty years and Janeth, twenty-seven. Elie explains that Janeth has been offered a longer sentence because her identification is definite—witnesses had seen her clearly. Ivy's ID is shakier. Despite the difference, Janeth wants to take the deal. She tells Adela, "When I get out, I'll be forty-five. I'll look like you—I'll be a little older than you, I can be like you."

Ivy thinks she deserves an even shorter sentence; she wants to hold out for sixteen years. Then her lawyer, as incompetent as ever, plants the seed that Ivy might walk. Ivy tells Janeth she wants to reject the deal altogether. The women are arguing constantly. It's a package deal—the two of them have to agree to accept it; they can't split the baby. Ivy turns down the deal, and the DA refuses to make another offer. Janeth is furious. When they appear together in court to set the date for the retrial, they start fighting. Bailiffs wind up having to separate them.

Despite the hostility between the two women, Adela visits Ivy and Janeth as often as she can. "I used to go to see them a lot. Ivy had suffered so much trauma—I saw it. She didn't even know what was good for her with the plea bargain. It was the same story. She didn't deal with the trauma she'd faced all her life and especially when she got involved with Pedro. He abused her. She was a mess—she couldn't think straight. And Janeth was so innocent and she was so immature. She was like a little girl who still needed her mother. Only her mother had totally abandoned her. Pedro was the one who was guilty. Pedro was the one who shot the deacon. So here were these two women, traumatized and scared out of their minds. And now they're both looking at a conviction."

Adela is not alone in her anxiety. Everyone worries what will happen in the second trial.

TWELVE

NEW LOVE

I wasn't ready for how lonely I'd feel when I got out of prison. I wasn't prepared for it. I was prepared to be poor, I was prepared not to work, I was prepared to have problems with my children. I wasn't prepared for missing my girl. It threw me way off balance.

—ANGELA WASHINGTON

A fter incarceration, there is one struggle women face that isn't easily addressed by changes in the law, public policy, or job placement services: their relationships with the partners they've loved and, in many cases, still love. Women's attachments and their search for affection and intimacy continues to play a role in their lives, alternately challenging and reinforcing their commitment to healing and empowerment. In her beautiful book *The Ex-Prisoner's Dilemma*, Andrea Leverentz describes how formerly incarcerated women "tried to balance a goal of independence with changing the ways in which they relate to others and the desire for strong, positive connections."[1] Leverentz explains how women resolve this dilemma as they tend to end former romantic relationships and friendships while preserving family ties. Additionally, most of the women "avoided romantic relationships or only engaged in casual relationships in order to focus better on themselves and their own recovery."[2]

This shed light on something I kept observing and didn't completely understand. While I was hearing a lot from women about all the issues they faced in their lives, there was a blank space when it came to certain topics: their relationships and their sexuality. Adela confided that she and Pati Zarate, the chef and founder of the Homegirl Café, had often talked about "becoming like nuns." I suspected that other women felt that way—but why? As Denise and Clara, along with so many others, explained, their relationships with men were part of what drove them deeper into gang life and crime, or precipitated their return to such a life during the vulnerable time of reentry. Adela reminded me of the example of Ivy and how her involvement with Pedro had short-circuited her recovery. It was important to learn who women cared about, who they were attracted to, and, just as significantly, how they negotiated sexuality as they reentered their communities. I also knew there was a very good reason why all this took a backseat—they had too much going on in their lives.

"I don't have time to think about a man. I don't have time to think about sex," Cynthia Diaz told me. "The only man I'm thinking about is my probation officer—and I'm not thinking about him *that* way. I'm thinking about how I gotta stay out of trouble." What Cynthia told me wasn't unusual. The women I knew felt overwhelmed with all the requirements they were trying to fulfill and all the obstacles they were facing.

But as we spent hours together, these same women grew tired of focusing on the problems they faced. They wanted to gossip and talk about the times they got to party or have fun and enjoy themselves. We'd talk about men, and they'd ask me endlessly about my marriage. Many of them started reminiscing about their past loves. Others wanted to talk about the significant relationships popping up in their lives. And then there was the small group of women who opened up about how incarceration had changed the way they viewed themselves and their sexuality.

The sexuality of women in prison has always been a source of curiosity and titillation. Over its seven seasons, the TV show *Orange Is the*

New Black explored the relationships that existed between women and how attraction, love, and loss occurred during lockup. As we talked, what I began to learn about women and sexuality was much more complex than anything that could be portrayed on a television series. I also knew that despite the time I'd spent with the women I knew, I still had very limited knowledge of the LGBTQIA community, a subject that warrants many books, particularly by those who have direct experience with gender-expansive identities.

The Prison Policy Initiative cited a study showing that 33 percent of incarcerated women identified as lesbian or bisexual, compared with less than 10 percent of incarcerated men.[3] But there's been limited examination of what happens with women's sexuality during incarceration, and even less study of women's sexuality *after* incarceration. It almost felt like no one really wanted to look too closely at sexuality, a reluctance reinforced by explicit and implicit homophobia. Maybe it's because sexuality wasn't the real issue. The real issue involved how relationships began and developed during incarceration and how that affected women when they returned home to their families.

Both men and women create structures for themselves in prison, and—no surprise—these structures are gendered. Incarcerated men's hierarchies are largely based on power, and that power is exerted through intimidation, illegal activities, gang rivalries, and rape. The last led to President George W. Bush's signing the Prison Rape Elimination Act into law in 2003, legislation aimed at protecting individuals from what was viewed as an epidemic level of prison rape.[4]

However, in prison women's hierarchies are based on attachments and relationships, often mirroring family structure; they also involve extensive caretaking. This was certainly what I learned from the women I interviewed. They formed strong bonds with one another while they were locked up but also after they were free.[5] Researchers have also found that women create what have been termed "pseudo-families" while in prison, where they tend to be locked up for longer stretches of time than in jail or other correctional institutions. While similar relationships occurred in men's prisons, with a stronger man "protecting" another man who becomes his lover, there's really no documented equivalent for these pseudo-families in men's incarceration. In creating these interdependent families and relationships women pair off with a sexual partner and care for younger women who represent children or kin in their care. The families offer support, attachments, and interdependent relationships. In many instances, these prison families are closer to an ideal family than the women's real families. Older women serve in a strong parental role, being deeply protective and acting as caretakers and mentors toward younger women. And just like their families outside prison, incarcerated women's relationships and roles are dynamic and change over time.[6]

Within these pseudo-families, sexual relationships are accepted; they're seen as just another part of life during incarceration. The idea that women would be "affectionate" or care for one another and how that might translate into sexual relationships has been studied somewhat inconsistently. Again, this is evidence of the implicit homophobia and bias that stalks research into prison behaviors. Still, some research has been done. One of the earliest studies of how women act on their sexuality while locked up was conducted in 1965 at Frontera Prison (now Chowchilla), at that time the only women's prison in California. Based on responses to a questionnaire, the researchers reported that 50 percent of the women there were involved in same-sex sexual activity.[7] Most of the time, this activity was for pleasure and wasn't viewed as meaningful. But occasionally, these interactions turned into serious relationships.[8] Over ten years later, in another study that used questionnaires administered in women's prisons, sociologist Alice Propper described the multiple reasons women gave for engaging in same-sex relationships while locked up: fun, to combat loneliness, needing companionship, and economic gain.[9] More recently, in 2014, a study found that consensual same-sex relationships were viewed as just part of life in prison for both men and women.[10] Maybe these attachments were best described by Kate Johns, a London lawyer who spent five years in prison after being convicted of tax fraud. She referred to such relationships using the familiar phrase "gay for the stay," explaining that they existed "out of pragmatism and as a counterbalance to loneliness."[11]

This scant published research was no substitute for the personal stories women told me. Adela brought up the subject one day spontaneously, bursting out, "One of the biggest things I remember about being in there was that I never saw so many lesbians in prison or anywhere else in my life. I was, like, what the heck? I'd only been in there for like two weeks and a new set of girls came in. Some of them were beautiful girls and some of them looked like *vatitos*, like boys. I thought this was only a women's prison. What were they doing here? Then I learned that these were girls who were straight-out looking like dudes. They cut their hair like guys—they walked like guys—they talked like guys. Oh my gosh, I just couldn't believe it. I had been around dykes with long hair. But nothing like this. These were women who looked like men. These other girls were taking care of them like their wives or girlfriends. I learned so much!"

Their relationships were subject to the same insecurities and jealousies that were part of romantic entanglements on the outside. Even though she didn't get involved, Adela was enlisted to keep an eye on women by their partners. "I remember one of them saying, 'Juarez, I trust you—is my girl being with anybody in your unit?'" Adela refused to cooperate, telling her, "Girl, you might trust me, but I'm not a snitch, so you're going to have to figure that out on your own. I don't get involved in your thing—your relationship—or whatever you got going on."

Rachel, Adela's "bunkie," soon got fed up with all the jealousy. She told Adela, "My husband cheated on me outside. So, I'm in here and I fall in love with Ella. Then I got thrown in the hole. I come back—she's with somebody else. It's the same shit—they promise you this and that, they're gonna wait for you—I come back, she's with somebody else." Adela viewed this all at a remove, refusing to get involved, refusing to be judgmental. "I thought it was cute in a way—these women, fighting for their women. In the end, I would benefit from it. I would get their makeup when they went to the hole for fighting."

So much of what Adela was talking about sounded like what's often called out as situational sexual behavior—when individuals engage in relationships that differ from their usual sexual preferences. Many women were open about it. Adela remembered, "My other bunkie, Juana, switched off. When she was on the unit, she'd be with a girl. She went home with her kids and boyfriend and came back on a violation. When she came back, I asked her, 'Are you going to be a lesbian again?' And she said, 'Fuck that, I'm not doing that again. I'm going to do my time and go home.'"

Adela never got involved in a relationship in prison, and Juana remained celibate until she was released. But not every woman was as clear about her sexuality. For some women, things get much more complicated when what starts out as a substitution actually translates to lasting change in a woman's life and identity. Incarceration led women to new discoveries about relationships and their sexual preferences. These women wondered if their newly discovered sexual attractions were just due to being locked up and in an environment that accepted gay relationships. Or were they the sign of something deeper?

Adela saw the doubts that women around her struggled to resolve. These uncertainties around their identity and sexual preferences affected women more strongly than any jealousy and possessiveness. Some women, believing they were truly in love for the first time, didn't know what do to. Because Adela wasn't involved and had the strength I would later observe at Homegirl, she was a source of support for the women in prison, particularly those who felt conflicted. "Girls would say, 'Don't judge me. I want to ask you, Do you think I'm wrong?' I'd say, 'I just feel you're confused.'" Adela knew these women had husbands or partners on the outside, and she thought they didn't really know what to do. "Rachel, my bunkie, was like that in the beginning. Then she realized that for her, it was all fake. She wasn't a lesbian. She stopped getting involved. But some of the girls were really mixed up. A lot of them—first they used a girl because they were lonely. Then they got confused. I saw these beautiful girls; they had a husband and children, and then they had a girlfriend. They were so mixed up inside. I think they were fluid, but we didn't have words like that back in the day."

Adela watched this happen over and over again. She also believed that the prison had a hand in it. At orientation women were told, "'All you girls who have someone out there, forget about them, do your time. Because right now, there's somebody else in your place.' We all looked at each other, like, what the heck?" Adela believed that this fear of betrayal by loved ones, along with loneliness and desire, drove women into relationships they didn't anticipate. And she admitted even she was surprised when she saw who women paired up with.

"I would trip out. I didn't understand how women could change who they wanted to be with permanently. There was this girl, she was with the *vatito* girl, then she got out and found out her *vatito* girl was cheating on her. She violated again *just to get back in*." Adela is laughing as she says this. "I couldn't believe it! This girl was beautiful. She's got a husband and kids. Why would she want to come back on a violation just to be with her *vatito*? There was another girl, and she was beautiful too; she had a girlfriend in here. During visiting day, I told my sister, 'When you walk out of here, give that girl's husband my number.' He was gorgeous."

Not everyone was as open as Adela in describing what happened in prison. For many, how their sexuality was expressed while incarcerated, and what occurred romantically after jail or prison was an area they shied away from discussing. Many women didn't hesitate to talk about violent acts they'd witnessed, including homicides, and they also described, in detail, complex criminal operations. Yet, they hesitated to discuss their sexuality unless it had something to do with their lives before being locked up. As time passed and we spent more time together, women ultimately opened up about how the attachments they made in prison and the relationships they engaged in often had far-reaching consequences for their lives.

Though they were few, some women acknowledged that they had always known they had feelings for the same sex. This had caused problems for them in their lives long before incarceration. But there were also women who didn't realize or didn't want to recognize the truth of their sexuality until much later in life. One of them began by saying candidly, "I'm forty years old now—and I can't believe I'm finally finding out who I am." Angela Washington told me this while we sat eating tacos at Danny Trejo's restaurant on La Brea. People stop to stare at Angela—her physical appearance is that arresting. She is tall and thin and has incredibly long legs. Her skin is a beautiful dark brown, reflecting her Caribbean and African American heritages. Angela's father was Black, her mother Puerto Rican, and, as she laughingly explained, "I'm just an American girl." She never knew her father and to this day has no idea where he is. He was a musician who romanced her mother when she worked as a cocktail waitress and he played in a house band at a club popular with Puerto Ricans in New York. After her mother gave birth to Angela, he abandoned the two of them. "My mother doesn't know where he went. All I've got is his last name and some photos of the two of them when they were young and in love. To this day, sometimes I think I see him in the streets. It's really just a dark-skinned man who's tall and thin. Once in a while, if I meet someone from New York, I ask them if they've ever heard of him. I don't really expect an answer. It's just a dream, just a fantasy. Besides, do you know how many Black men are named Washington?" Angela laughs again as she says this, while her eyes fill with tears.

Angela's mother eventually did marry, a man named Enrique, and they had two sons together. Her mother insisted they were all one family, but Angela always felt like an outsider. Enrique developed an addiction to cocaine and began to abuse her mother, beat the boys, and threatened Angela that he was going to kick her out. "I knew I had to get the hell out of there as fast as I could."

When she was seventeen, her boyfriend offered her the opportunity she needed. "Kenny and I were in love, and I got pregnant, so we got married." There was one problem: the couple had absolutely no money. But Kenny had two brothers in business in Los Angeles, and the couple soon decided to join them.

Once they arrived in LA, it wasn't long before Angela discovered that the family "business" was drug dealing. "I was pregnant and just decided I didn't want to know." While Angela remained in a state of willful ignorance, Kenny was making money. She gave birth to a son and, eighteen months later, found herself pregnant again. Within three years, she'd gone from being a girl in love to the mother of two sons. The family graduated from an apartment to a small house with a yard and a patio. Despite their success, there was turmoil. Angela begged Kenny to stop dealing drugs; she worried about the arsenal of firearms he was accumulating in their closet.

"And then it all came crashing down," Angela told me. "Kenny didn't come home one night—I didn't think much about it. He was gone two or three nights sometimes; he had to go out to get more 'product'—that's all he told me. Then, when he was gone for more than a week, I started to worry." Her concern was well founded. Ten days after she last saw her husband, his brother Mikey told her that Kenny had been killed, in Colorado. "It was crazy," she said. "I still don't know if he really got killed or if he just ran away. It didn't matter. All I knew was, I was on my own."

She tried to find work, but there was no one to watch the kids, so, she went on welfare and food stamps. Even then, there was never enough money. "I really tried," Angela insisted. "The only other job I could get was in a club—serving drinks or being an exotic dancer." In the end, she asked Kenny's brothers to cut her into the family business. Angela refused to deal what she considered hard-core drugs—meth and heroin. "Mostly it was pot, cocaine, and crack. I kept thinking, 'I'll just do this until I get the boys through school.'"

She kept a low profile and was only arrested occasionally for drug possession; she'd end up spending a week or two in the LA County jail. By then, her sons were teenagers and could fend for themselves while she was locked up. When she turned forty, the boys were finally out of the house, and working; one was a truck driver and one stocked shelves at Costco. "I was proud of my boys," she told me. "They never joined a gang, and both of them finished school. I went to two high school graduations. All that time, I stayed home with them, I know I did the right thing."

Her sons were the center of Angela's life. She never remarried. "I'd meet guys, but there were never any sparks," she told me. "After Kenny was gone, I'd tell guys I thought he might come back. Now I know, I really wasn't interested in being with a man." Her older son, Trayvon, had a girlfriend, as they had a baby; Angela loved being a grandmother.

Around this time, she scaled back her drug dealing. She started selling clothes, jewelry, and other items out of her apartment. Everything went well until an LA County sheriff showed up at her door with a warrant for her arrest for receiving stolen property. They also had a search warrant and soon discovered the small cache of drugs she kept on hand to sell. Now her case was turbocharged and wouldn't be straightened out by a few nights in jail. Angela panicked. "I was scared. I *knew* I wasn't a criminal, and I didn't have money for a lawyer. And the charges were serious." At the urging of her public defender, Angela did the only thing she could: she agreed to a plea bargain and ended up with two strikes and two years in the Central California Women's Facility, or, as it is better known, Chowchilla.

Chowchilla is the largest women's prison in the United States, covering 640 acres, with an operating budget of $140 million. It's notorious for its high-profile residents, including Kristin Rossum, whose story was documented on television's *48 Hours*, and former Manson family member Susan Atkins, now deceased. Despite its large budget and size, it's overcrowded. Designed to house 2,004 women, by 2020, Chowchilla was housing 2,640—132 percent of its official capacity.

Despite the crowding and her fears, Angela soon learned that if she adjusted to the routines and avoided getting into trouble, she'd be eligible for Chowchilla's early release program. She also learned something else: she was attracted to women.

"All my life, I'd been with men, from the time I was fourteen and lost my virginity. When I was locked up everything changed. I met a woman there, Ronnie. She said she'd take care of me. There were women who hooked up with other women. They said they did it to get through prison. For a while, that's what I said too. It turned out for me, this wasn't just a way to get through prison. I fell in love with Ronnie."

There were problems. Ronnie was locked up for multiple murders: her sentence was twenty-five years to life. "I was getting out in a year or less. I knew if I couldn't be with Ronnie, I wanted to be with a woman.

I'd never been so happy with anyone as I was with Ronnie. None of this bisexual bullshit. I was a lesbian. It was crazy. I hated every minute in prison, but I also finally learned about myself."

Angela was lucky. The women in Chowchilla told her about a place in Claremont, Crossroads Halfway House. She went there when she was released. Located about forty miles east of LA, Crossroads traced its beginnings to a couple running a dairy farm next door to the California Institution for Women. They routinely supplied the prison with milk. One day, after a conversation with the prison warden, the couple agreed to take in a foster child whose mother was incarcerated. After her release from CIW, the mother moved in as well, until she and her child were able to live on their own. The couple, seeing how meaningful their support was, continued taking in women after incarceration for ten years, until Crossroads "officially" opened a small home for six women in Claremont in 1975. With its mission "to provide housing, education, support, counseling, and employment training in a homelike environment for women who have been incarcerated," it's still considered "the best-kept secret in Claremont."[12]

By the time Angela arrived, Crossroads had grown, sheltering twenty-four women in two houses—California bungalows under big shady trees. Angela loved the program and the woman who ran it, Sister Terry Dodge. Sister Terry understood reentry; her brother had cycled through jail and prison for over a decade.

I'd been introduced to Sister Terry by one of my students and was immediately struck by her compassion, humor, and commitment to the women she served. Crossroads flourished under her leadership. Its model shares similarities with ANWOL, but there are differences as well. While it's not a faith-based organization, it's largely underwritten by donors associated with the Catholic Church, operating on a very limited budget. Also unlike ANWOL, it's affiliated with the California Department of Corrections and Rehabilitation. The Crossroads program emphasizes women's autonomy and financial sustainability. Once her case manager determines a woman is ready, she is placed in a paying job and required to save 75 percent of her earnings for moving out. This all works and, according to self-reports, 86 percent of the women who have graduated from Crossroads don't reoffend or relapse into criminal behavior and are "self-sustaining after six years."[13]

Although Angela missed Ronnie, she settled into Crossroads and focused on getting better—she wanted to be financially independent through legal activities. She was also eager to be up-to-date. When she compared herself to other residents who'd never even used a cell phone, she "was happy I wasn't that far behind, and I wanted to learn. Everyone was talking about Facebook. I wanted to catch up."

Angela blossomed at Crossroads, but she also knew she had to move on. Claremont was different from Los Angeles—a quiet town. She missed her sons and her friends. After six months in the program, she found work as a receptionist at a small nonprofit in South LA. A coworker told her about an apartment next door to where she was living that was for rent, and Angela grabbed it. Her coworker became more than a neighbor.

"It was easy to fall in love with Simone," Angela said. "The hard part was telling my boys. They'd visited me in prison, but they'd never met Ronnie. I knew I was gonna have to tell them what happened one day. My relationship with Simone made that one day come faster." Her older son, Trayvon, was fighting with his girlfriend—they'd broken up and she wouldn't let him see his little boy. Preoccupied with his own problems, he took what Angela told him in stride. "He joked that he couldn't understand why I'd want to be involved with a woman after he was having so much trouble with his baby mama, and we both laughed. He also told me he figured something was up because I'd never had a serious boyfriend. He said lots of men had wanted me, and I didn't seem to want them. I guess he knew more than I did."

Trayvon's reaction didn't prepare Angela for how her younger son, Tyrone, would respond. When Angela explained that Simone was moving in, Tyrone angrily told her he'd *never* visit her as long as they lived together. "He called me all kinds of names and said I was sick in the head. I was heartbroken." Angela tried to reach out to him, and in the process told more people about her new life. "In the beginning, it was hard. You know the Black community sometimes has its troubles with gay men and lesbians. Two of my friends thought I just had to get prison out of my system." Angela shook her head as she told me this.

She tried to joke with me about the impact of "coming out at forty-three," but the truth was that she felt transformed. "I know now the people that loved me are gonna go on loving me. I'm hopeful about Tyrone too, and I know it's gonna be baby steps." He'd finally answered the phone when she called him and accepted her invitation to dinner.

Angela felt deeply fulfilled with the relationship she'd started after incarceration. I didn't know if other women had the same experience. Beyond their struggles with economics and children, their anguish and their joy, what happened to women after incarceration in their search for love? Many had told me they didn't have time to think about romance while trying to rebuild their lives, but maybe they felt the way Angela did: "I just want what everyone wants—someone to love who loves me."

THIRTEEN

LOVE IN THE
TIME OF REENTRY

*I want to find someone to love me. I do. But who's got the
time? I gotta think about getting a roof over my kids' heads;
I gotta think about getting food on the table. I gotta think
about getting a job, meeting my PO. When can I find the
time to do a relationship?*

—NITA JANNSSON

I'm trying to talk my husband into going to Watts to sit down with a
former gang member who wants to "pick his brain" about the LAPD.
Although he's been retired from the force for fourteen years—in recovery, as I love to say—he works alongside many residents of South LA
who have come to trust him and talk to him about the police. But it's
a quiet Sunday afternoon and he wants to watch the Dodgers game.
I'm getting ready to drive down to Watts, alone, when my cell phone
chimes and my anxiety kicks in. Over the years, I've developed my
own version of the national warning system. Late-night calls are never
good. Weekend calls are also not good, especially Sundays. A Sunday
afternoon call is the red alert of warnings. There's no number on the
readout, just the name: Carmen. "Oh dear God! What's happened
now?" I wondered.

Carmen had survived childhood sexual abuse, gang involvement, and the revolving door of Los Angeles County probation camps and jails to finally land in downtown Los Angeles, working in a tourist kiosk. She had long been part of my chosen family, and I was the godmother, co-madre, to her third child. I knew very few women who possessed her kind of resilience. Carmen had succeeded in surviving—undocumented—in Los Angeles while racking up a series of encounters with government institutions from which she always managed to emerge unbroken. About two years before, after a particularly gruesome incarceration that included delivering her fifth child while she was locked up in the LA County jail, she told me she was going straight, promising, "I'm never dealing drugs again, and I'm never getting locked up again." Making good on that promise, she was hired by a local entrepreneur to sell T-shirts, souvenirs, and memorabilia. She went to work six days a week, wearing her thick ebony hair in a braid coiled on top of her head and colorful eye makeup; thin and dressed dramatically all in black, she looked like Frida Kahlo's twin sister. At her Olvera Street souvenir stall, Carmen hawked "I [Heart] Olvera Street" T-shirts and mariachi puppets, while selling jewelry and accessories on the side.

The gift stall thrived as a combination monument to Los Angeles and a swap meet all in one, with Carmen capably managing the business with the same entrepreneurial skills that had contributed to her past success as a drug dealer. If you bought something from the gift stall and Carmen knew you, she'd open up her tote bag to show off new earrings or baubles she had for sale. She once enthusiastically tried to sell me a "beautiful purse—it's pure leather," and I barely managed to resist her sales pitch.

Carmen succeeded with the world view of a professional gambler—calculating the risks then making her move, which almost always turned out all right. Now, despite some of her sketchier business ventures and her alignment with active gang members, she'd won her latest bet: she hadn't been arrested in over two years. Her juvenile record was sealed and her adult record had been expunged, primarily because none of her crimes were violent. There was only one place her luck didn't hold:

when it came to men, her choices invariably led to heartbreak, failure, and worse. Carmen was drawn to Black men who'd been involved with gangs and criminal activity. She was often told, even by her friends, "Stay with your own kind!"

Yet, ultimately, the problems with the men she chose had nothing to do with their color or their dangerous behaviors—instead, it always came down to their miserable treatment of her. All of them cheated assiduously, one beat her bloody, one had a child with another woman, then tried to enlist Carmen's help taking care of the newborn, and one failed to show up at the baby shower that a group of women—myself included—threw for her when she was eight months pregnant with their second child together. But that didn't stop her. Carmen kept searching for love—and by the time she was forty years old, she had a series of wrecked relationships and five children, along with the son of her former boyfriend, all dependent on her. Things had ended badly with her last boyfriend, Kevin. Despite some initial misgivings, Carmen managed to press charges, and he was found guilty of domestic abuse and attempted murder after he pushed her out of their car onto the San Diego Freeway.

Still, Carmen kept going. After Kevin was locked up, she moved right into her next relationship, with Brian, a gang-connected drug dealer. "He's the one, Jorgee, he loves me!" Carmen confided. Then, a month after professing his love for her, he was arrested for racketeering and drug distribution, eventually taking a plea bargain for five years in state prison. And it was there that Carmen finally accomplished what she'd longed for her entire life: in a beige dress, with the assistance of a prison chaplain and her five children present, she got married. She was officially a wife and delighted in using the words "My husband, Brian." In some ways it was an ideal situation: she had all the legitimacy and status of marriage without any of the responsibilities. She could live her life freely, no longer worried about finding or keeping a man.

Carmen's work commitments attested to how well this new arrangement suited her. She moved on from Olvera Street and was now a case manager at a nonprofit program for homeless mothers and their children. Her coworkers adored her and the families she worked with all lined up to see her, even spending time with her after hours, drinking coffee and eating cookies at her Section 8 housing. Carmen wanted to become a credentialed social worker, and together we investigated community colleges where she might take classes.

The one obstacle to her career advancement—and her personal safety—was her undocumented status. But Carmen, ever resourceful, had connected with an immigration attorney who'd figured out a way to help her obtain a green card legally. She wasn't paying $5,000 to acquire a fake ID! This was legitimate. She'd be able to stop looking over her shoulder and focus on the future. The executive director she worked for at the nonprofit was already mentoring her and we'd shared our ideas about Carmen's pathway into college and when she could enroll in classes. The stars were aligned.

I learned early on working with men who'd been gang members that just when their lives started to stabilize and they encountered some degree of success, they would actually commit a crime or relapse back into substance abuse or suddenly, inexplicably, stop showing up for work—as if to wreck their good fortune. Homeboy Industries used to bestow an "Employee of the Month" award until it became apparent that every time someone won the award, they would recidivate, relapse, or just disappear. "It's just too much pressure," one gang member told me when I went to visit him in jail. I was confused. Didn't doing well, winning an award, motivate him to keep going? "I couldn't take it, miss. The award, everything. It was just too good. I didn't deserve it."

I don't know if Carmen thought she didn't deserve the upward turn her life was taking—she was calling on this Sunday afternoon to tell me she'd been arrested. She'd managed to be released within a few hours after reaching out to my unofficially adopted daughter, Joanna Carillo, who, just as she'd done for so many others, had raised the bail money for her. Now, her opening line was a lulu. "You are family, Jorgee, and I trust you. And I am going to tell you the truth."

I knew exactly what this meant. Whenever someone who was caught up in criminal activity says they are going to tell me *the truth*, it was a signal to brace myself for a series of lies, usually revolving around their innocence and their total ignorance of any crime that was committed. This kind of lying certainly wasn't the norm. So many of the women and men who reached out to me had *not* committed the crimes of which they were accused. But when they had and they lied, I truly understood why—there was shame along with the belief that someone like me couldn't really understand the obstacles they faced. Carmen was no exception, and her narrative involved some supersized deceit.

"You know, I went to see Brian with the kids. I was sitting with him at a table, and someone had left their drugs there. I would never bring drugs into the prison. I'm not that stupid. You know me, Jorgee. I would *never* do anything like that." She waited for me to agree, but I was silent.

"The deputies found the drugs on the table, and then they accused me of trying to smuggle drugs in to Brian, into the prison. They said they were gonna call DCFS to take my kids away if I didn't sign a confession. So, I signed it. I swear, Jorgee, I didn't do it. And I need a lawyer. And *not* some public defender—a real lawyer. I need you to help me, Jorgee. I need you to write a letter saying I am of good character. Please!"

Once I regained the power of speech, I told her I'd call her after I talked to Elie. Elie would know. Elie would help her. Again, the mantra, "Wait for Elie."

I already knew certain things without any doubt. Carmen most certainly had tried to smuggle drugs into a state prison during visiting hours. There were no drugs "left behind" on the table—no one in their right mind did such a thing. The California state prison system is riddled with drugs supplied by two major sources: prison guards and families of the incarcerated. Sometimes, the two worked together: Nita Jannsson had a longtime drug-smuggling business that involved guards at a state prison—she was on the outside, her husband was on the inside, and one guard was their connection. Compared to Nita, Carmen was an amateur. None of this would stop my helping her, but before I did anything, I needed to find out just what the charges against Carmen were.

I also knew that there was no way she could afford a private attorney, even if she didn't trust the public defender. This was an attitude shared by lots of people, including my partner in Project Fatherhood, Elder Michael "Big Mike" Cummings, a former gang member turned community activist who often referred to the public defender as the "public pretender." These widely held, highly unfair attitudes were based on the belief that PDs never defended their clients, that they pushed clients to accept plea bargains rather than go to court. This was far from true and reflected a confusing range of factors, all of them leading to the reality that prosecutorial culture and practice reigned supreme with the scales hopelessly tipped in favor of the district attorney's office.

I also knew that the sheriff's deputies hadn't threatened Carmen with children's protective services so much as they'd used the law coercively, in their favor. They'd probably "educated" Carmen about what was about to occur. If she was in custody and said she had no family to take the kids—and for Carmen, there was no one—they'd be placed in foster care pending the outcome of her criminal case. As a teenager, Carmen had lived in a foster home; she didn't want history to repeat itself. This could all be avoided if she simply agreed to the charges, said she was guilty, and promised to be in court on a date to be determined. That's the document she signed. Which brought her to me.

I called Elie.

"Well, you know she's lying to you."

I sighed in acknowledgment.

"And you know she's going to ask you for something—to testify or to write her a letter of recommendation. That's risky—you're going to stake your reputation on someone who tried to bring contraband into a state prison." I wasn't worried about this—I would testify if it came to that. I was more worried Carmen wouldn't go to court but instead would deal her rights away as part of a plea bargain.

"So, what can we do for her? She's desperate *not* to have a public defender."

"That's exactly the lawyer she should have," Elie was adamant. "She can't afford an attorney. Anyone she finds will probably try to cheat her. I need to look up her charges. Why'd she do this?"

That was the one thing I did know: *Carmen wanted her new husband to love her.* More than anything, she wanted to make sure he wouldn't abandon her—even while he was in prison. Weeks later she admitted to me that he'd asked her to bring the drugs into prison. By that time, Elie had found out exactly what Carmen had been charged with, and the news wasn't good. She'd been caught trying to transfer marijuana and heroin to Brian for distribution inside the prison. Brian wasn't going to let being incarcerated put a dent in his business activities. According to Elie, Carmen could serve time for this offense, and she'd be unable to visit a state prison again. Ever. Elie had recently filed an appeal for a woman who'd attempted to smuggle drugs into a prison ten years earlier. Since that time, the woman had lived an exemplary life. Her son was now locked up and she'd been diagnosed with stage 4 cancer; she wanted to see her son one more time before she died. The court denied her appeal. But there was additional bad news in store for Carmen: she would most certainly be fired from her job at the nonprofit and stood to lose her Section 8 housing—jobless, homeless, with five kids. Her efforts to get a green card would be totally derailed. We were living in Donald Trump's America at the time, and she might even be deported.

Once again, Carmen would not be broken. She called, furious, after her arraignment and told me the public defender was "horrible, a monster; he wanted me to plead guilty." She then pleaded with me to send her money for a private attorney. I called Elie and asked if she could find someone honest to take the case pro bono. But Elie was unflappable.

"It wasn't her attorney representing her at the trial; it was just the supervisor from the PD. She has to calm down and wait. She'll get a good PD to help her. Don't give her any money."

Elie was too late. I'd already told Carmen that I was going to send her $200. I also broke the news to her that I couldn't find her a private attorney.

"That's okay, Jorgee. Thank you for the money. I'll find an attorney."

"Why don't you call Elie?"

"Oh, I think she's gonna yell at me. I don't want her to yell at me. I can't take it."

And she's going to call you out for lying, I thought.

A day later Elie called to tell me she'd heard from Carmen.

"I told her to stick with the public defender. It will be okay."

"What do you think is going to happen to her?" This was always my refrain.

"I don't know. She was just a few weeks away from getting her green card. She really blew it."

I knew Elie was right. I also knew Carmen had done all of this for love.

I kept thinking about how I could help. Elie counseled caution. My daughter, Shannon, in her first year of law school, loved Carmen and, while still a legal novice, predicted, "She'll probably be okay; it's a non-violent offense. They'll make her wear an ankle monitor." Surprisingly, Elie echoed her evaluation. Carmen called to tell me the housing agency had placed her on administrative leave. She knew they were getting ready to fire her. "I'm gonna run out of money, and my kids and I are going to be homeless. I was only trying to help Brian."

Carmen was only "trying to help" her husband. But over the years, I'd never seen any evidence of men "trying to help" their incarcerated wives or girlfriends. The men who these women believed would protect them all too frequently abandoned them once they faced jail or prison. "We wanna believe men are gonna wait for us," Nita told me, "and we're havin' a fantasy." Men don't have any problem finding women who will wait for them.

There are even formerly incarcerated women who deliberately marry "lifers."

When I ask one woman why she married a lifer, she was quick to explain: "We have conjugal visits, and I know where he is every night—I don't know a lot of girls who can say that." I would say that sets the bar pretty low in terms of marital commitment, but many of these women express satisfaction with their lives.

I had heard stories of women who took the bus from Los Angeles to Corcoran Prison, 220 miles and four hours away, just so they could see their man. Yet when I put together all the material on the women I'd interviewed, laughed with, spent time with—all eighty of them—*not a single woman told me she was visited by a spouse, partner, or boyfriend while she was locked up.* There were also no accounts of men who brought children to visit their mothers. Instead, these women saw their children when grandmothers or other family members or social workers brought them to visit. Once they were released from prison, the vast majority of women were alone. A small number of them—six in all—started up again with the men they'd been involved with in the past. But for most of the women, there was no one waiting and no future possibilities. "Who's gonna want me?" Nita asked me. "I'm old, I'm tired, I've been locked up, I've got three mouths to feed, and I don't have a job. I don't even want me. We're 'after prison women,' and with men, we got a big problem."

The big problem was love. Most of these women, even after incarceration and despite their uncertainties, still wanted an intimate relationship; they wanted someone to take care of them. These were the same desires that often had led them into the criminal justice system in the first place. And even on their journey out, many admitted they still longed to find someone to live with and love. This longing and the search for its fulfillment was what guided them and often conflicted with their commitment to change. "I want a relationship," one woman told me, "but it can't interfere with my recovery. There's nothing more important than that." Her words not only described her challenges; they reflected the experiences many women face after incarceration. They wanted relationships, yet after being locked up, they were also determined to change. The majority of the women I'd gotten to know didn't want to repeat their past mistakes. "I don't want the same kind of man, I don't want an abuser, I don't want a hustler," an older woman who'd finished serving seventeen years at Chowchilla, explained. "I've been married twice—they were both no good. I want a good man now. I'm just not sure I can find one."

Over the past decade, I've discovered only one thing for certain: there is no single pattern to post-release relationships. This is yet another example of how, after being locked up, women differ profoundly from men. There's no sugarcoating it—it's much easier for men who have been incarcerated to find women and build relationships after they've been in jail or prison than it is for women. They're able to maintain relationships even *while* they're in jail or prison. This is absolutely not to deny the intense barriers men face after incarceration. Their stories and struggles are real in terms of psychological, sociocultural, and economic obstacles. But the one area where men don't contend with post-incarceration challenges is personal relationships.

For five years, I listened to the men in Project Fatherhood describe in detail their relationships with their wives, ex-wives, girlfriends, and casual hookups; they talked about their women almost as much as they talked about their children. The men complained about the women who wanted to possess them, the women who wanted to control them, the women who wanted them to be faithful, the women who cheated on them. And then I realized, no one complained about not having a woman (or, in several cases, women). What the men uniformly encountered and even expected was women *wanting* them and waiting for them. Very few of the women I spent time with experienced that. Despite the fragmentation of families of color and Black families, within marginalized communities, men appear to have a better chance than women of maintaining personal relationships when they are incarcerated.

Social stigma against women who are incarcerated and the negative consequences surrounding their relationships and family life appear to be much more profound for women than for men. Yet, despite all of these issues and others, the search for love and intimacy is part of women's lives. No matter what they've experienced, none of the women I know wanted to be alone. The question is, just who did they choose as partners once their lives were changing after incarceration? And how far were they willing to go for love?

I was thinking about this when Adela called, asking if we could meet up at Alma Backyard Farms, in Compton. She'd been volunteering for this worthwhile program, which helps formerly incarcerated men and women learn about urban agriculture, carpentry, and landscaping through working in an enormous community garden. By connecting with the land and plantings, Alma fosters healing and creates a relationship between nature and community.[1] It was the perfect place to meet and talk during the Covid-19 pandemic. A week later, Adela and I were in the open air, wearing masks, sitting some feet apart from each other. Still, despite our social distance, this was one of the most intimate moments in all our years of talking. She began, "I wanna tell you about my relationships. It's time."

Adela had insisted, more than once, that she didn't want to be involved with men anymore. Despite what she said, that declaration *still* surprised me—a reaction that was clearly idiotic on my part. When I'd known her at Homegirl, men were falling all over her. All the homies, no matter what age, would hit on her, ask her out, bring her presents, try to win her favor. She'd smile softly and turn them away. "I'd been married twice. Both of my husbands, first Sleepy and then Lefty, were gang members. They both ended up in prison. So, I had a rule: I was never dating a gang member again. I didn't want to get involved with anyone who was caught up." She stuck to her rule for years. But all that changed when her second husband, Lefty, was released from prison.

At first, she only saw Lefty when they were making custody arrangements for sixteen-year-old Julia, co-parenting with suspicion on both sides. But they soon began to spend time together, hiding it from their daughter. Then Adela discovered she was pregnant. She hadn't planned on another child and wasn't sure what to do. She'd had an abortion in the past and she wasn't against having one again. She and Lefty were fighting, and she felt unsettled, uncertain. One day, she started bleeding and doubled over in pain. She had to ask Julia to drive her to the hospital. At the ER, Julia stayed by her side while the doctor examined her and said, "I'm sorry, you're having a miscarriage. You've lost the baby." The minute Julia heard this, she got upset. She couldn't believe her parents had been together—and they hadn't told her! That night she told Lefty, "You've done enough to hurt my family, leave us alone." Still, even after their breakup, Adela acknowledged how good it felt to be wanted, good to be desired.

Lefty started calling her again. He still wanted her back, but along with wanting to control Adela, he was angry at her. He'd threatened her, although he hadn't done anything physical. Yet. "I was afraid of him, even though he said he'd never hurt me. I wasn't gonna wait and see," Adela told me. "I told Julia we needed to go to a shelter because I was afraid of what he would do. I realized that either I stayed with Lefty in that lifestyle or I got out." Adela thought about Ivy and how she'd warned her about Pedro, telling her to leave him, that he was abusing her emotionally and physically. She remembered another homegirl she'd helped leave an abusive marriage and, in desperation, called her for advice. The woman told Adela how much she'd helped her. This made Adela's request for help with an abusive relationship even more difficult. "I remember I said, 'I'm ashamed. I'm going through something, and I don't know what to do.'" The woman immediately called the shelter she'd lived at, and the next day Adela was contacted by a counselor from Interval House, a nearby shelter for women and their children. "She asked me 'Are you ready?' I said, 'I don't know—but I feel like I am.'"

The next morning, Adela and Julia moved into Interval House. Adela followed their program, which included counseling and classes about domestic violence. "I started learning what abuse was. This was in 2017. I believed I wasn't there because I was adjusting to life after prison. I was there because I needed to learn."

At first, Adela had a hard time adjusting to her newfound knowledge—she felt a sense of shame and uncertainty. "I kept thinking, they're not going to understand me, they're going to judge me. But they welcomed me with open arms and helped me get through it. I started to understand that, with Lefty, I was emotionally abused. I also understood that in the past I'd been physically abused. I can't tell you what I felt like when I realized that. I'm still learning what happened to me. I guess I was ready to understand—I hadn't been ready before."

This was beautiful Adela, the woman who'd always been in control, finally learning that she too had been hurt, she too had suffered. So much of the trauma she endured had been stuffed deep down inside of her. She'd pushed all of this away so she could go on—working, caring for her children, taking risks, running her business, getting through prison. She thought she'd settled her losses, but until she went to the shelter and spent this time healing herself, she never even understood what those losses were.

Adela is now a counselor at Interval House. She works closely with the women there, talking to them about what she experienced, accompanying them to court when they are filing temporary restraining orders or dealing with child custody issues. None of this is surprising to me. Adela and Interval House are a perfect fit, just as the Homegirl Café had been earlier in her life. Both share a similar philosophy about women helping women, although in many ways, this shelter also resembles ANWOL, but without the focus on incarcerated women. From the time it was founded in 1979, Interval House established its unique identity as the first "survivor-led" program in the US, staffed entirely with individuals who have dealt with and overcome trauma, violence, and homelessness. Its mission, "to ensure health, safety and self-sufficiency for victims of domestic violence and individuals at risk for abuse and homelessness," is reinforced by its practice of "training from within."[2] Its approach is culturally sensitive and diverse—services are available in over seventy languages. Embodying the mission, its executive director, Carol Williams, wisely recognized that Adela could help so many others if she joined the Interval staff.

Today, Adela is at peace. Along with a woman who was incarcerated with her in federal prison, she now plans to open a domestic violence shelter that specifically helps women who've been incarcerated. Because of what she experienced, Adela believes women who've been locked up may not realize what traumas they endured until years after they get out of jail or prison.

"I think about these women," she tells me. "I was one of them. I could have been Ivy or Janeth. I wonder what would have happened if someone really knew what the two of them had gone through. Ivy and Janeth didn't want to get in trouble; they were lost. They both were abused. And it was all because they wanted someone to love them."

INTERLUDE

By the time their second trial begins, Ivy and Janeth are barely speaking. Again, the trial lasts a little over a month. This time the jury finds both women guilty. Each is sentenced to a longer term of incarceration than she would have faced if they'd accepted the plea deal. Janeth's sentence is forty years to life, and Ivy, who held out believing she would walk, is sentenced to sixty years to life. I'm not sure why there's a difference. Is it because Janeth is younger? Because Ivy was on parole?

As usual, Elie explains everything.

Janeth receives an "aggregate indeterminate" term in state prison of forty years to life. "Aggregate" means that her sentences are combined: fifteen years to life for second-degree murder, plus twenty years for the firearm-use enhancement, and a concurrent term of life for an attempted premeditated murder. However, her sentence is also indeterminate because it carries the hope that prison might rehabilitate her. If Janeth is determined to be rehabilitated, she will be paroled closer to (but not less than) her minimum term of forty years. In other words, the one thing Janeth can hold on to is the idea that she might get out in forty years.

Ivy also receives an aggregate, indeterminate sentence totaling sixty years to life. Out the gate she receives more time because when the crime took place, she was already on parole for a serious felony that brought with it one strike. This automatically *doubles* her sentence for the homicide. Ivy, too, is found guilty of second-degree murder, which ordinarily carries a sentence of fifteen years to life, but Ivy gets thirty years. She also receives twenty-five years to life for a firearm-use enhancement and five years for a previous felony conviction. Her chances on appeal are very weak, but, luckily, she will be able to obtain a new lawyer to help with her appeal.

Ivy cries and keeps saying, "I should've taken the deal. Now I'm never going to see my son." Strangely enough, Janeth has more faith, telling Adela, "I'm gonna to be free one day. It might be a minute, but I'm gonna to get out eventually." Her attorney, who is still devotedly working for Janeth, promises they'll file an appeal and immediately begins looking for an expert to assist her.

A few days later, Janeth renews her plea that Adela adopt Angelina. At this point, Adela knows that DCFS is involved, and she warns Janeth that the paternal grandmother, Myra, will put up a fight. "She knew I was right, so she asked me to reach out to Myra and help her to keep a relationship with Angelina."

Ivy and Janeth are both sent to Chowchilla state prison. Honoring Janeth's wishes, Adela starts to build a relationship with Myra. Eventually that relationship becomes so strong that Myra calls Adela for help finding an attorney to represent her youngest son, Alberto, when he's arrested. Adela always asks how Angelina is, and Myra says she's "doing good, growing up strong," adding, "I can't take her up to Chowchilla; it's too far for me. Angelina talks to Janeth on the phone. She knows her mom is in prison. And she knows one day she's coming home."

Ivy struggles to maintain a relationship with her son, Jessie, fearing she'll be gone a long time and will have to let go. She tells Adela, "It will be like I'm dead. He'll never really know me." Ivy's trauma has deepened, but Janeth still feels an unshakeable sense of hope.

FOURTEEN

REDEMPTION BABY

I knew when I got out I had to have some sort of symbol of hope—some sign that things were going to change, that my life would be better. So, when I got pregnant I knew, I was a redemption mama and this would be my redemption baby.

—ROSA LUCERO

In the beginning of winter, there is joyful news. Denise gives birth to a healthy baby girl, Elizabeth. Three months later, she's in my office, showing me an iPhone full of baby photos. Her eyes fill with tears.

"I never believed I could love anyone so much. It hurts me, how much I love her."

I just nod and reach out to squeeze her arm.

"G-ma, I just can't tell you how I feel . . ."

Denise has long called me G-ma—godmother. It's the sweetest acknowledgment of both my caring and the power differential in our relationship. Today, she's eager to tell me about the baby, the changes she's experiencing, and how it's all affecting her husband, Leroy. I know Denise has been married for several years, even though she rarely talks about Leroy. Today is different—she opens up. Leroy loves Elizabeth, but it's hard for him to understand how Denise is feeling. She isn't paying attention to him—the baby is everything. Her hormones are bouncing all over the place, and right now she's wondering if she can take care of Elizabeth and go to graduate school at the same time. Admissions decision letters will be out in a month, and she's worried UCLA will reject her. She's also worried UCLA will accept her. I try to reassure her, telling her to wait until she receives the letter and then make plans.

"In the meantime, just enjoy being with Elizabeth."

A few days later, after texting me even more photos, Denise adds her thoughts. Sometimes, it's easier for Denise to text what she's feeling than to express it in person. She's not alone in this. Over the years, women have texted me deeply personal messages. Often, it's something that's happened that they're too ashamed or too afraid to talk about face-to-face. They want me to know what's been going on, but they're worried how I'll react. "It's easier to have courage on a text," Denise begins. "After Elizabeth was born, I got to thinking about everything. There's lots of stuff going on inside of me. I seem to uncover more damage in my life than I originally anticipated. The revelation/epiphany has been forcing me to enlarge my circle. I guess you need to know—and tell everybody—the struggle to heal is real."

I text back that I'm here for her if she needs me. I don't want to text that I understand—there's no way I can truly understand. I don't know what it's like to have experienced trauma, substance abuse, and the wounds of incarceration. Anyone who says they do without having experienced it is a liar. Still, I want to bear witness to her struggle and make sure her words are heard.

"I love Elizabeth so much but when I consider the possibility of inadvertently subjecting my daughter to the same situation because I lack the tools to protect her if the situation arose is more devastating than I can articulate. Now I'm trying to be honest. Write that in your book . . . Jorja."

Elizabeth is the center of Denise's world. She's also a symbol of hope for her. While this is Denise's first baby, she shares a feeling that many women who've given birth post-incarceration have expressed: a baby is a sign that a new life is starting for them as well. This is part of the reason many women have a child after incarceration, irrespective of how many children they already have. The new child is a sign of their hope for a new life. Nita, who had two children after serving seven years in state prison, told me, "These are the babies I want to raise without children's services."

Whatever their ages or birth order, children play a critical role in the lives of system-involved women. Overall, research has shown that being separated from their children is one of the greatest "stressors" that women who are incarcerated experience. As if we needed research to tell us what we already know. However, there are two sides to this coin: family reunification is also a crucial motivator for women to get out of prison and put their lives back together.

The desire to reunite with her children created the turning point in Rosa's life. Although she struggled with trauma from being trafficked and being abused and then the work of recovering from substance abuse, there was no question that she'd ever go back to the rage and destruction she'd been caught up in. That life was over and she was focused on the future. But she faced a new struggle: with child welfare services.

"You've got no idea how crazy the system is. I knew that to get my kids back I was going to have to be more than a good mother; I was going to have to be a perfect mother," Rosa explained, her voice urgent as she recalled what it took to reunite with her two sons and her daughter. Because of her drug use, she'd cycled in and out of jail multiple times. In the end, the fallout from the revolving door of lockup was more devastating than incarceration itself. What nearly shattered Rosa was her fight with the Department of Children and Family Services. "You know how Trump keeps saying the system is rigged? I wanna tell someone DCFS is rigged—and it's rigged against mothers who've been locked up. I know lots of mothers who do worse things to their kids than I did and nothing happens to them. Because they haven't been locked up."

I knew a lot of those mothers too, and many of them struggled with substance abuse for years. It was impossible to believe they escaped unscathed. But Rosa was right: incarceration added an additional and often insurmountable burden to mothers trying to reconnect with and regain custody of their children. The chances a mother would actually succeed depended on where the children lived while she was locked up, what kind of relationship she experienced with them while she was in jail or prison, and what resources were available once she was released.[1] The social justice activist Renny Golden offered this sadly realistic description of the dilemmas that women face as they fight to reunite with their children as part of reentry:

> How can a mother without a work history or a home previous to incarceration immediately find a job when she may lack a permanent address, has most likely *not* been in a drug rehab program in prison, and must negotiate reuniting with children who are troubled, angry or withdrawn? Finally, if she finds work, how can she possibly afford day care, rent and food on an $8 per hour job?[2]

Rosa's life was a case study of the frustrations and inequities of the child welfare system. It was also a case study in strength and determination. First, she concentrated on her own drug rehab and recovery. When she was released, clean and sober after finishing rehab, her first call was to DCFS to find out how she could visit her children and, more importantly, how she could get them back. But what was about to happen added a new chapter in the criminalization of trauma. Rosa's drug abuse could be traced in a straight line to the trauma of being sexually trafficked; now she was experiencing further trauma, courtesy of the child welfare system. It was all in the name of family reunification.

Family reunification is the "key goal" of child welfare agencies throughout the United States. It starts with the idea that if children are at risk, usually because of neglect or abuse, they should be *temporarily* removed from their families to ensure their safety. When they are, government agencies, like DCFS, are supposed to work with the parents to address the problems that brought the family to the attention of the child welfare system in the first place. Ideally, they work together to build family strengths so that children can eventually go back home. As part of this process, family reunification means that parents, usually mothers, are expected to fulfill various court-mandated expectations:

being drug-free, attending parenting classes, having a job, providing a place to live. It all sounds like a great idea—in theory. For some families, the requirements are smoothly fulfilled: parenting courses are completed, counseling is ongoing, and children go back home. But this isn't so easy for the women who describe this process to me—in fact, the requirements often prove to be completely unattainable. The deadline for fulfilling these requirements adds even more pressure to the mothers who long to have their children return to them. As the criminal justice scholar Suzanne Godboldt puts it so aptly, these women are literally "racing against the clock" to obtain employment and housing before their parental rights are automatically terminated.[3] Formerly incarcerated women already have their hands full with more problems than child welfare can even track. They have probation officers on their backs, they have restitution to pay, they have to fight stigma on a daily basis. And on top of all that, here is yet another set of obstacles.

In addition, women have to make their peace with the people their children have been living with once they are placed in foster care. The child welfare default is "kinship care"—ideally, children are sent to relatives while parents get their lives together. "Ideally" is the key word here because there are problems with kinship care out of the gate. Often, extended family and relatives are part of a multigenerational pattern of neglect and abuse. The last people Rosa wanted taking care of her children were her mother and stepfather—they'd trafficked her! In her case, kinship care was out of the question, and so DCFS went to its next option: foster care, with strangers, in a system whose quality is, at best, inconsistent. There are tremendous foster parents who love children. One of my former students, Heather Fier, and her husband, Joe, had been foster parents to a baby girl for over a year. They were both happy and heartbroken when she was reunited with her birth mother and have remained in touch with the child. But not everyone is like Heather and Joe. Many foster parents "provide" only minimal shelter and food, as Clara Vasquez experienced when forced to live in her foster home's backyard.

Although the extremes of Clara's childhood were unique, the very mention of foster care frightens so many incarcerated women, with justification. It's not just the anxiety of where their children will live—women are terrified they'll lose their children forever. Half the states in the US have legislation that allows for the termination of parental rights if the parent with custody—usually the mother—is incarcerated.[4] Beyond this, even the foster-care placement system is gendered: 11 percent of the children of incarcerated mothers are placed in foster care, in contrast to only 2 percent of the children of incarcerated fathers.[5]

Rosa wouldn't allow herself to even think about losing her children. She was confronting enough of what social workers called "challenges." Rosa's three children were split up between foster homes, which made reunification even more difficult. But she was dedicated to doing what she had to—she wanted her children back. Just as she was beginning to work with her DCFS case manager on a family reunification plan, she discovered that she was pregnant.

"You would think this was a bad thing," she told me, "but it wasn't. I knew this was the start of a new life for me. This was my redemption baby. It was a sign I was going to get my kids back."

As I listened to Rosa, I wondered if she'd considered abortion. In California, it would have been available and affordable, even free for someone in her circumstances.[6] Across the country, a survey of the availability and cost of abortion presents a mixed picture. In sixteen states, including California, New York, and even Montana, public funding covers all or most medically necessary abortions. California requires insurance providers, including public insurance options, to cover abortion costs, regardless of medical necessity.[7] Other states, including most southern states and some in the American West, have restrictions in place that severely limit the availability of abortions, even if they remain legal nationally. For example, thirty-eight states require a licensed physician to perform an abortion, even though studies demonstrate that first-trimester abortions are equally safe when nurses, physician assistants, and midwives perform them.[8] Eighteen states require a woman to be counseled about the fetus's ability to feel pain, a purported link between abortions and breast cancer, and the long-term mental health consequences of an abortion before she is able to obtain an abortion.[9]

Twenty-five states require women seeking abortions to wait twenty-four hours between counseling and the abortion.[10] All of these laws, whether states have just one or a combination of them, create additional barriers for women seeking abortions. These laws also exacerbate already unequal access to medical care, alongside the historical discrimination that the healthcare system has inflicted upon poor women, women of color, and especially Black women (across all socioeconomic levels) and women—overrepresented in each of these categories—who've been incarcerated.[11]

The vast majority of the formerly incarcerated women I met with were adamantly pro-choice; several had described times in their lives when they'd chosen to have an abortion. But a handful were clear that they could *never* have an abortion—even though they believed in a woman's right to choose. Their ability to hold these two ideas was true for both Black women and women of color who'd been incarcerated. Only three out of all the women I interviewed were anti-abortion, telling me it was a sin and explaining that their pro-life beliefs were forged out of faith they'd discovered while in prison. One woman told me she'd had an abortion before finding God, adding, "I know she understands and forgives me."

Rosa later told me she'd never considered an abortion. She was overjoyed about having this baby. But balancing pregnancy and reunification wasn't going to be easy, and DCFS had a long "to-do" list for Rosa. She applied for Section 8 subsidized housing and also put her name on the list for a unit in a public housing development, aware that she could wind up living anywhere in Los Angeles County. She attended counseling religiously and submitted to random drug testing, carefully peeing into the cup her PO provided. The bright spot in her week was the supervised visits with her children. This was what she lived for.

And she went back to work at Homeboy Industries. There were delays in her case while she waited for government-subsidized housing to kick in. At Homeboy, she was happy to be part of a community. "I give thanks to Father Greg and Homeboy Industries every day of my life," Rosa told me. She never worked as a waitress at the Homegirl Café, instead settling into administrative work within the main program. It was there she began to find her voice. "I got to know people who were just genuine, like Marissa." Marissa Gillette was the curriculum director at Homeboy Industries, but, like all of the senior staff, she was much more than that. My ongoing research showed that the secret to Homeboy's success went far beyond the job training that was part of the "Industries" in its name. HBI's impact was largely due to the staff, who built deep relationships with the homies and homegirls, creating a community of kinship with everyone who walked through their doors. "Marissa broke down that wall. I would tell her, 'Leave me the fuck alone; this is too much.'" Understanding her mistrust, Marissa would tell Rosa how much she valued her, how much she loved her. When Rosa would ask, "How can you love me?" Marissa would tell her how much strength she had, how gifted she was, and what incredible qualities she saw in her.

Marissa wasn't just talking. Rosa definitely possessed great strength and resilience to deal with the overwhelming process of family reunification. Trying to meet the expectations and confront the bureaucracy of the child welfare system is in and of itself a full-time job. It took nearly a year and a half, but Rosa succeeded and was reunited with all three of her children, after welcoming her fourth child, Isabel, her redemption baby, into the world. Together, they made up a family: her eldest son, Arturo, was now twelve years old; her daughter Pahola was nine; and her son Daniel was seven; all three adored their new little sister.

Still, Rosa knew it would take a long time before both she and her family healed from the wounds of her incarceration. In 2018, the US Department of Health and Human Services reported that children whose parents have been incarcerated are at "increased risk of mental health conditions, including anxiety and depression. In adulthood, they have higher rates of asthma, migraines, high cholesterol, and HIV/AIDS, and are more likely to use illicit or prescription drugs." The same report revealed that incarceration had an equally dire economic impact—adolescent boys with incarcerated *mothers* "are 35% more likely to drop out of school, and have a higher chance of ending up incarcerated themselves."[12]

Ironically, although the child welfare system poses all sorts of legal and institutional obstacles, the biggest obstacle women who've been incarcerated face is rebuilding their relationships with the children they've been separated from, often for many years. Their substance abuse issues, their crimes, and their incarceration have all cost them precious time with their children. And the pain and loss those children have endured are difficult to repair.

No child responds the same way to the loss of their mother. But for every child, rage and desire exist side by side. Children blame their mother for what happened, but they long to see her again. This is what Adela faced. Although she never had to contend with children's services, Adela had to confront enduring problems with both her children that began the moment she was arrested.

Adela still remembers the trauma of her arrest. It was a morning like any other. After telling her son, Joshua, and her daughter, Julia, to hurry up and get their lunches so she could drive them to school before she went to work, she walked out to her car. "I would go warm up the car and wait for them. They'd gather up their things, and they knew: the last one closes the door. It was December, it was cold, my car had ice and snow on it. The next thing you know, I see DEA, FBI—everybody surrounded me. I asked them, 'What are you guys doing?' They read me my rights. I kept saying, 'I haven't done anything.' They had guns to my head, they had guns on my children. I begged them, 'Please don't point guns at my children.'" As she tells me this story, nearly fifteen years after it happened, Adela's eyes fill with tears and her voice starts to shake. "I was angry because of the way they had treated my children—like criminals. I asked them what were they doing. I couldn't believe it."

After she was sentenced to two years of incarceration, the judge gave Adela three weeks to make plans for her children before surrendering herself to the federal penitentiary. She decided that her son, Joshua, who was thirteen, would live with her sister who had two sons; he'd fit in there. She made different plans for Julia, seven years old at the time. Her father, Lefty, had convinced Adela that their daughter should stay with his mother. When the time came to explain what was happening, Adela told Joshua the truth about her sentence but lied to Julia, saying she was going to a camp for dental assistants. "She asked how long I'd be gone, and I said two years. She said, 'That's a long time to go to camp.'"

These memories still hurt Adela. "After I came home, my daughter told me that she looked out the window and saw me walk away; she watched me get into the car to go to prison. Her grandma came into the room and asked, 'What did your mom tell you?' Julia said, 'She told me she's going to a dental camp.' Then her grandma said, 'Your mom lied to you. She's going to prison.' Julia couldn't believe it. Why was her mom going to prison? Her dad was already in prison—she'd grown up hearing that her dad's in prison because he's a bad man. Now her mom is going to prison—how could her mom do bad?"

Adela was furious at Lefty's mother. "It was my place to tell Julia, and I wasn't ready to let her know. She had looked at me like her hero." Still, her grandmother also tried to help Julia, taking her to church and to a pastoral counselor. In the meantime, Adela didn't want her children to see her locked up. This was easily accomplished since the prison was far away, in Dublin, six hours from where the children were living.

Despite her deep emotional pain, Adela adjusted to prison. "I made up my mind . . . I was getting out and I would never be back in that situation again." Listening to Adela's story, I knew that her real struggle would begin once her incarceration ended.

After serving her sentence, then being released from the halfway house, Adela went to her sister's. Both Celia and her husband, Sam, were willing to make Adela and her children part of the household. Adela knew she was lucky—very few incarcerated women find family who can offer financial and emotional assistance for any length of time. But even with her sister's support, there were problems almost immediately.

"It was a difficult transition." Adela shook her head as she said this. "It was hard because I didn't feel like I knew how to be a mother. . . . How am I going to tell them not to do things, when I felt like I was going to be judged all the way around—because they were hurt. I tried to make the best of it. Then, they started becoming rebellious toward me. I think Julia was nine and Joshua was fifteen or sixteen. At those ages, I felt like how am I going to do this? I didn't know how to talk to them. It was getting worse and worse as they were becoming more and more rebellious. One day, I said, 'I'm done trying to kiss you guys' ass. I know I'm far away from perfect—I committed a crime and I paid for it. I don't feel like I've got to pay you guys for it too. I think we should start clean, like fresh from the beginning. It's overwhelming me emotionally because I don't know what else to tell you two. I don't know how else to be a mother. You either want to be with me or you don't want to be with me. We lost each other once. We gotta work on it.' Once I had the conversation, things started to be better for a minute. Then other things started happening."

Adela faced unique issues with each child. Her son was in high school by this time, and he'd started smoking weed. Her daughter was ditching school. Adela felt sadness. "I was losing control, and I didn't know what to do as a mother anymore. I'm not going to beat them— what do I do?" All the responsibility for the kids was on her shoulders. She'd contacted each of her ex-husbands, Sleepy and Lefty, who were both still incarcerated, and told them she was out, that the kids would be fine. "I felt like I'd been through the same thing they felt each day, being in prison, worrying about my kids. I wanted them to feel better and not worry too much. They both thought, 'Now mom is home, she's got this.' Too bad it wasn't true."

Adela worried that Joshua really needed his father. Her son's dope smoking persisted until he wound up in a hospital ER after having a series of seizures. The doctors warned that he'd suffer more seizures if he continued to smoke dope. Joshua said he'd quit, but Adela feared marijuana would be a gateway drug to "something stronger."

Their relationship continued to be troubled, and Adela suggested they go to counseling. Even though they went several times, Joshua felt uncomfortable sharing his feelings with a stranger. "I told him that's okay, and we stopped. It's been hard for Joshua. We're not as close as I am with Julia. I don't know if it's because he's a boy." It's difficult for Adela to talk about her son; her voice drops, her speech becomes halting. But despite her pain—or maybe because of it—her son has grown into a good man, avoiding any kind of trouble. He explained to Adela that he loved her, that she was strong compared to her brothers, who were stupid. They were in and out of prison, and, he said, he "didn't want to go down the same pathway."

When she became a teenager, Julia posed much more of a challenge for Adela because, as she explained, "I see myself in her." The problems in the mother-daughter relationship really became apparent when the family moved from her sister's house forty miles back to LA. Adela was working full-time at Homegirl. "That's when her rebellion started. She started wearing dark lipstick, she was goth, she started to dress different." Julia would promise to bake cookies for Adela, then ask what time she'd be home. "If I told her six, she would get there about five thirty. Pretty soon, I caught on to it." At Homegirl, Adela told Erika she had to leave early so she could spy on Julia. Hiding in wait, what she saw shocked her. "She was dressed like a little *cholita*, wearing clothes I'd never seen." Adela followed Julia into a liquor store and confronted her. "I said, 'Damn what kind of weed is that? You guys smell strong.' Her friend was like, 'Oh shoot!' I told Julia, 'Say goodbye to your friend— you're never going to see her again.' She said, 'You can't do this to me,' and I said, 'Oh yeah? Just watch me.'"

The next day, Adela met with the school principal and Julia's guidance counselor. She learned that Julia had been ditching class and getting into fights. "She was out of control." Even though they hadn't always gotten along, Adela called Lefty's mother and told her what was happening. She immediately said, "Bring her now." Adela didn't waste any time, driving Julia to her grandmother's "with only the clothes on her back." Adela laughs as she remembers. "She told me, 'I hate you! I hate you!' and I said, 'You're gonna hate me right now but you're gonna love me tomorrow.' I told Erika I needed some time off—I was taking Julia to another school. Everyone at Homegirl was so supportive."

Adela started spending more time with Julia; they went to counseling together. "I felt like I had to make up for those lost years—all the time I was locked up and I wished I was with my daughter." Adela's words are sadly familiar. Many mothers lament the years with family they can never make up—and every one of them described to me their fears and worries over how their incarceration would affect their children in the long term.

Meanwhile, the number of children affected by women's incarceration grows every year.

According to the Prison Policy Initiative, 80 percent of the women locked up in local jails are mothers. In one calendar year, jails will separate 2.3 million mothers from their children.[13] The Sentencing Project has reported that in the US, the number of children with a parent in prison increased 80 percent in the sixteen years from 1991 to 2007. These separations have serious long-term consequences for families. It has long been believed that it would be better for mothers, families, and communities if there were community-based alternatives to incarceration—but where are these? Along with this deficit, there are very few reentry programs like ANWOL, that allow women to live with their children.

In the midst of my latest round of interviews focusing on mothers and their children, my phone started ringing. It was Susan Burton, telling me we were going to New York to sit down with formerly incarcerated women on the East Coast and talk about their experiences. Along with that, there were some programs she wanted to visit, and she'd be speaking about her memoir at a bookstore and meeting with several foundations. I was exhausted just listening to her, yet I also knew she was constantly developing new ideas, searching for ways to help while she advocated for incarcerated women everywhere.

Six weeks later, in New York, our first stop was Hope House, a transitional home in the Bronx modeled after ANWOL. Susan believed so deeply in this effort that she'd actually given part of her savings to the founders of Hope House, Topeka Sam and Vanee Sykes, to set up this small, immaculate townhouse offering housing and programs for five women at a time. From its founding in 2017, Hope House had progressed, offering a clear-cut example of how the ANWOL model could be replicated in other cities. This was Susan's plan: to create a model for reentry homes that could be replicated all over the country. What she was putting together may have looked obvious, yet it was brilliant. I couldn't believe she was the first one to do this. But she was, and it was to have far-reaching implications for formerly incarcerated women—something I would soon discover as I traveled alongside Susan, literally and figuratively.

I spent a lively afternoon with Vanee, learning how she and Topeka met while incarcerated at Danbury Federal Prison and put together their plan to open a reentry home for women. Tragically, two years later, Vanee would die of Covid-19, but not before Hope House and her work with Topeka was well on its way.

Our time at Hope House was a prelude to our visit the next day to Hour Children, the well-known women's reentry program based in Queens.[14] The program's several buildings were located in the center of Long Island City, a blue-collar community filled with fast-food restaurants, auto repair centers, and small bodegas. It was four miles and a world away from Manhattan. I could see smoke stacks and frame houses next door to pizza joints. In the midst of a working-class neighborhood, Hour Children appeared to have a handle on how to support women and their children as they struggled to heal from the impact of incarceration. It also had an approach that was completely different from anything I'd experienced in my efforts to understand the world of formerly incarcerated women.

The minute we walked in, I felt at home—there were children everywhere. The materials on display in their main office told the whole story. A poster with a mission statement proclaimed, "With most reentry programs focused on men, Hour Children provides valuable services to women and their children, helping them to reunite and establish stable lives and a future filled with hope." There were additional placards explaining, "Our mission is to help incarcerated and formerly incarcerated women and their children successfully rejoin the community, reunify with their families and build healthy, independent and secure lives." This was a mission statement that was clear and all-encompassing and promised a lot more than referrals and monitoring.

Hour Children traced its history back to the groundbreaking work of Sister Elaine Roulet, a Roman Catholic nun who devoted her life to serving mothers during and after incarceration. Her basic belief still stands as a guide to enlightened public policy for incarcerated women: that women should have consistent visits with their children along with receiving parenting lessons to end the cycle of familial trauma. Although this seems like such a simple idea, the activities involved in putting that belief into practice have been nothing short of radical. Sister Elaine was the guiding force behind the Children's Center at the Bedford Hills Correctional Facility in New York, which because of her efforts ultimately became a place where mothers could live with their newborns and play with their older children instead of "visiting" through glass.

This innovative work all began as a result of the partnership between Sister Elaine and Elaine Lord, the superintendent at Bedford Hills. Their first step was creating a program that allowed mothers to live with their babies for the first year to eighteen months of their lives, a critical period in terms of infant attachment. Hour Children runs a residential nursery at the Bedford Hills Correctional Facility, where infants and mothers can stay together. Women are expected to stick to their mandated prison program, so during the day, while the mothers work or attend classes, their infants are cared for by Hour Children employees and other incarcerated women, who staff the Child Development Center.

But a dilemma remained: while infants can stay with their mothers, what about older children? So many are lost, living with relatives or placed in foster care in homes that don't understand their deep need to connect with their incarcerated mothers. In 1986, Sister Elaine put what was termed "an open request" to the Catholic community for help.

Sister Tesa Fitzgerald answered the call. Along with four other members of her order, she set up a small home in Long Island City to care for children whose mothers were incarcerated at Bedford Hills. Once the first group of children was in residence, the staff, led by Sister Tesa, brought them to visit their mothers in prison. This activity had an unexpected consequence: in conversations with the incarcerated women, Sister Tesa soon understood that these mothers wanted desperately to reunite with their children once they were released, yet all too often they lacked the supports and the resources to do so. It was the familiar list of needs: housing, job training, counseling, help with parenting. Six years later, in 1992, Hour Children was founded to help these women and their children "reunite, stabilize and transform their lives." This meant providing transitional and permanent housing, job training, and job placement. Most significantly, the Hour Women program focused on women pursuing careers, not just low-wage jobs. The program's success in these efforts was notable; women were able to walk into careers as head chefs, dental technicians, computer programmers, and paralegal professionals.

This was a fresh approach to helping women negotiate life after incarceration, with potentially far-reaching impact. Most agencies and organizations, from halfway houses to the Homegirl Café to ANWOL, focused on the issue of employment. Their emphasis was on getting formerly incarcerated women *jobs*—the higher the pay, the better. Homeboy Industries had multiple individuals working full-time on work-force development and job training. Formerly incarcerated women signed up for the Homeboy businesses, and their training very often led to long-term employment in the outside world, but this was not a career. Shayna Welcher had come face-to-face with this dilemma once she left the Homegirl Café and went to work in a popular LA restaurant, where she'd interned for six months. A year later, during an economic downturn, the restaurant went out of business, and Shayna struggled to find another job. The importance of these job placement efforts was clear—women had to satisfy their probation officers and children's services agencies: their focus was on making a living and getting their children back, not starting out on a career.[15] The difference with Hour Children was how it stressed that women didn't need to sacrifice meaningful work to meet administrative and economic demands. In fact, according to the career-placement staff, emphasizing careers, rather than just jobs, helped women and their children much more in the long run, allowing them to avoid low-wage jobs that would lead to the long-term pressures experienced by the working poor.

Hour Children is committed to making sure that women receive the support they need to "plan for their professional future, which includes setting expectations and developing a set of attainable goals." Their staff engage in "one-on-one education and career planning." Additionally, the organization secures mentors who provide guidance and support for women, helping them "to develop as working professionals." These services, all reinforcing the goal of career development, offered something different and significant—which really was the identity of Hour Children.

I'd wondered where this incredible organization got its name and kept checking if I even had it right—was it "our" children? I was reassured that it was "hour" and learned that the name referred to the many pivotal hours in a child's life: the moment of the mother's arrest, the time allowed for visits, the time of the mother's release. These moments formed the vision of Hour Children and gave it its structure: it made sure children were taken to visit their incarcerated mothers, and it provided programming for incarcerated mothers and support for children and teenagers waiting for their mothers to return. Once women came home, there were apartments and small houses where a mother and her children could live comfortably, cooking meals for the family with food obtained from the agency's food pantry. This food pantry was another testimony to Hour Children's effectiveness and its innovative approach. In keeping with the culture of the organization, the food pantry emphasized safety and *dignity.* When a staff member told Susan and me that she'd be taking us to visit the food pantry, I'd expected to see a small back room stocked with canned goods. Instead, we entered a building the size of a Trader Joe's, with a large inventory of healthy and nutritious food and home products. It had, in fact, more to offer than a Trader Joe's, and if you told me I was viewing a local gourmet market, I wouldn't have blinked.

The food pantry was initially created to "address hunger and health-related issues" that impact formerly incarcerated women and their children, along with the low-income families in the surrounding Long Island City community. But the pantry also helped to connect the women and families it serves with the surrounding community. Today, these efforts are reinforced through educational workshops, cooking demonstrations, and partnerships to extend resources. The Hour Children food pantry also works with Visiting Nursing Services of New York and the Food Bank for New York City, ensuring that women, their families, and nearby residents can seek out resources and services to help sustain their lives. Food and hunger are long-term problems in Long Island City for many seniors, the homeless, and all those confronting the deprivations that accompany chronic poverty. Hour Children's business model doesn't see those problems and the needs they create as a reason to deprive individuals of healthy food. The supermarket-style "business" is staffed by volunteers and draws upon donations for funding. It offers fresh organic vegetables and fruits, meat and fresh fish, dairy products, canned goods, pasta, rice, whole grains, granola, and healthy cereal—all consistent with cultural tastes and preferences.

However, there are no cash registers: everything is free. Hour Children reported that annually almost ten thousand people shopped at their sites. Those astonishing numbers and the use of the plural are correct. Their services have expanded to all five New York boroughs, connecting formerly incarcerated women to the outside world, as well as building the health and capacities of the communities around them. Shoppers come from surrounding neighborhoods. There's no admission requirement—it's accepted that only needy individuals shop at the food pantry.

Although Susan and I were visiting their main site, Hour Children has bases in several communities throughout Queens where, every year, it provides housing to almost two hundred families. There are six "communal" homes where women live with their children. At these homes, women are helped in finding career-track work and, ultimately, moving on to permanent affordable housing—also obtained through Hour Children. There is therapy, case management, and ongoing support to help navigate the challenges of the child welfare system and the process of family reunification. Finally, just as at ANWOL, there is no expiration date for help. This means that mothers and their children are given all the time they need to heal and adjust, each woman receiving housing and services specifically tailored to her needs and the needs of her children.

Susan and I sat with Sister Tesa in her cluttered office while she called different women in and introduced us, explaining how each plays a vital role in the program's functioning. Her staff is deeply committed, as well as being multiracial, multicultural, and multitalented. Sister Tesa also explained that the Children's Center, founded by Sister Elaine Roulet, continues to function. I found the details of all this work—once again—to be new and completely different. I should have gotten used to the fact that Hour Children consistently challenged the usual ways of working with currently and formerly incarcerated women. There has been so much research on the importance of the bonds between incarcerated women and their children. Hour Children figured out and has sustained so many ways of fostering this critical attachment.

In addition to the ongoing activities of the Children's Center, during the summer, Hour Children supervises eighty children who spend a week visiting with their mothers at both the Bedford Hills and Taconic Correctional Facilities. These children live throughout the state of New York and sometimes even in neighboring states, but that's not viewed as an obstacle to keeping them connected to their mothers. Hour Children provides transportation for every single child, picking them up wherever they might live and bringing them to each of the prisons. The children spend time with their mothers during the day; once visiting hours end, the children stay with local families who serve as their "hosts." These host families are an integral part of the summer program, acting as "the glue that holds this program together, year after year." All host families are volunteers, and some welcome children into their homes both during the summer and over school breaks and holiday weekends.

The results of all these efforts to keep children actively involved with their incarcerated mothers have been significant: Hour Children reports that women in their programs were six times less likely to return to prison; their recidivism rate within three years was less than 5 percent. Every program Hour Children creates drives toward their goal of increasing women's chances for success once they exit jail or prison. Integral to that success is supporting and building mothers' relationships with their children. I wondered what it would have been like for Clara to have stayed connected to her children and how much pain she and so many others would have been spared.

At the end of the day, sitting in Sister Tesa's office, I listened to her plans to expand the program and to continue to help women confront the endless demands of public bureaucracy. The work was frustrating: keeping families together served everyone's interests, but government policies and child welfare services kept placing obstacles in the way of women, while Hour Children wanted to give them support and resources, to help them to heal and succeed. After our meeting, when we walked out into the late-afternoon sunshine, Susan looked back at the building and quietly observed, "Every woman who's been locked up deserves this. They just need a chance—to be with their children and start a new life."

FIFTEEN

THE LIGHT

I knew if I could just hang on long enough, things would change. I had to believe in hope, I had to believe in myself, I had to believe in the light.

—SHAYNA WELCHER

D enise is sitting in my office with six-month-old Elizabeth. The baby is happily managing to break everything she can reach, although I've put anything dangerous out of harm's way. She is a beautiful child with a round face, big brown eyes, and the signs of teeth beginning to form a joyful smile. She's also energetic, curious, and not easily contained. "She's a wild baby," Denise says, laughing and stating the obvious. "I hoped for a quiet baby, but I think she's like me—she's not gonna sit still." I play with Elizabeth and talk about what classes Denise will be taking in the fall. A week ago, she received an email from UCLA graduate division—she'd been accepted into the MSW program.

"I never thought this day would come. You know, G-ma, I never really thought I'd get in."

"Why?"

"I don't know. . . . I just didn't believe it would work out. You know, I feel happy and scared at the same time. Do you think I can do it? Really? Really? I want to make sure I can."

I wait for her to finish before reassuring her. By this time, I'm used to Denise's staccato rhythm of speaking. She'll ask questions without waiting for an answer. Then she'll free-associate about whatever is worrying her. On the precipice of realizing a dream, she's afraid it won't come true.

I understand why Denise feels the way she does, even though her case for admission to the MSW program was a strong one. I wrote a letter of recommendation for her, but I didn't intervene in the admissions process. Every faculty member at one time or another has advocated on behalf of a student who didn't have perfect qualifications for admissions—it is the nature of social welfare. Sometimes it works out; sometimes it doesn't. In Denise's case, her acceptance was straightforward. Her undergraduate record was strong, her letters of recommendation—in addition to mine—were stellar. There wasn't a doubt in my mind that she belonged in the social work profession. But I also understood her anxiety. It all seemed too good to be true.

This is why Susan Burton is a role model for women like Denise. While I might tell Denise she'll make it, that things will work out, I just didn't have the same credibility as Susan. Susan has faced loss, substance abuse, and incarceration—she's the walking, talking proof that Denise and other women who've been locked up can make it. Still, Susan and others like her aren't sitting around waiting for their admirers to kiss the ring. They're all engaged in sustaining the movement that will ensure that public policy and trauma-informed programming will meet the needs of women currently and formerly incarcerated.

This commitment to sustaining the movement on behalf of women who've been incarcerated is part of the reason leadership and advocacy have always been among the key building blocks of A New Way of Life. At ANWOL, Susan contributes to the efforts of the Los Angeles chapter of a national advocacy effort, All of Us Or None, a grassroots organizing campaign designed to reverse the discriminatory policies and practices affecting formerly incarcerated individuals. As part of this, ANWOL is training women to be leaders and organizers in this national movement. Susan isn't alone in these efforts. There are other devoted leaders, including Kim Carter, the founder and executive director of the Time for Change Foundation; Leyla Martinez, the founder and executive director of the Beyond the Box Initiative; and Cheryl Wilkins, the senior director of education and programs at Columbia University's Center for Justice and the Justice in Education Initiative. All of these women and others alongside them are dedicated to changing policy, altering systems, and making sure that long-neglected women receive the services they need. It's also critical to note that this movement is being led by Black women and women of color, many of whom have been incarcerated; all of them have confronted major obstacles in their own lives.

It's the end of 2019, and Susan Burton is launching plans for the coming year. We're sitting in her office, but she keeps jumping up to greet a woman arriving at ANWOL for the first time or to answer a question posed by one of the staff. She sits down in the extraordinary chair that the designer Frank Gehry gave to her only long enough to start talking about "some guy named Chris Martin who wants to give a concert to raise money for us." While her communications manager, Christin Runkle, and I begin hyperventilating, Susan quickly turns her attention to the subject of racism and systemic change. She has no interest in Coldplay right now. Instead, she talks of her impatience with elected officials and policymakers who aren't moving fast enough to fund more community-based options for the formerly incarcerated.

"I'm not convinced policy is the way to go," she announces. "I don't see it working fast enough to change lives in any way. I don't see it reaching the people in power. I think we're gonna have to do things differently. I think we're gonna have to look at community organizing—bringing people together to demand that there be real change in our criminal justice system—what we do to people, women in jail and prison and what we do to them once they get out. We need to demand a better life and I think the best way to do that is through organizing."

I know she's right. I think back to the first time I saw Susan at the philanthropists' tour of the women's jail back in 2013. That seems like a million years ago, but her words are still fresh in my mind. She urged—no, exhorted—the group to think about the fact that most of the women incarcerated were awaiting trial, that the only thing they were guilty of was not being able to afford bail. The most pressing concern of these women and most of the women who were incarcerated was their children. In the short term, they were disconnected from their children, who couldn't even visit them. In the long term, they faced the prospect of losing their children forever, in so many cases to the child welfare system. And running like a thread through all of these concerns was the utter lack of funding or programming to support women while they were locked up and afterward, when they tried to reenter their families and their communities, struggling to change and facing a list of obstacles that would stop most of the people touring the jail in their tracks.

Over the years since that tour, I have learned about efforts like Hour Children, which seeks to unite and strengthen the bonds between incarcerated mothers and their children, and I have seen firsthand the ongoing miracle of the Homegirl Café, which works to create and sustain a community of women helping one another. And, under the guidance and vision of Susan Burton, I've documented her efforts to establish a national network of SAFE houses for women reentering society after incarceration. These initiatives run parallel to the national movement to "Ban the Box," so that men and women will not have to indicate that they've been incarcerated when applying for jobs. Finally, the movement to end money bail culminated in a series of ballot measures in the 2020 elections. All of these represent efforts to address some of the obstacles currently and formerly incarcerated women confront and reform the systems that created them.

But there is more work to be done on a number of fronts.

First, although California's 2020 ballot measure to end cash bail failed, and so far, reform legislation in a handful of other states hasn't been successful, the indiscriminate use of money bail must end, to be replaced by a system of determining who represents a risk to the community that offers assessments free of racism and explicit and implicit bias. Right now, the United States spends *$10 billion* each year to incarcerate people in pretrial detention.[1] This costly investment yields absolutely nothing; research continually demonstrates that pre-trial detention increases rates of recidivism, breaks families apart, punishes poverty, and disproportionately impacts women, Black people, and people of color. The most recent research study took me back to where my work began, at the Los Angeles County women's jail. Here was the embodiment of the problem: because women experience higher rates and longer time periods of pretrial detention than men, they are especially susceptible to these collateral consequences.[2]

Until recently, Washington, DC, was the only jurisdiction in the US that had effectively eliminated cash bail, except in certain instances. Given the stated purposes of pretrial detention—to reduce the risk to community safety, ensure individuals are present at their court dates (as opposed to fleeing), and preserve pretrial liberty—Washington, DC's leadership on this issue has proved to be highly effective. Nearly fifteen years after the nation's capital banned the practice, 94 percent of defendants have been released pretrial without cash bail, and 88 percent of these individuals have shown up to all of their court dates. Additionally, while free without cash bail, 86 percent were not arrested for any criminal offense.[3] For those who were rearrested, less than 2 percent involved arrests for crimes of violence.[4] Despite these positive outcomes, as of March 2021, Illinois was the only state with plans to completely prohibit cash bail, as set out in the Illinois Pre-Trial Justice Act, which will go into effect in 2023.[5] Other states have made piecemeal reforms to cash bail, but not enough to constitute real change.

In the meantime, unless cash bail is eliminated nationally, taxpayers will continue to spend billions basically to incarcerate individuals for open-ended periods of time when they are presumed to be innocent. And in the cases of so many women, this often means bringing child protective services systems into the picture, decimating families and costing taxpayers even more. This all happens as authorities insist they're addressing a problem that simply doesn't exist. Washington, DC's success has demonstrated that people charged with a crime don't pose a threat to the community and still show up for their day in court.

Needlessly separating women from their families and their communities only creates more problems and more costs for individuals and society as a whole. There is an alternative to punitive and costly cash bail: effective risk assessment tools can determine whether or not a woman can stay with her family while awaiting trial. Used alongside investment in pretrial services, risk assessment tools that are individualized to the particular person, independently validated on a routine basis, and evaluated to be free of racial, gender-based, and class bias can safely and effectively replace pretrial incarceration.

Second, if a woman is sentenced either after pleading or being found guilty, alternatives to incarceration make rehabilitative and financial sense. For most crimes, a system of community-based alternatives to incarceration, including diversion and supervision, should be established and sustained. Such an approach would allow women to remain with their children, ultimately strengthening families and communities. Because so many crimes that women are accused of involve drugs, many diversion programs for drug-related and nonviolent crimes have been created, allowing women to engage in substance abuse treatment programs. Expanding these programs to include trafficking-related and other gender-based crimes would also help reduce the rising numbers of women who are incarcerated every year. In what world does it make sense for a woman who's been trafficked to then have to serve time? Instead, it's both humane and critical to create courts that exclusively hear specialized cases and sentence women to alternatives to incarceration. One effective example of this occurs in California, which has instituted a Girls' Court within the juvenile justice system for young women who have a history of trauma or exploitation or are at risk of either of these.[6] Los Angeles County has also established a special program in LA County Superior Court to defer sentences while providing services for the victims of sex trafficking, most of them underage girls. Known as STAR Court, the program's full name, the Succeeding Through Achievement and Resilience Court, actually describes the services and positive outcomes it provides through multidisciplinary teams that offer healing in place of incarceration.

For women who are no longer juveniles, the Los Angeles County court system has also created the Second Chance Women's Reentry Court (WRC), facilitated by Prototypes, a community-based organization. WRC is designed for women charged with felonies, even if they have past convictions. This alone represents a new approach, in contrast to most diversion programs, which tend to limit eligibility to individuals with misdemeanors and "clean" prior records. Women who are eligible for WRC receive three years' probation, along with placement in a residential treatment program, followed by an outpatient treatment program and after-care services. Women can bring two children under twelve years old to live with them in these residential programs.[7] The services women receive are designed—using gender-responsive and trauma-informed, evidence-based models— to match their histories of trauma, substance use or dependence, cycles of incarceration, homelessness, and poverty. As part of their probation supervision, women must submit to drug testing, and they face sanctions if they violate any of their terms of supervision. But an emphasis on treatment, not punishment, is the guiding strategy of WRC.

A patchwork of these alternative courts and diversion programs exists in jurisdictions across the country. In 2010, the Philadelphia courts implemented the Project Dawn Court Diversionary Program, which is designed to offer alternatives to punishment for women charged with sex work and sex trafficking crimes.[8] Women with a history of sex work convictions and no history of violent crimes are eligible—at the district attorney's discretion—for their case to be processed through this alternative court. The Project Dawn Court Diversionary Program focuses on treatment and reentry services, including trauma counseling for abuse and treatment for substance abuse.[9] Participants must remain clean through the duration of the program and, just as in WRC, women are subject to sanctions if they don't comply with the terms of their supervision.

In developing these diversion programs, gender-aware courts, and alternatives to incarceration, it's critical that practitioners adopt strength-based and trauma-informed approaches that provide the necessary conditions for women to succeed. Often, this means that the most effective programs minimize barriers to qualification, including fines and fees, and streamline the connection between women and the community-based services they require.[10] Successful programs also provide an individualized approach, working to meet every woman where she is at, address her particular needs, and invest in her strengths.[11]

It's critical to note, however, that each of these efforts still represents a reactive approach to what women and girls experience. Investing in girls, women, and their communities *before* they come into contact with the criminal justice system would do wonders in preventing the increasing and disproportionate incarceration of girls and women, especially Black women and women of color.

This approach doesn't need to be limited to what currently exists. More counties can independently create their own "girls' courts" and "women's courts" that focus on providing services and gender-specific, trauma-informed care, rather than punishment. Right now, current efforts tend to focus on girls—an insensitive limitation, for traumatized women of all genders and all ages should be eligible for such judicial responses. Extending programs like these into adulthood would redirect women from the criminal justice system into a diversion program that would address the underlying conditions that propelled them into the system.

Third, programming for women that allows them to remain securely attached and relating to their children and their communities while they're incarcerated needs to be expanded and funded. Hour Children's efforts represent a collaboration between a nonprofit program and a prison that enables women to stay connected to their children while they're incarcerated and helps them once they leave prison to reenter their families and communities. Happily, Hour Children is not a unique model. There are already indications that other programs are engaging in such efforts. For example, the Washington State Residential Parenting Program, offered at the Washington Corrections Center for Women, is cast from the same mold as Hour Children. The program allows women who enter prison pregnant, are convicted of nonviolent offenses, and will be released before their child turns thirty months old to live with their child during the course of their incarceration.[12] Though the program is certainly a step in the right direction, its impact is limited, given its restricted acceptance criteria.

Finally, more than anything, the approaches described in the second part of this book must become part of a sustained effort to address the needs of women reentering their families and their communities after incarceration. The Prison Policy Initiative has identified four major areas policymakers must focus on to undercut obstacles and ensure women successfully reenter mainstream life. The list is no surprise; the items are interwoven with the narratives of the women in this book and include (1) addressing the economic marginalization and poverty that formerly incarcerated women experience; (2) investing in housing and helping women establish housing stability; (3) investing in trauma-informed and gender-responsive services to prevent future recidivism; and (4) reuniting families with care and support after the trauma of family separation.[13] Along with what the Prison Policy Initiative has identified, there are also huge gaps that haven't even begun to be addressed, involving the challenges faced by non-binary individuals and trans women during and after incarceration. Once again, through the work of Susan Burton and the incredible efforts of Black and Pink, a national organization that partners with ANWOL, a light is finally being shed on these individuals and how programs and services must expand to address their needs. All of this points to the reality that there is much work left to be done.[14]

In the end, government, philanthropy, and private partners must band together to address one of the questions that has burned in my brain as I wrote this book: Why aren't there enough reentry programs across the country to address the specific issues formerly incarcerated women face? With eighty-one thousand women released from state prisons annually, we can't afford to wait.[15] We don't need any additional research studies to prove that the costs to society of failing to support these women are far greater because of the inevitable recidivism that occurs without strong support. Even those who describe themselves as "tough on crime" must acknowledge that it's more fiscally and socially responsible to support women and prevent future crime than to keep locking them up. Of course, fundamental to this entire discussion is the commitment to investing in these women and their communities *before* they become involved with the criminal justice system.

What I've encountered and described here are some of the models for meaningful support services, and there are more. Future public, private, and philanthropic efforts to create programs for women should be informed by the best practices established through the work of A New Way of Life in Los Angeles, Hour Children in New York, the Center for Women in Transition in St. Louis, Angela House in Houston, and the handful of similar programs that exist throughout the United States. These programs all represent new and innovative approaches to serving the specific needs of women and to provide wraparound services to holistically meet their needs when they return home. Additionally, these programs demonstrate that the ideas and models that effectively serve women actually do exist and justify the further investment in these programs that is profoundly needed.

Finally, the ANWOL Sisterhood Alliance for Freedom and Equality or, as Susan Burton branded it, the SAFE Housing Network, as well as other efforts aimed at establishing housing and reentry support for formerly incarcerated women, require dedicated funding streams. These undertakings create positive outcomes for women, children, public safety, and human well-being and should be supported by public-private partnerships in a sustained manner.

It's also important to prepare for the unexpected. Over the past year, the global pandemic has made the cliché of strategic planning a reality. By May 2020, Susan Burton was spending very little time sitting in her Frank Gehry chair. While the pandemic raged, as most people were tearing their hair out over the rate of infection and the availability of toilet paper, she was hard at work raising more money to remodel a former convent where she could shelter the women whom she lobbied LA County and the State of California to release from incarceration.

The *New York Times* covered her efforts, describing how she was "racing against the clock to shelter those freed early because of the surge of coronavirus cases in prisons."[16]

To this day, her work during the pandemic continues unabated. I'm helping her plan an online training to add more partners to the SAFE Housing Network. Once a month, ANWOL hosts a Zoom meeting where network members gather to talk, brainstorm, and bolster one another. Susan Burton continues organizing, advocating, fundraising, and standing as a hero to women in prison systems from the United States to Kenya, Norway, and Japan.

There have been many changes in the lives of the women this book has followed. In the summer of 2021, almost six years after their guilty verdict, Ivy and Janeth's case is on appeal, while they both serve their sentences at Chowchilla, the state prison three and a half hours from Los Angeles. Ivy's sentence has already been reduced by five years because the judge made a mistake and added too many years to the original sentence. However, there are even more important developments in their appeal, which is pending before the California Supreme Court. Ivy's is an important case because it's testing a new California law based on Senate Bill (SB) 1437, which reverses what's long been known as the natural and probable consequences theory. "My brain hurts when I think about this theory," Elie Miller tells me, but as soon as she explains the new law, it makes sense. Ivy's and Janeth's original guilty verdicts were based on a law that said that during the time a felony is committed, if someone dies, the charge is murder and *everyone* involved can face first-degree murder charges. So, as in the case of Ivy and Janeth, you could face murder charges even if you never actually killed anyone. Under SB 1437, you can be charged with first-degree murder only if you're the person who actually killed someone or if you actively helped someone else kill that person. You have to be a major participant in the crime, playing an active role helping someone kill another person. Anyone who successfully appeals their sentence on a previous crime can have the time they serve reduced, because they avoid felony murder charges. In many cases, other murder charges end up with sentences of fifteen years to life. Of course, there's been lots of opposition to SB 1437 and the changes in sentencing. Luckily, efforts to oppose the law's constitutionality have all failed. Janeth and Ivy's appeal is scheduled to go forward, and there's a reason for hope.

For Janeth, there's an additional promising development. Due to a new ruling in case law, she will be eligible for what's known as a "youth offender parole hearing." The law states that if an individual was under the age of twenty-six when they committed the "controlling offense"—the crime that earned the longest sentence—then they qualify to be considered a youth offender. Janeth was twenty-two when she was charged, so she's eligible to be considered a youth offender. Until recently, youth-offender parole dates could not be moved forward because of what are called "conduct credits." This has now changed: conduct credits can advance a parole date. This means that an individual who's been involved in an activity such as getting an education earns credits that can translate to taking years off of their sentence. Janeth has already qualified for conduct credits. Her original parole eligibility date was 2039, but it was advanced to 2036. This doesn't mean she'll automatically be released that year, but if she keeps out of trouble while she's in Chowchilla, she has a chance of her parole eligibility date being advanced again.[17]

While they await the outcome of their appeal, both women remain far from their children. Ivy's son is being raised by his paternal grandparents, and Janeth's daughter has been adopted by the child's paternal grandmother, Myra. Adela is in touch with all the grandparents, making sure the memory of Ivy and Janeth stays alive with their children. Erika has stayed in touch with Jessie's grandparents and is certain of their love for him, telling me, "Sonia loves him so much, she loves him as if he were her own. He's been with her since Ivy was locked up—she has given him the unconditional love he needs."

Denise Marshall is well into her first year of the MSW program at UCLA, and her daughter is flourishing. Rosa Lucero is working part-time at Homeboy Industries and has applied to a vocational training program to learn to write computer code. After receiving two years' probation, Carmen and her children still live in subsidized housing. With her usual resilience, she is working at a new job, as a case manager for a Covid-relief program. Adela Juarez continues her work on behalf of women at Interval House and is moving forward with plans to open her own shelter. To raise funds for this effort, we're already gathering material on a book about her life, with proceeds to go to fund the shelter. Angela Washington and her partner, Simone, are still together and she is now joyfully reconciled with her son Tyrone, whose girlfriend is expecting their first child.

And then there is Clara Vasquez.

I'd planned to end Clara's story as she finished community college and applied to a four-year university. But when I reached out to see how she was doing, I changed my mind. She'd applied to three California state universities—Northridge, Los Angeles, and Long Beach—and was accepted at all three. She chose Cal State Long Beach because it had a specific program for sign language interpretation.

School was exciting, although the pandemic had changed things, as Clara explained: "I'm hands-on—I need the professor right there in front of me. I know now, I have a learning disability and it's challenging being online. I can survive in the street with my eyes closed, but school is different. I love learning—my problem is retention. Now I know, it's not that I'm stupid; it's just that I learn differently."

Clara and I were talking on the phone—even with masks available, we didn't want to take the chance of meeting in person. Despite all these limits, she was just as open as she'd been during our past "in-person" conversations, telling me how she felt unsure of herself when she first stepped on campus, far from her comfort zone in community college. She enrolled in advanced courses and then had to drop two classes and enroll in their prerequisites. "I kept going, even though I made mistakes. I was determined to do it."

In the end, the most difficult problem she faced had nothing to do with school: her daughter Veronica had started acting out and running away. While she protected Veronica's privacy and stayed away from giving me the details, Clara told me, "A lot of things happened, and she was placed in foster care."

That was devastating news. Clara had thought the child welfare system was all behind her, but, unbelievably, she was once again dealing with DCFS and the family reunification process. "I was fighting for custody, I was going to parenting class, I was going to counseling. Plus, I was adjusting to school. So, it was just a little overwhelming for me."

Just a little overwhelming? I got anxious even listening to Clara. The strength, the resilience, the will to get her daughter back—again—was shining through her account. As a formerly incarcerated woman, she carried the weight of her past traumas and how they affected her daily life, including her children. Yet, there was no stopping her. I thought about Rosa, I thought about Adela, I thought about Denise. These women all continued undaunted in the face of so many obstacles. I feel in awe of them.

"What kept me going was that I didn't want her to continue in my footsteps. I was sticking to that purpose," Clara told me. "At the same time, my sister passed away. She committed suicide—she'd had mental health issues. Then my boyfriend got deported. I felt like, my God, why is this happening? I had to break myself in ten pieces so I could take care of everything."

She didn't do as well as she wanted in her courses, passing two and failing one, but she stayed in school. That in itself was an accomplishment. And Veronica returned home. "She came back to me right before Thanksgiving. Even the judge told me, 'Congratulations, you did everything in five months. You're a great mother.' All I could think was, I did it! I reunified my family!"

Veronica was happy to be home—the experience strengthened her and Clara's relationship. The two of them went to therapy, and Clara "reached out to her school to get her the help that she needs so she can succeed." While she focused on helping Veronica, Clara also encountered new economic pressures. Her boyfriend had been a large source of financial support; once he was deported, she feared she would be evicted. She was notified that she had to move and couldn't believe she was going to be homeless again. Reluctantly, she reached out to a social worker at the House of Ruth, who helped her apply for government aid. Despite feeling ashamed at first, she went ahead, reasoning, "I've worked since I was fifteen years old. I've paid taxes, so I'm allowed to apply for help whenever I need it."

Once she started receiving TANF (Temporary Assistance for Needy Families) funds, as well as funding from CalWorks, she budgeted carefully, going to food banks for fresh food and milk. She was hired as a student worker at school, which spurred her to become involved with several on-campus programs, including the Guardian Scholars, an organization for formerly incarcerated students. "After my first semester, I was getting the hang of university life. Then my counselor at Guardian Scholars asked me why I wasn't in the Equal Opportunity Program. I told her, 'I don't know. I applied, and they denied me.' She said I should have been in it from the start! So, she helped me get into EOP." Her counselor then sent her to the Bob Murphy Access Center, a program for students with disabilities, which helped with her learning disability. There, the counselor recommended she stick to three classes a semester. Clara was into her second semester when the pandemic struck. The idea of a school year attending classes online intimidated her as she confided, "I'm scared of failing. And my girls are my priority."

She drew encouragement to continue from her daily life. "When this whole quarantine happened, there were long lines at the grocery store. There was a deaf lady trying to get in and the security guard was trying to communicate with her, and of course, they weren't understanding each other. I stepped in to help. The lady was so grateful, it just made me feel so good, like *yes*! This is my passion, this is my calling. I will do it—with school or without it." Clara is dedicated to being trained and plans to apply to an interpreter program once she has accumulated enough credits. "I'm going to try," she tells me. "I mean, the worst thing they can say is no. And then I can apply next year." There is steel in her voice, even as she giggles. "I'm taking this slow. I joke around and tell my kids, 'By the time I finish school, it will be time for me to retire.' Then they laugh and say, 'Hey, Mom, but at least you got your degree. You got what you wanted.'"

I soon learn why Clara was referring to multiple kids: her oldest daughter, Theresa, has moved in. She'll graduate community college in a year, the same time that Veronica graduates from high school. Theresa's baby, Juana, Clara's first grandchild, now seven years old, rounds out the family—three generations of women under one roof. Theresa is applying to transfer to UCLA and plans to one day be a history professor; the impact of Clara's love and example lives through her. "She told me, 'Mom, you're an inspiration to me. Because of everything you've been through—and you're still staying in school.'"

Clara has never let go of Aracely, either. She is now twenty and living in Bakersfield with one of her father's sisters. Continuing her education in community college, she calls Clara every week and sometimes every day for information and support. "Our relationship is getting stronger—she'll always be my daughter—and I love advising her about school!" Clara laughs with pleasure. All three of her daughters deeply value education and are committed to succeeding in school. This is Clara's legacy.

Ivy and Janeth's legacy is heartbreaking. Their trauma, never fully addressed, continues to shadow their lives, undoubtedly growing more severe while they are incarcerated. Through all of these accounts, their story serves as a reminder of how women desperately need gender-sensitive, trauma-informed support and services to change. Elie Miller is adamant about this, telling me, "Those two women should never have been locked up. They needed help, they needed services, they needed to heal." But all of the other women whose stories make up this book are the jewels at the bottom of Pandora's box: hope. Not one has returned to prison or jail. Their strength, their lives, and those working to give them a fair chance, offer the promise of a pathway forward into the light.

ACKNOWLEDGMENTS

This book would never have been written without the help of the eighty women who shared their lives with me. Over the past fourteen years, as I've talked with them, giggled, gossiped and cried with them, all the time learning their stories of courage and resilience, I've never stopped being both in awe and grateful for everything they've given me. My debt to them is incalculable. Their lives and their stories have changed me forever.

I am honored that Adela Juarez, Rosa Lucero, Denise Marshall, and Clara Vasquez allowed me into the most intimate parts of their lives. Their strength and honesty was—and is—the heart of this work. Denise once explained, "I like the idea of owning my life for a change." Whatever the motivation for the candor and authenticity you four have blessed me with, words fail as I try to express my gratitude. Thank you.

Susan Burton is connected to all of these women and so many others. As this book strives to make apparent, she is a leader, a role model, and an advocate all rolled into one. Her devotion to the cause of formerly and currently incarcerated women globally is unparalleled. It was my good fortune that Dr. Bob Ross and the California Endowment connected the two of us all those years ago, allowing me to begin working with A New Way of Life. That organization and the people who comprise it—including co-directors Michael Towler and Pamela Marshall, Ingrid Archie, Claire Arce, and Margaret Dooley-Sammuli—continue to inspire me with their devotion to the lives of formerly and currently incarcerated women everywhere. I will forever be committed to ANWOL.

This parallels my commitment to Homeboy Industries and the women of the Homegirl Café. To this day, they are a singular part of my life. While my beloved Pati Zarate, Shannon Smith, and Erika Cuellar have moved on to new projects, the soul of the café remains unchanged with Arlin Crane "now leading its efforts." I remain in contact with and steadfastly admire all of the women I grew to know and love through its work and Homeboy Industries' mission to provide "hope, training and support to formerly gang involved and recently incarcerated men and women, allowing them to redirect their lives and become contributing members of our community." I continue to deeply respect the contributions of all the Homeboy leadership staff, including my friends Tom Vozzo, Shirley Torres, and Hector Verdugo. I am also in awe of the loving dedication of Myrna Tellez.

It's impossible to think or write about Homeboy Industries, the Homegirl Café, and the struggles of women who have come of age in the shadow of gangs and incarceration without thinking of the one person who has taught us all about kinship and compassion. There is no one on this earth like Father Greg Boyle. He has been and will always be a constant source of knowledge, reassurance, and delight. Understanding that women's struggles are born of trauma and pain, he continues to be part of my journey as I bear witness to women's stories in the spirit of kinship and humility. His love, wisdom, and friendship are all one of the great joys of my life.

The truism "it takes a village" was never more apparent to me than throughout the stages of writing this book, which spanned a global pandemic and the ongoing demand for racial and social justice ignited by the murder of George Floyd. From the beginning, Helene Atwan at Beacon Press served as both an insightful editor and a great source of support. She is simply extraordinary. I'm also indebted to Pam Mac-Coll, Beth Collins, Susan Lumenello, and Katherine Scott. This is my third book to be published by Beacon Press, words I am honored to write. Their commitment to social justice and the quality of the works they publish have served as an inspiration to so many readers—including me.

I'm deeply indebted to my friends and colleagues at the UCLA Luskin School of Public Affairs and the Department of Social Welfare. While they're too numerous to name, I'm grateful to Rosina Becerra for taking a chance on me thirty years ago and to Laura Abrams, whose research and guidance is part of this work. I'm also thankful for Dean Gary Segura, Michael Dukakis, Anastasia Loukaitou-Sideris, Ian Holloway, Gerry Lavinia, Susana Bonis, Ann (F-Ann-Tastic) Kim, Jianchao Lai, Monica Macias, and Livier Guttierez. Although Annalisa Enrile teaches at "the other school" (USC), her scholarship and insights have deeply informed efforts to achieve justice and equity for women all over the globe. Along with Marcia Cunha, she's the best boss lady I know! The amazing Whitney Gouche helped turn this manuscript into a well-organized piece of work.

At UCLA, I also met the man who changed my professional life. Todd Franke is a gifted professor who cares deeply about his students. He is also the most brilliant research methodologist I've ever known. I'm so grateful that he took me by the hand almost twenty years ago and taught me more about research and evaluation than I ever could have imagined. I'm grateful every day for the role he continues to play in my life.

My village is also populated by the friends and chosen family that surround and support me, whom I simply could not live without. I am so grateful for the love and wisdom of my Watts family, including my mommy, Betty Day, my forever partner, Elder Michael Cummings, Donny Joubert, Deborah Riddle, Perry Crouch, John King, Kathy Wooten, Amada Valle, and the men and women who participate in the Watts Leadership Institute. My appreciation for and support of the men of Project Fatherhood and the women of Motivated Moms is enduring; their devotion to their families and to Watts is a source of both hope and awe. I've also been inspired by a talented collection of individuals who care deeply about the communities of both men and women who live in the shadow of violence and incarceration. With deep respect, I am grateful for Connie Rice, Sandy Jo MacArthur, Emada and Phil Tingirides, Aqeela Sherrills, my wonderful E—Elizabeth Ruebman, David Kennedy, Melvyn Hayward, Aquil Basheer, Ben Owens, Blinky Rodriguez, Robert "Bobby" Arias, Gerald Cavitt, Skipp Townsend, Fernando Rejon, Andre Christian, Reginald Zachery, Jose Rodriguez, Alex Sanchez, my brother Kenny Green, and my daughter forever, Bertha Cordova.

My partner at the UCLA Watts Leadership Institute who also serves as the director of the Social Justice Research Partnership, Karrah Lompa, deserves all the praise I can heap upon her and so much more. Over the years we have worked with a remarkable group of community researchers and scholars, including Susana Bonis, Callie Davidson, Sergio Rizzo-Fontanesi, Crystal Thomas, Adriana Ariza, Samantha McCarthy, Sophia Bilodeau, and Katie Saenz. Stephanie Benson was integral to the work at ANWOL, and her efforts in that endeavor were second to none.

I cannot begin to describe what my friend Carol Biondi means to me. I constantly draw upon her strength and steadfastness; her friendship is a gift I could never have imagined. Bill Resnick and Michael Stubbs have served as thought partners in this endeavor, and their support for formerly and currently incarcerated women is a living example of compassion and philanthropy. In all of this, Alexis Rizutto has answered the phone, helping me as a true friend and sounding board as I thought about what this work should encompass.

My beloved second father, therapist, friend, and mentor, Dr. Joseph Rosner, is ninety-nine years old and warned me that I had to finish this book before he turned one hundred. I needed that "encouragement" just as I drew upon the support of my two brothers and their families: Tony and Margie, and Chris and Kim. My heart belongs to them and to the members of my chosen family whose love and support I treasure every day of my life: Shelly Brooks and Ben Goff, Tina Christie and Michelle Parra, Gerry Chaleff, Joe and Malinda Kibre, Nina Bende, Penny Fuller, Larry Pressman, my GT Marcia Berris, Anne Taylor Fleming,

Ann Herold, Julio Marcial, my beloved Greek sister, Sofia Liosis, John and Nicolette Skrumbis Phillipopoulos, Jack Rosner, Heather and Joe Fier, Robert Green, Katie Sparks and David Jackson, Gail Egstrom Clarke, Marcy Jones Erickson, and the incredible Sean Kennedy.

Along with the incomparable and brilliant lawyer Elie Miller, the journalist and scholar Celeste Fremon is my "justice sister." Her intellect and humor are a constant in my life. Both of these women have sustained me through many struggles.

Like so many other individuals, the global pandemic affected my personal life. I am grateful beyond words for the care and compassion of Dr. Cheryl Charles and Dr. James Caplan. Their efforts reinforce the significance of affordable healthcare for all women, honoring the memory of two women I loved deeply: my Thea Ernie—Virginia Manos Pappas—and the irreplaceable Beatriz Solis.

Finally, there are the two people who are, quite simply, the center of my world. My husband, Mark, and my daughter, Shannon, have given me a dream of life. Together they have taught me the meaning of unconditional love.

NOTES

CHAPTER 1: SLEEPWALKING

1. Hector Becerra, "Widow of Church Deacon Killed by Tagger Asks Public for Help," *Los Angeles Times*, Nov. 9, 2012, www.latimesblogs.latimes.com/lanow/2012/11/church-widow.html.

CHAPTER 2: PARTY BUS

1. "The Custody Division Mission Statement," introduction, *Custody Division Manual*, Section 1-00/000.00, Los Angeles County Sheriff's Department (July 2021), http://pars.lasd.org/Viewer/Manuals/14249/Content/12551.

CHAPTER 3: PERSONAL STATEMENT

1. Christine White, "Putting Resilience and Resilience Surveys Under the Microscope," *ACEs Too High News*, Feb. 5, 2017, https://acestoohigh.com/2017/02/05/__trashed-4.

2. Ira Glass, "Back to School," *This American Life*, NPR, Sept. 14, 2012, https://www.thisamericanlife.org/474/transcript.

CHAPTER 4: I DIDN'T HAVE ANY TEARS

1. Jorja Leap, *Project Fatherhood: A Story of Courage and Healing in One of America's Toughest Communities* (Boston: Beacon Press, 2015).

2. Jorja Leap, Stephanie Benson, and Callie Davidson, *A New Way of Life Reentry Project: A Case Study* (Los Angeles: California Endowment, 2016).

3. Jason Baker et al., "Mother-Grandmother Co-Parenting Relationships in Families with Incarcerated Mothers: A Pilot Investigation," *Family Process* 49, no. 2 (June 2010): 164–84.

4. Joyce Arditti and April Few, "Maternal Distress and Women's Reentry into Family and Community Life," *Family Process* 47, no. 3 (2008): 303–21.

5. Annalisa Enrile, *Ending Human Trafficking and Modern-Day Slavery: Freedom's Journey* (Los Angeles: Sage, 2017).

CHAPTER 5: I THOUGHT HE WOULD TAKE CARE OF ME

1. Gini Sikes, *8 Ball Chicks: A Year in the Violent World of Girl Gangsters* (New York: Anchor Books, 1997).

2. "Gender" is used as a binary concept. While this reflects the past organization of gang activity, it will be important to consider nonbinary views of gender in future gang research. Karen Joe and Meda Chesney-Lind, "Just Every Mother's Angel: An Analysis of Gender and Ethnic Variations in Youth Gang Membership," *Gender & Society* 9, no. 4 (1995): 408–31; Tara Sutton, "The Lives of Female Gang Members: A Review of the Literature," *Aggression and Violent Behavior* 37 (2017): 142–52.

3. Joe and Chesney-Lind, "Just Every Mother's Angel."

4. Sam Quinones, "The Queen of Florencia," *Los Angeles Magazine*, Sept. 25, 2017, https://www.lamag.com/longform/arlene-rodriguez-queen-of-florencia.

5. Rachel Snyder, *No Visible Bruises: What We Don't Know About Domestic Violence Can Kill Us* (New York: Bloomsbury, 2019).

6. Snyder, *No Visible Bruises.*

7. Joanne Belknap, *The Invisible Woman: Gender, Crime, and Justice* (Boulder, CO: Wadsworth, Cengage, 2007).

8. Sarah Halpern-Meekin et al., "Relationship Churning, Physical Violence, and Verbal Abuse in Young Adult Relationships," *Journal of Marriage and the Family* 75 (2013): 2–12; Johanne Vézina and Martine Hébert, "Risk Factors for Victimization in Romantic Relationships of Young Women: A Review of Empirical Studies and Implications for Prevention," *Trauma, Violence, and Abuse* 8, no. 1 (Jan. 2007): 33–66.

9. Victoria Folette et al., "Cumulative Trauma: The Impact of Child Sexual Abuse, Adult Sexual Assault and Spouse Abuse," *Journal of Traumatic Stress* 9, no. 1 (Jan. 1996): 25–35.

10. Azmaira Maker, Markus Kemmelmeier, and Christopher Peterson, "Child Sexual Abuse, Peer Sexual Abuse, and Sexual Assault in Adulthood: A Multi-Risk Model of Revictimization," *Journal of Trauma Stress* 14, no. 2 (Apr. 2001): 351–68.

11. David Fergusson, Joseph Boden, and John Horwood, "Exposure to Childhood Sexual and Physical Abuse and Adjustment in Early Adulthood," *Child Abuse & Neglect* 32, no. 6 (2008): 607–19; Terri Messman-Moore and Patricia J. Long, "Child Sexual Abuse and Revictimization in the Form of Adult Sexual Abuse, Adult Physical Abuse, and Adult Psychological Maltreatment," *Journal of Interpersonal Violence* 15, no. 5 (May 2000): 489–502.

12. Tamerra Moeller, Gloria Bachmann, and James Moeller, "The Combined Effects of Physical, Sexual and Emotional Abuse During Childhood: Long-Term Health Consequences for Women," *Child Abuse and Neglect* 17, no. 15 (1993): 623–40.

13. Alytia Levendosky et al., "Trauma Symptoms in Preschool Age Children Exposed to Domestic Violence," *Journal of Interpersonal Violence* 17, no. 2 (2002): 150–64.

CHAPTER 6: BABY PRISON

1. In 2010, the LA County Probation Department initiated a new program at Camp Scott to meet young women's needs for trauma-informed care. Despite positive responses from the young women detained there, at the same time problems at the camp site emerged, including a crime involving a probation officer who was convicted of molesting four young women detained at the camp. See James Queally, "L.A.

County Probation Officer Pleads Guilty to Assaulting Inmates at a Juvenile Hall," *Los Angeles Times*, Sept. 20, 2017, https://www.latimes.com/local/lanow/la-me-ln -probation-officer-sexual-assault-20170920-story.html.

2. Paul Colomy and Martin Kretzmann, "The Gendering of Social Control: Sex Delinquency and Progressive Juvenile Justice in Denver," in *Governing Childhood*, ed. Anne McGillivray (Aldershot, UK: Dartmouth, 1997), 1901–27.

3. Kimberly Flemke and Katherine Allen, "Women's Experience of Rage: A Critical Feminist Analysis," *Journal of Marital and Family Therapy* 34, no. 1 (2008): 58–74, https://doi.org/10.1111/j.1752–0606.2008.00053.x; Kimberly Flemke, "Triggering Rage: Unresolved Trauma in Women's Lives," *Contemporary Family Therapy* 31 (2009): 123–39, https://doi.org/10.1007/s10591–009–9084–8.

4. Flemke, "Triggering Rage."

5. Flemke, "Triggering Rage."

6. Meda Chesney-Lind, "Imprisoning Women: The Unintended Consequences of Mass Imprisonment," in *Invisible Punishment: The Unintended Consequences of Mass Imprisonment*, ed. Marc Mauer and Meda Chesney-Lind (New York: Free Press, 2002), 79–94.

7. John Dilulio, "The Coming of the Super-Predators," *Washington Examiner*, Nov. 27, 1995, www.washingtonexaminer.com/weekly-standard/the-coming-of-the -super-predators; Carroll Bogert and Lynnell Hancock, "Superpredator: The Media Myth That Demonized a Generation of Black Youth," Marshall Project, Nov. 20, 2020, www.themarshallproject.org/2020/11/20/superpredator-the-media-myth-that -demonized-a-generation-of-black-youth.

8. Eileen Poe-Yamagata and Jeffrey Butts, *Female Offenders in the Juvenile Justice System, Statistics Summary* (Washington, DC: US Department of Justice, Office of Justice Programs, Office of Juvenile Justice and Delinquency Prevention, June 1996), https://www.ncjrs.gov/pdffiles/femof.pdf.

9. Margaret Zahn et al., *The Girls Study Group—Charting the Way to Delinquency Prevention for Girls*, report (Washington, DC: US Department of Justice, Office of Justice Programs, Office of Juvenile Justice and Delinquency Prevention, 2008), https://www.ncjrs.gov/pdffiles1/ojjdp/223434.pdf.

10. Meda Chesney-Lind, "Girls and Violence: Is the Gender Gap Closing?" VAWnet.org, National Online Resource Center on Violence Against Women, National Resource Center on Domestic Violence (NRCDV), Aug. 2004, https://vawnet .org/material/girls-and-violence-gender-gap-closing.

11. Melissa Sickmund et al., *Easy Access to the Census of Juveniles in Residential Placement* (Washington, DC: US Department of Justice, Office of Justice Programs, Office of Juvenile Justice and Delinquency Prevention, 2017).

12. American Civil Liberties Union, "Casey A., et al. v. Robles, et al.," Mar. 16, 2011, https://www.aclu.org/cases/casey-et-al-v-robles-et-al.

13. Solitary confinement in federal prisons for youth was banned by President Barack Obama in 2016. However, as of 2020, only eleven states and the District of Columbia prohibit or limit solitary youth confinement; the remaining thirty-nine states have some form of solitary confinement. See Eli Hager, "Ending Solitary for Juveniles: A Goal Grows Closer," Marshall Project, Aug. 2, 2017, www.themarshall project.org/2017/08/01/ending-solitary-for-juveniles-a-goal-grows-closer; Anne Teigen, "States That Limit or Prohibit Juvenile Shackling and Solitary Confinement,"

National Conference of State Legislatures, Jan. 29, 2020, www.ncsl.org/research/civil-and-criminal-justice/states-that-limit-or-prohibit-juvenile-shackling-and-solitary-confinement635572628.aspx.

14. Chesney-Lind, "Girls and Violence: Is the Gender Gap Closing?"

15. Chesney-Lind, "Girls and Violence: Is the Gender Gap Closing?"

CHAPTER 7: CROSSOVER KIDS

1. Dorothy Roberts, "Prison, Foster Care, and the Systemic Punishment of Black Mothers," *Faculty Scholarship at Penn Law* 432 (August 2012); Eli Hager and Anna Flagg, "How Incarcerated Parents Are Losing Their Children Forever," Marshall Project, Dec. 3, 2018, www.themarshallproject.org/2018/12/03/how-incarcerated-parents-are-losing-their-children-forever.

2. Mary Dodge and Mark Pogrebin, "Collateral Costs of Imprisonment for Women: Complications of Reintegration," *Prison Journal* 81, no. 1 (2001): 42–54; Ross Parke and K. Alison Clarke-Stewart, "Effects of Parental Incarceration on Young Children," in *From Prison to Home* (Washington, DC: US Department of Health and Human Services, Dec. 1, 2001), https://aspe.hhs.gov/basic-report/effects-parental-incarceration-young-children.

3. Stephen Demuth, "Racial and Ethnic Differences in Pretrial Release Decisions and Outcomes: A Comparison of Hispanic, Black, and White Felony Arrestees," *Criminology* 41, no. 3 (2003): 873–908, https://doi.org/10.1111/j.1745–9125.2003.tb01007.x.

4. Mikaela Rabinowitz, *Incarceration Without Conviction: Pretrial Detention and the Erosion of Innocence in American Criminal Justice* (New York: Routledge, 2021).

5. Wendy Sawyer and Peter Wagner, *Mass Incarceration: The Whole Pie 2020*, report, Prison Policy Initiative, Mar. 24, 2020, www.prisonpolicy.org/reports/pie2020.html.

6. Wendy Sawyer and Wanda Bertram, "Jail Will Separate 2.3 Million Mothers from Their Children This Year," Prison Policy Initiative, May 13, 2018, www.prisonpolicy.org/blog/2018/05/13/mothers-day-2018.

7. Sawyer and Bertram, "Jail Will Separate 2.3 Million Mothers from Their Children This Year"; Lauren Glaze and Laura M. Maruschak, "Parents in Prison and Their Minor Children," US Department of Justice, Bureau of Justice Statistics, 2008; Pew Charitable Trusts, *Collateral Costs: Incarceration's Effect on Economic Mobility*, report (Washington, DC: Pew Charitable Trusts, 2010); Sarah Schirmer, Ashley Nellis, and Marc Mauer, *Incarcerated Parents and Their Children: Trends 1991–2007* (Washington, DC: Sentencing Project, 2009), www.sentencingproject.org.

8. Throughout this book, the words "gang," "hood," "neighborhood," and "barrio" are used interchangeably, depending on the individual's terminology.

9. "Connections with Youth in the Child Welfare System," Youth.gov, https://youth.gov/youth-topics/juvenile-justice/connections-youth-child-welfare-system.

10. MacLaren Hall Survivors, "About Us," April 15, 2011, www.maclarenhallsurvivors.wordpress.com/about.

11. Eli Hager and Anna Flagg, "How Incarcerated Parents Are Losing Their Children Forever," Marshall Project, December 3, 2018, www.themarshallproject.org/2018/12/03/how-incarcerated-parents-are-losing-their-children-forever.

12. Hager and Flagg, "How Incarcerated Parents Are Losing Their Children Forever"; Steve Christian, "Children of Incarcerated Parents," National Conference of

State Legislatures, 2009; Susan George et al., "Incarcerated Women, Their Children, and the Nexus with Foster Care," *PsycEXTRA Dataset* (2011), https://doi.org/10.1037 /e725792011–001.

CHAPTER 8: SELF-MEDICATION

1. Sarah Stillman, "America's Other Family Separation Crisis," *New Yorker*, Oct. 29, 2018, https://www.newyorker.com/magazine/2018/11/05/americas-other-family -separation-crisis.

2. Wendy Guastaferro and Laura Lutgen, "Women with Substance Use Disorders Reentering the Community," in *Female Offenders and Reentry: Pathways and Barriers to Returning to Society*, ed. Lisa Carter and Catherine Marcum (New York: Routledge, 2018), 76–107.

3. Barry Krisberg, Susan Marchionna, and Christopher Hartney, *American Corrections: Concepts and Controversies* (Los Angeles: Sage, 2014), 293.

4. Meda Chesney-Lind, "Girls and Violence: Is the Gender Gap Closing?" VAWnet.org, National Online Resource Center on Violence Against Women, National Resource Center on Domestic Violence (NRCDV), Aug. 2004, https://vawnet .org/material/girls-and-violence-gender-gap-closing.

5. Ruben Castaneda, "Why Do Alcoholics and Addicts Relapse So Often?" *U.S. News & World Report*, Apr. 24, 2017, https://health.usnews.com/wellness/articles /2017–04–24/why-do-alcoholics-and-addicts-relapse-so-often.

6. Stillman, "America's Other Family Separation Crisis."

7. Ann Loper and Elena Tuerk, "Parenting Programs for Incarcerated Parents: Current Research and Future Directions," *Criminal Justice Policy Review* 17 (2006): 402–7; Joyce Arditti, *Parental Incarceration and the Family: Psychological and Social Effects of Imprisonment on Children, Parents and Caregivers* (New York: New York University Press, 2012).

8. Angela Moe and Kathleen Ferraro, "Criminalized Mothers: The Value and Devaluation of Parenthood Behind Bars," *Women & Therapy* 29, no. 3–4 (2007): 135–64.

CHAPTER 9: HALFWAY IS JUST THAT

1. Audrey Begun, Theresa Early, and Ashley Hodge, "Mental Health and Substance Abuse Service Engagement by Men and Women During Community Reentry Following Incarceration," *Administration and Policy in Mental Health and Mental Health Services Research* 43 (2016): 207, https://doi.org/10.1007/s10488–015–0632–2.

2. Nora Wikoff, Donald Linhorst, and Nicole Morani, "Recidivism Among Participants of a Reentry Program for Prisoners Released Without Supervision," *Social Work Research* 36, no. 4 (2012): 296, https://doi.org/10.1093/swr/svs021.

3. Catherine Fuentes, "Nobody's Child: The Role of Trauma and Interpersonal Violence in Women's Pathways to Incarceration and Resultant Service Needs," *Medical Anthropology Quarterly* 28 (2013): 85–104, https://doi.org/10.1111/maq.12058.

4. For additional research, see Kyle Ward and Mary Evans, "Mental Health Needs and Treatment," in *Female Offenders and Reentry: Pathways and Barriers to Returning to Society*, ed. Lisa Carter and Catherine Marcum (New York: Routledge, 2017).

5. Barry Krisberg, Susan Marchionna, and Christopher Hartney, *American Corrections: Concepts and Controversies* (Los Angeles: Sage, 2014), 309.

6. Wendy Sawyer, "Who's Helping the 1.9 Million Women Released from Prisons and Jails Each Year?" Prison Policy Initiative, briefing, July 19, 2019, https://www.prisonpolicy.org/blog/2019/07/19/reentry.

7. Todd Minton and Zhen Zeng, "Census of Jails (COJ)" (Washington, DC: US Department of Justice, Bureau of Justice Statistics, 2019), https://bjs.ojp.gov/data-collection/census-jails-coj.

8. According to PPI, five states—Connecticut, Delaware, Hawaii, Rhode Island, and Vermont—did not report jail data because jail systems are completely integrated into the state prison system.

9. Krisberg, Marchionna, and Hartney, *American Corrections*, 312.

10. "Women Released from Prison: Where Is Their Support?," A New Way of Life, http://anewwayoflife.org/wp-content/uploads/2019/10/SAFE-Housing-Network.jpg. The five states are Colorado, Connecticut, Maine, Massachusetts, and Rhode Island.

11. For trans and gender-expansive individuals, the situation is even more dire. The plight of such individuals is beyond the scope of this book, but reliable information can be found at https://www.blackandpink.org.

12. Begun, Early, and Hodge, "Mental Health and Substance Abuse Service Engagement by Men and Women During Community Reentry Following Incarceration," 207.

13. California Department of Corrections and Rehabilitation, Alternative Custody Program, "Female Offender Programs and Services," https://www.cdcr.ca.gov/adult-operations/acp.

14. The State of California gives each formerly incarcerated individual $200, an amount unchanged since 1973. Other states give less or nothing. See "What Gate Money Can (and Cannot) Buy," Marshall Project, Sept. 10, 2019, https://www.themarshallproject.org/2019/09/10/what-gate-money-can-and-cannot-buy.

15. Roxanne Daniel and Wendy Sawyer, "What You Should Know About Halfway Houses," Prison Policy Initiative, Sept. 3, 2020, https://www.prisonpolicy.org/blog/2020/09/03/halfway.

16. Ida Johnson, "Women Parolees' Perceptions of Parole Experiences and Parole Officers," *American Journal of Criminal Justice* 40, no. 4 (2014): 785–810, http://dx.doi.org/10.1007/s12103-014-9284-0.

17. Begun, Early, and Hodge, "Mental Health and Substance Abuse Service Engagement by Men and Women During Community Reentry Following Incarceration," 207.

18. Fuentes, "Nobody's Child," 85–104.

19. Diane Fields and Laura Abrams, "Gender Differences in the Perceived Needs and Barriers of Youth Offenders Preparing for Community Reentry," *Child and Youth Care Forum* 39, no. 4 (2010): 266, http://dx.doi.org/10.1007/s10566-010-9102-x.

CHAPTER 10: THE HOPE OF REENTRY

1. Stephanie Covington, "Women and the Criminal Justice System," *Women's Health Issues* 17, no. 4 (2007), https://doi.org/10.1016/j.whi.2007.05.004.

2. Jorja Leap, Stephanie Benson, and Callie Davidson, *A New Way of Life Reentry Project: A Case Study* (Los Angeles: California Endowment, 2016).

3. Pati Zarate eventually moved on to open her own restaurant, a long-held dream, and she was ably succeeded at Homegirl by Arlin Crane.

CHAPTER 11: THE STRUGGLES OF LIFE
1. Wendy Sawyer, "Who's Helping the 1.9 Million Women Released from Prisons and Jails Each Year?" Prison Policy Initiative, briefing, July 19, 2019, https://www.prisonpolicy.org/blog/2019/07/19/reentry, citing Holtfreder et al. (2004).

2. Sawyer, "Who's Helping the 1.9 Million Women Released from Prisons and Jails Each Year?"

3. Marilyn Brown and Barbara Bloom, "Reentry and Renegotiating Motherhood: Maternal Identity and Success on Parole," *Crime and Delinquency* 55, no. 2 (2009): 313–36, https://doi.org/10.1177%2F0011128708330627.

4. Sawyer, "Who's Helping the 1.9 Million Women Released from Prisons and Jails Each Year?"

5. Brown and Bloom, "Reentry and Renegotiating Motherhood."

6. Renny Golden, *War on the Family: Mothers in Prison and the Families They Leave Behind* (New York: Routledge, 2005).

7. Brown and Bloom, "Reentry and Renegotiating Motherhood."

8. American Civil Liberties Union, "Facts About the Over-Incarceration of Women in the United States," https://www.aclu.org/other/facts-about-over-incarceration-women-united-states.

9. Jorja Leap, Stephanie Benson, and Callie Davidson, *A New Way of Life Reentry Project: A Case Study* (Los Angeles: California Endowment, 2016).

10. Andrea Leverentz, *The Ex-Prisoner's Dilemma: How Women Negotiate Competing Narratives of Reentry and Desistance* (New Brunswick, NJ: Rutgers University Press, 2014), 138.

11. Leap, Benson, and Davidson, *A New Way of Life Reentry Project*.

CHAPTER 12: NEW LOVE
1. Andrea Leverentz, *The Ex-Prisoner's Dilemma: How Women Negotiate Competing Narratives of Reentry and Desistance* (New Brunswick, NJ: Rutgers University Press, 2014), 138.

2. Leverentz, *The Ex-Prisoner's Dilemma*, 138.

3. The same study reported that lesbian and bisexual women are likely to receive longer sentences than straight women. See Aleks Kajstura, "Women's Mass Incarceration: The Whole Pie 2019," Prison Policy Initiative, Oct. 29, 2019, https://www.prisonpolicy.org/reports/pie2019women.html.

4. "Prison Rape Elimination Act," National PREA Resource Center, https://www.prearesourcecenter.org/about/prison-rape-elimination-act. Passage of the legislation does not mean that rape of incarcerated women does not occur. There is a long-documented history of rape and molestation committed by guards and corrections officers in women's juvenile and adult facilities. However, that subject is beyond the scope of this book. For a sensitive case study and discussion of this issue, see Celeste Fremon, "When LA County Probation Officials Got Repeated Reports That a Staff Member Sexually Assaulted a Teenager, Why Did They Do Nothing?" WitnessLA, July 8, 2021.

5. Cristina Rathbone, *A World Apart: Women, Prison and Life Behind Bars* (New York: Random House, 2005).

6. Christopher Hensley and Richard Tewksbury, "Inmate-to-Inmate Prison Sexuality: A Review of Empirical Studies," *Trauma, Violence, and Abuse* 3, no. 3 (2002): 226–43, https://doi.org/10.1177/15248380020033005.

7. Given attitudes toward sexuality and the stigma placed on same-sex relationships in the 1960s, the number of same-sex relationships was most likely underreported.

8. Angela Perdue, Bruce Arrigo, and Daniel Murphy, "Sex and Sexuality in Women's Prisons: A Preliminary Typological Investigation," *Prison Journal* 91, no. 3 (2011): 279–304, https://doi.org/10.1177/0032885511409869.

9. Perdue, Arrigo, and Murphy, "Sex and Sexuality in Women's Prisons."

10. Ava Vidal, "Women Prisoners: Sex in Prison Is Commonplace, the Male Inmates Just Hide It More Than Girls," *Daily Telegraph*, Feb. 26, 2014, https://www.telegraph.co.uk/women/womens-politics/10662145/Women-prisoners-Sex-in-prison-is-commonplace-the-male-inmates-just-hide-it-more-than-girls.html.

11. Kate Johns, "Many Prison Inmates Are 'Gay for the Stay,'" *Independent*, May 6, 2013, https://www.independent.co.uk/voices/comment/many-prison-inmates-are-gay-stay-8605173.html.

12. "Crossroads," *Charity Matters*, May 2, 2020, https://charitymatters.com/2020/05/03/crossroads.

13. Most small organizations and halfway houses such as Claremont self-report rates of recidivism. They cannot afford program evaluation but at some point will require it. The source of this statistic and information about the program can be found at Crossroads, http://www.crossroadswomen.org/program.

CHAPTER 13: LOVE IN THE TIME OF REENTRY

1. Alma Backyard Farms, 2020, https://www.almabackyardfarms.com.

2. Interval House, http://www.intervalhouse.org/about.php.

CHAPTER 14: REDEMPTION BABY

1. Suzanne Godboldt, "Reunification with Family and Children During the Reentry Process," in *Female Offenders and Reentry: Pathways and Barriers to Returning to Society*, ed. Lisa Carter and Catherine Marcum (New York: Routledge, 2018), 203–22.

2. Renny Golden, *War on the Family: Mothers in Prison and the Families They Leave Behind* (New York: Routledge, 2005), 118.

3. Godboldt, "Reunification with Family and Children During the Reentry Process," 215.

4. Jenni Vainik, "The Reproductive and Parental Rights of Incarcerated Mothers," *Family Court Review* 46 (2008): 640–94.

5. Sarah Schirmer, Ashley Nellis, and Marc Mauer, *Incarcerated Parents and Their Children: Trends 1991–2007* (Washington, DC: Sentencing Project, 2009); Christopher Mumola, "Incarcerated Parents and Their Children," information bulletin, Aug. 30, 2000, US Department of Justice, Bureau of Justice Statistics.

6. "An Overview of Abortion Laws: As of July 1, 2021, State Laws and Policies," Guttmacher Institute, https://www.guttmacher.org/state-policy/explore/overview-abortion-laws.

7. "California Abortion Coverage in Medi-Cal and Private Insurance," National Health Law, https://healthlaw.org/storage/documents/NHeLP-CAAbortionCoverage FactSheet-Web.pdf.

8. "An Overview of Abortion Laws"; Tracy Weitz et al., "Safety of Aspiration Abortion Performed by Nurse Practitioners, Certified Nurse Midwives, and Physician Assistants Under a California Legal Waiver," *American Public Health Association* 103 (2013), https://ajph.aphapublications.org/doi/full/10.2105/AJPH.2012.301159; Elizabeth Fernandez, "Study: Abortions Are Safe When Performed by Nurse Practitioners, Physician Assistants, Certified Nurse Midwives," University of California San Francisco, Jan. 17, 2013, https://www.ucsf.edu/news/2013/01/13403/study-abortions -are-safe-when-performed-nurse-practitioners-physician-assistants.

9. "An Overview of Abortion Laws."

10. "An Overview of Abortion Laws."

11. An in-depth discussion of the history of race and reproductive justice can be found in Dorothy E. Roberts, *Killing the Black Body: Race, Reproduction, and the Meaning of Liberty* (New York: Vintage Books, 1998).

12. Sarah Stillman, "America's Other Family-Separation Crisis," *New Yorker*, Oct. 29, 2018, https://www.newyorker.com/magazine/2018/11/05/americas-other-family -separation-crisis.

13. Wendy Sawyer and Wanda Bertram, "Jail Will Separate 2.3 Million Mothers from their Children This Year," Prison Policy Initiative, May 13, 2018, https://www .prisonpolicy.org/blog/2018/05/13/mothers-day-2018.

14. "Who We Are: Hour Story," Hour Children, https://hourchildren.org.

15. "Hour Working Women Program," Hour Children, https://hourchildren.org /how-we-help/hour-working-women-program.

CHAPTER 15: THE LIGHT

1. *Pretrial Justice: How Much Does It Cost?* (Pretrial Justice Institute), https:// university.pretrial.org/HigherLogic/System/DownloadDocumentFile.ashx?Document FileKey=c2f50513-2f9d-2719-c990-a1e991a57303&forceDialog=0, accessed July 23, 2021.

2. Wendy Sawyer, "Who's Helping the 1.9 Million Women Released from Prisons and Jails Each Year?" Prison Policy Initiative, July 19, 2019, https://www.prisonpolicy .org/blog/2019/07/19/reentry.

3. "The State of Bail Reform," Marshall Project, Oct. 30, 2020, https://www .themarshallproject.org/2020/10/30/the-state-of-bail-reform; Melissa Block, "What Changed After D.C. Ended Cash Bail," *Weekend Edition*, NPR, Sept. 2, 2018, https:// www.npr.org/2018/09/02/644085158/what-changed-after-d-c-ended-cash-bail.

4. Block, "What Changed After D.C. Ended Cash Bail?"

5. Cheryl Corley, "Illinois Becomes 1st State to Eliminate Cash Bail," NPR, Feb. 22, 2021, https://www.npr.org/2021/02/22/970378490/illinois-becomes-first-state -to-eliminate-cash-bail.

6. "Girls' Courts/CSEC Courts Overview," California Courts, Judicial Branch of California, https://www.courts.ca.gov/37353.htm.

7. "Treatment Courts," Law Offices of Los Angeles County Public Defender, https://pubdef.lacounty.gov/treatment-courts.

8. "Diversion and Reentry Programs," City of Philadelphia, https://philadelphiada.org/diversion-reentry-programs.

9. "Diversion and Reentry Programs."

10. Jamie Gullen et al., "Supporting Women in the Criminal Legal System Through Access to Diversionary Programs," Community Legal Services, https://clsphila.org/wp-content/uploads/2021/02/Diversionary%20Programs%20Report%20(3).pdf.

11. Gina Fedock and Stephanie Covington, "Strengths-Based Approaches to the Treatment of Female Offenders," Center for Gender and Justice, in press, https://www.centerforgenderandjustice.org/site/assets/files/1514/8-30-18_revised_fedock_covington_with_suggested_edits_8_30_2018.pdf.

12. Melissa Santos, "'I Really Want Him to Have a Different Life': How Some Female Inmates are Raising Babies Behind Bars," *News Tribune*, Mar. 25, 2017, https://www.thenewstribune.com/news/politics-government/article140712783.html.

13. Sawyer, "Who's Helping the 1.9 Million Women Released from Prisons and Jails Each Year?"

14. As noted previously, information about Black and Pink National can be found at https://www.blackandpink.org.

15. Sawyer, "Who's Helping the 1.9 Million Women Released from Prisons and Jails Each Year?"

16. Patricia Leigh Brown, "Leaving Gun Towers and Barbed Wires for a Healing House," *New York Times*, Aug. 7, 2020.

17. I am indebted to Christopher Hawthorne, clinical professor of law and director of the Juvenile Innocence and Fair Sentencing Clinic at Loyola Law School, for this information.

INDEX